VOLUME 2

Since the Fifteenth Century

THINKING THROUGH SOURCES FOR
Ways of the World

A Brief Global History

FOURTH EDITION

Robert W. Strayer
The College at Brockport: State University of New York

Eric W. Nelson
Missouri State University

bedford/st.martin's
Macmillan Learning
Boston | New York

For Bedford/St. Martin's

Vice President, Editorial, Macmillan Learning Humanities: Edwin Hill
Program Director for History: Michael Rosenberg
Senior Program Manager for History: William J. Lombardo
History Marketing Manager: Melissa Rodriguez
Director of Content Development: Jane Knetzger
Assistant Editor, History: Stephanie Sosa
Content Project Manager: Lidia MacDonald-Carr
Senior Workflow Project Supervisor: Joe Ford
Production Supervisor: Robin Besofsky
Senior Media Project Manager: Michelle Camisa
Media Editor: Tess Fletcher
Manager of Publishing Services: Andrea Cava
Project Management: Lumina Datamatics, Inc.
Composition: Lumina Datamatics, Inc.
Photo Editor: Christine Buese
Photo Researcher: Bruce Carson
Text Permissions Manager: Kalina Ingham
Text Editor: Mark Schaefer, Lumina Datamatics, Inc.
Director of Design, Content Management: Diana Blume
Text Design: Heather Marshall, Lumina Datamatics, Inc.
Cover Design: William Boardman
Printing and Binding: LSC Communications

Cover Photo: **Top,** Panel, third quarter of the 15th century (silk cut & uncut voided velvet, brocaded with gold-metallic wefts), Italian School, (15th century)/Museum of Fine Arts, Boston, Massachusetts, USA / Gift of Philip Lehman in memory of his wife Carrie L. Lehman/Bridgeman Images. **Bottom,** Literacy, by Diego Rivera (1886–1957), detail from the Ministry of Education frescoes (1923–1928), Mexico City. Mexico, 20th century. De Agostini Picture Library/M. Seemuller/Bridgeman Images © 2018 Banco de México Diego Rivera Frida Kahlo Museums Trust, Mexico, D.F./Artists Rights Society (ARS), New York.

Copyright © 2019, 2016 by Bedford/St. Martin's.

All rights reserved. No part of this book may be reproduced, stored in a retrieval system, or transmitted in any form or by any means, electronic, mechanical, photocopying, recording, or otherwise, except as may be permitted by law or expressly permitted in writing by the Publisher.

Manufactured in the United States of America.

1 2 3 4 5 6   23 22 21 20 19 18

For information, write: Bedford/St. Martin's, 75 Arlington Street, Boston, MA 02116

ISBN 978-1-319-17020-2 (Volume 1)
ISBN 978-1-319-17025-7 (Volume 2)

Acknowledgments

Text acknowledgments and copyrights appear at the back of the book on pages 372, which constitutes an extension of the copyright page. Art acknowledgments and copyrights appear on the same page as the art selections they cover.

Preface

Designed specifically to be used with all versions of *Ways of the World*, Fourth Edition, this collection of sources—both primary and secondary—complements and extends each chapter of the parent textbook. As the title of the collection suggests, these source projects enable students to **"think through sources"** and, in turn, begin to understand the craft of historians as well as their conclusions. Readers explore in greater depth a central theme from each chapter, using both documentary and visual sources as well as brief extracts from works by recent historians and other scholars. Each Historians' Voices feature and every primary source includes a brief headnote that provides context for the source and several questions to consider. The primary source projects include a series of integrative and probing essay questions appropriate for in-class discussion and writing assignments.

In addition to this print volume, we are delighted to offer *Thinking through Sources* in LaunchPad, Bedford's online learning platform. In LaunchPad, these features are surrounded by a distinctive and sophisticated pedagogy of auto-graded exercises. Offering immediate substantive feedback for each rejoinder, these exercises help students learn even when they select the wrong answer. These unique exercises guide students both in assessing their understanding of the sources and in drawing useful conclusions from them. In this interactive learning environment, students will enhance their ability to build arguments and to practice historical reasoning.

More specifically, a short **quiz after each primary source and Historians' Voices feature** offers students the opportunity to check their understanding of materials that often derive from quite distant times and places. Some questions focus on audience, purpose, point of view, limitations, or context, while others challenge students to draw conclusions about the source or to compare one source with another. Immediate substantive feedback for each rejoinder creates an active learning environment in which students are rewarded for reaching the correct answer through their own process of exploration.

At the end of each Thinking through Sources exercise, a **Draw Conclusions from the Evidence activity** asks students to assess whether a specific piece of evidence drawn from the sources supports or challenges a conclusion related to a **Guiding Question**. Collectively, these assignments create an active learning environment in which reading with a purpose is reinforced by immediate feedback and support. The guiding question provides a foundation for in-class activities or a summative writing assignment.

To learn more about the benefits of LaunchPad and the different versions of *Ways of the World* to package with LaunchPad, visit macmillanlearning.com/catalog.

New in This Edition

The major new element in this edition of *Thinking through Sources* is a feature we call **Historians' Voices**. At the end of each chapter, two brief statements from contemporary scholars present varying viewpoints on the larger theme addressed by the primary sources. An explicitly integrative question invites students to make use of both primary and secondary sources. In Chapter 4, for example, two religious scholars express their varying understandings of the historical Jesus. In Chapter 19, two historians of Japan focus on different factors that help to explain Japan's modern transformation during the later nineteenth century.

Beyond these Historians' Voices extracts, some entire primary source projects are new in this edition. Chapter 22, for example, now provides a range of commentary on the astonishing technological innovations of the past century, while Chapter 23 explores the experience of migration during the same century.

Acknowledgments

We extend our thanks to Senior Program Manager William Lombardo, Senior Development Editor Heidi Hood, Media Editor Tess Fletcher, Developmental Editor Stephanie Sosa, and Content Project Manager Lidia MacDonald-Carr of Bedford/St. Martin's.

> Robert Strayer, La Selva Beach, California
> Eric Nelson, Springfield, Missouri

Contents

Preface ... iii

12 Early Encounters, First Impressions ... 178

Source 12.1 Cadamosto in a West African Chiefdom: Alvise da Cadamosto: *On Meeting with Budomel*, 1455 ... 178

Source 12.2 Vasco da Gama at Calicut, India: *A Journal of the First Voyage of Vasco da Gama*, 1498 ... 181

Source 12.3 Celebrating da Gama's Arrival in Calicut, *Tapestry Depicting the Arrival of da Gama at Calicut*, Early sixteenth century ... 184

Source 12.4 Columbus in the Caribbean: Christopher Columbus: *Letter to Ferdinand and Isabella*, 1493 ... 186

Source 12.5 Columbus Engraved: *Columbus Arriving on Hispaniola*, 1594 ... 189

HISTORIANS' VOICES: Assessing Christopher Columbus and His Legacy ... 191

Voice 12.1 Zvi Dor-Ner on Christopher Columbus's Legacy, 1991 ... 191
Voice 12.2 Charles Mann on Remembering Columbus, 2012 ... 192

13 The Spanish and the Aztecs: From Encounter to Conquest (1519–1521) ... 193

Source 13.1 The Meeting of Cortés and Moctezuma: A Spanish View: Bernal Díaz: *The True History of the Conquest of New Spain*, Mid-sixteenth century ... 193

Source 13.2 The Meeting of Cortés and Moctezuma: An Aztec Account: Fray Bernardino de Sahagún: *The Florentine Codex*, Mid-sixteenth century ... 196

Source 13.3 Images of Encounter: ... 198
  Moctezuma and Cortés, 1560
  The Massacre of the Nobles, 1581

Source 13.4 Conquest and Victory: The Fall of Tenochtitlán from a Spanish Perspective: Francisco de Aguilar: *Brief Record of the Conquest of New Spain*, ca. 1560 ... 202

Source 13.5 Defeat: The Fall of Tenochtitlán from an Aztec Perspective: Fray Bernardino de Sahagún: *The Florentine Codex*, Mid-sixteenth century ... 203

v

Source 13.6	Depicting the Seizure of the Aztec Capital: *The Conquest of Tenochtitlán*, Seventeenth century	205
Source 13.7	Lamentation: The Aftermath of Defeat: *Cantares Mexicanos*, Late sixteenth century	207

HISTORIANS' VOICES: Conquest, Disease, and Demographic Collapse in the Aztec Empire — 209

Voice 13.1	Alfred Crosby on the Impact of Disease on the Conquest of the Aztec Empire, 1972	209
Voice 13.2	Philip Hoffman on the Roles of Disease, Social Disruption, and Technology in the Conquest of the Aztecs, 2015	210

14 Voices from the Slave Trade — 211

Source 14.1	The Journey to Slavery: Olaudah Equiano: *The Interesting Narrative of the Life of Olaudah Equiano*, 1789	211
Source 14.2	The Business of the Slave Trade: Thomas Phillips: *A Journal of a Voyage Made in the Hannibal of London*, 1694	214
Source 14.3	The Slave Trade and the Kingdom of Kongo: King Affonso I: *Letters to King João of Portugal*, 1526	217
Source 14.4	The Slave Trade and the Kingdom of Asante: Osei Bonsu: *Conversation with Joseph Dupuis*, 1820	219
Source 14.5	Images of the Slave Trade: *Sale of Slaves in West Africa*, 1796 *The Slave Ship* Wildfire, 1860 *Advertisement for a Slave Auction in Charleston, South Carolina*, 1769	221
Source 14.6	Data: Patterns of the Slave Trade: *Voyages and Slave Rebellion: An Aggregate Statistic* *Changing Patterns of the Slave Trade* *Percentage of Slave Arrivals by Destination*	225

HISTORIANS' VOICES: Describing the Middle Passage — 227

Voice 14.1	Lisa Lindsay on Conditions Above and Below Deck during the Middle Passage, 2008	227
Voice 14.2	Johannes Postma on Mortality during the Middle Passage, 2003	228

15 Renewal and Reform in the Early Modern World — 229

Source 15.1	Luther's Protest: Martin Luther: *Table Talk*, Early sixteenth century	229
Source 15.2	Calvinism and Catholicism: *Engraving of Calvinists Destroying Statues in a Catholic Church*, 1566	232

Source 15.3	Progress and Enlightenment: Marquis de Condorcet: *Sketch of the Progress of the Human Mind*, 1793–1794	234
Source 15.4	Art and Enlightenment: Joseph Wright: *A Philosopher Giving a Lecture on the Orrery*, ca. 1766	236
Source 15.5	The Wahhabi Perspective on Islam: Abdullah Wahhab: *History and Doctrines of the Wahhabis*, 1803	238
Source 15.6	The Poetry of Kabir: Kabir: *Poetry*, ca. late fifteenth century	240
Source 15.7	Religious Syncretism in Indian Art: *Kumbhaka (breathing exercises)*, ca. 1600	241

HISTORIANS' VOICES: Reform and Renewal in the Christian and Islamic Worlds — 245

Voice 15.1	R. W. Scribner on the Evangelical Agenda in Protestant Germany, 1986	245
Voice 15.2	Natana DeLong-Bas on the Teachings of Ibn Abd al-Wahhab, 2004	246

16 Claiming Rights — 247

Source 16.1	The French Revolution and the "Rights of Man": *The Declaration of the Rights of Man and Citizen*, 1789	247
Source 16.2	Representing the Declaration: Jean-Jacques Le Barbier: *Declaration of the Rights of Man and Citizen (Painting)*, ca. 1789	249
Source 16.3	Rights and National Independence: Simón Bolívar: *The Jamaica Letter*, 1815	251
Source 16.4	Rights and Slavery: Picturing "Reason and Nature": *All Mortals Are Equal, It Is Not Birth But Virtue That Makes the Difference*, 1793	253
Source 16.5	Rights and Slavery: An African American Voice: Frederick Douglass: *What to the Slave Is the Fourth of July?*, 1852	255
Source 16.6	The Rights of Women: Depicting a Revolutionary Woman: *Frenchwomen Freed*, 1793	257
Source 16.7	The Rights of Women: An American Feminist Voice: Elizabeth Cady Stanton: *The Solitude of Self*, 1892	259

HISTORIANS' VOICES: Origins and Echoes of the American Revolution — 261

Voice 16.1	Dorinda Outram on Enlightenment Ideas in the American Revolution, 1995	261
Voice 16.2	Carl Guarneri on British Expansion Redirected, 2007	262

17 Experiencing the Early Industrial Revolution — 263

- **Source 17.1** The Experience of an English Factory Worker: Elizabeth Bentley, Factory Worker: *Testimony*, 1831; William Harter, Mill Owner: *Testimony*, 1832 — 263
- **Source 17.2** Urban Living Conditions: Friedrich Engels: *The Condition of the Working Class in England*, 1844 — 265
- **Source 17.3** Another View of Factory Life: Eyre Crowe: *Outside the Factory*, 1874 — 267
- **Source 17.4** A Weaver's Lament: *The Weaver*, 1860s — 269
- **Source 17.5** Poetry from the Factory Floor: Ellen Johnston: *Poetry*, 1867 — 270
- **Source 17.6** Railroads and the Middle Class: *The Railroad as a Symbol of the Industrial Era*, 1870s — 274
- **Source 17.7** Inequality: John Leech: *Capital and Labour*, 1843 — 276

HISTORIANS' VOICES: Children and Family during the Industrial Revolution — 278

- **Voice 17.1** Elinor Accampo on Migration, Industry, and the Loosening of Parental Control, 1989 — 278
- **Voice 17.2** Louise Tilly and Joan Scott on Daughters and Industrial Work, 1978 — 278

18 Colonial India: Experience and Response — 280

- **Source 18.1** Images of Colonial Rule: — 280
    J. Bouvier: *A British Breakfast in India*, 1842
    Tiger Hunting in Colonial India, 1860s
    The British and Indian Princes, ca. 1820
    Blowing from a Gun, 1858
- **Source 18.2** Seeking Western Education: Ram Mohan Roy: *Letter to Lord Amherst*, 1823 — 285
- **Source 18.3** The Indian Rebellion: Prince Feroze Shah: *The Azamgarh Proclamation*, 1857 — 286
- **Source 18.4** The Credits and Debits of British Rule in India: Dadabhai Naoroji: *Speech to a London Audience*, 1871 — 288
- **Source 18.5** Gandhi on Modern Civilization: Mahatma Gandhi: *Indian Home Rule*, 1909 — 291

HISTORIANS' VOICES: The Great Indian Rebellion — 294

- **Voice 18.1** Stanley Wolpert on British Innovations and Indian Grievances, 1965 — 294
- **Voice 18.2** D. R. SarDesai on the Greased Cartridges Incident, 2008 — 295

19 Japan and the West in the Nineteenth Century 296

Source 19.1 Continuing Japanese Isolation: *An Edict of Expulsion*, 1825   296
Source 19.2 The Debate: Expel the Barbarians: Tokugawa Nariaki: *Memorial on the American Demand for a Treaty*, 1853   297
Source 19.3 The Debate: A Sumo Wrestler and a Foreigner: Yoshiku Utagawa: *Throwing a Frenchman*, 1861   298
Source 19.4 The Debate: Eastern Ethics and Western Science: Sakuma Shozan: *Reflections on My Errors*, Mid-1850s   300
Source 19.5 Westernization: Toyohara Chikanobu: *Women and Westernization*, 1887   302
Source 19.6 A Critique of Westernization: Honda Kinkichiro: *Critique of Wholesale Westernization*, 1879   304
Source 19.7 War and Empire: Chomatsu Tomisato: *Japan, Triumphant*, 1904   305
Source 19.8 Japan in the Early Twentieth Century: Okuma Shigenobu: *Fifty Years of New Japan*, 1907–1908   307

HISTORIANS' VOICES: Explaining Japan's Transformation   309

Voice 19.1 James Huffman on Japan's Historical Legacy and Its Meiji Leaders, 2010   309
Voice 19.2 James L. McClain on the International Context of Japan's Transformation, 2002   310

20 Experiencing World War I 311

Source 20.1 Experiences on the Battlefront: 311
Julian Grenfell: *Letter from a British Officer in the Trenches*, November 18, 1914
John Nash: *Painting: Over the Top*, 1918
Hugo Mueller: *Letter from a German Soldier on the Western Front*, 1915
Behari Lal: *Letter from a Soldier in the British Indian Army*, 1917

Source 20.2 On the Home Front: 315
British Propaganda Poster: *Women of Britain Say — "Go!"*, 1915
Lena Guilbert Ford: *Keep the Home Fires Burning*, 1915
Editha von Krell: *Recollections of Four Months Working in a German Munitions Factory*, 1917
Berlin Police Reports, 1915

CONTENTS

Source 20.3	In the Aftermath of the Great War: Otto Dix: *Painting: "Prague Street,"* 1920 Erich Maria Remarque: *All Quiet on the Western Front*, 1929 Nar Diouf: *A Senegalese Veteran's Oral Testimony*, 1919	319
HISTORIANS' VOICES: The Legacies of World War I		323
Voice 20.1	John Keegan on the Legacies of World War I, 2000	323
Voice 20.2	Peter Frankopan on World War I and the Decline of Empire, 2015	323

21 Articulating Independence 325

Source 21.1	Declaring Vietnam's Independence: Ho Chi Minh: *Declaration of Independence of the Democratic Republic of Vietnam*, September 2, 1945	325
Source 21.2	An Image of Vietnam's Independence: Fifty Years Later: *Fiftieth Anniversary of Vietnamese Independence*, 1995	327
Source 21.3	India's "Tryst with Destiny": Jawaharlal Nehru: *Independence Day Speech*, August 14, 1947	329
Source 21.4	Another View of India's Struggle for Independence: *Gandhi and the Fight against British Colonialism*, ca. 1930–1931	331
Source 21.5	One Africa: Kwame Nkrumah: *Africa Must Unite*, 1963	333
Source 21.6	South African "Independence": *Photograph of the First Post-Apartheid South African Election*, 1994	334
Source 21.7	Independence as Threat: Alvim Pereira: *Ten Principles*, 1961	336
HISTORIANS' VOICES: Assessing African Independence		338
Voice 21.1	Basil Davidson on the Promise of Independence, 1978	338
Voice 21.2	George Ayittey on the Betrayal of Independence, 1992	339

22 Reflections on Technology 340

Source 22.1	Postcards of the Future: A French Artist Imagines Technological Change: Maximilian Villemard: *Air Battles and Air Freight in the Future*, 1910 Maximilian Villemard: *The Horse as a Curiosity*, 1910 Maximilian Villemard: *The School of the Future*, 1910 Maximilian Villemard: *A Video-Telephone in the Year 2000*, 1910	340
Source 22.2	Depicting Communist Technology: *Soviet Industry and Technology*, 1933	345
Source 22.3	Nehru and Gandhi on Technology and Industry: Jawaharlal Nehru, *The Discovery of India*, 1946	347

Source 22.4	"Technology with a Human Face": E. F. Schumacher, *Small Is Beautiful*, 1973	349
Source 22.5	Nuclear Technology and Fears of a Nuclear Holocaust: "The Climatic Effects of Nuclear War," 1984 Jonathan Schell: *The Fate of the Earth*, 1982	351
Source 22.6	Technology and Climate Change: Piers Forster: *Reversing Climate Change . . . Technologically*, 2014 Jeffrey T. Kiehl: *Facing Climate Change*, 2016	353
HISTORIANS VOICES: Technological Change in the Twentieth Century		357
Voice 22.1	Trevor Williams on the Impacts of Technology in the First Half of the Twentieth century, 1982	357
Voice 22.2	J. R. McNeill on Challenges Overcome and Challenges Created in the Twentieth century, 2000	358

23 Experiencing International Migration 359

Source 23.1	Hana in Holland: Hana: *Adapting to Holland*, 2016	360
Source 23.2	Ayaan Hirsi Ali in Holland: Ayaan Hirsi Ali: "From a Letter to My Grandmother," 2010	361
Source 23.3	Left Behind: J. Nozipo Maraire: *Zenzele: A Letter for My Daughter*, 1996	362
Source 23.4	The Politics of Immigration: A Cautious Welcome in Europe: Angela Merkel: *Speech to the European Parliament,* October 7, 2015	363
Source 23.5	The Politics of Immigration: Resentment and Resistance in Europe: Geert Wilders: *Speech at the "Europe of Nations and Freedom" Conference*, 2017	364
Source 23.6	From the Holocaust to Israel: *Fund-Raising Poster from Israel*, 1950	366
Source 23.7	The Palestinian Diaspora: *"The Catastrophe" Memorialized*, 2015	368
HISTORIANS' VOICES: Immigration to the United States and Europe		370
Voice 23.1	Konrad Jarausch on Europe's Shift from Emigration to Immigration, 2015	370
Voice 23.2	Tobias Brinkmann and Annemarie Sammartino on American and German Attitudes toward Immigration, 2010	371

Acknowledgments 372

CHAPTER 12

Thinking through Sources

Early Encounters, First Impressions

During the fifteenth century on the remote far western end of the Eurasian landmass, the government of Portugal initiated a series of maritime explorations that had profound implications for the entire world. Spain and other European powers soon followed suit. Their voyages down the coast of West Africa, around the Cape of Good Hope to India, and across the Atlantic to the Americas, set in motion a pattern of European expansion that by 1900 had enveloped most of the peoples of the planet—with incalculable consequences that continue to echo to this day. In that epic process, the peoples of Europe and those of Africa, Asia, and the Americas encountered one another in new ways and often for the first time.

Here we examine three of these early encounters and the impressions they generated. The limitations of available sources means that we know much more about how Europeans experienced these encounters than we do about how the people they met viewed the strangers who had suddenly appeared on their shores. None of them, however, could imagine the enormously transforming, and often devastating, outcomes of these early interactions.

SOURCE 12.1 Cadamosto in a West African Chiefdom

At the beginning of the fifteenth century, no one could have predicted that the small and poor kingdom of Portugal, operating at the margins of European life, would become a major international power over the next two centuries. But building on a long seafaring tradition in Mediterranean and North African waters, the Portuguese royal family sponsored a series of maritime voyages that took the kingdom's ships down the coast of West Africa and in 1498 all the way to India. A global Portuguese empire began to take shape. It was driven by a familiar mixture of motives—to seek a sea route to the luxury goods of the East; to outflank, defeat, and if possible convert Muslims; to ally with any Christians they could find to continue the crusades; and to provide aristocratic warriors an opportunity for military glory and social promotion. These voyages produced any number of first encounters between Europeans and various African societies as the Portuguese explored the region, constructed trading posts and forts, sought gold and slaves, and made modest efforts at missionary activity.

Among the earliest and the most carefully recorded of these first encounters occurred in 1455, when the Italian trader and explorer Alvise da Cadamosto, sailing for Portugal, encountered Budomel, the ruler of a small chiefdom within the Wolof-speaking state of Cayor in what is now Senegal. The two men apparently hit it off, for Budomel soon invited Cadamosto to visit his residence, located approximately 25 miles inland. Observant and open-minded, Cadamosto later wrote an account of his month-long visit, which has become an important source for historians of fifteenth-century West Africa. In doing so, he also recorded one of the earliest encounters between European explorers and west Africans.

- How would you describe Cadamosto's posture toward Budomel and his society? What did he admire? What did he criticize? In what ways was he judging it by European standards?
- How might Budomel have written about his encounter with Cadamosto?
- What could historians learn from this account of a West African society in the mid-fifteenth century? Consider the role of slavery, the position of women, the political system, economic transactions, the penetration of Islam, and relationships with a wider world.

ALVISE DA CADAMOSTO | *On Meeting with Budomel* | 1455

This is what I was able to observe.... First, I saw clearly that, though these pass as lords, it must not be thought that they have castles or cities....The King of this realm had nothing save villages of grass huts, and Budomel was lord only of a part of this realm.... Such men are not lords by virtue of treasure or money, for they possess neither, but on account of ceremonies and the following of people they may truly be called lords; indeed they receive beyond comparison more obedience than our lords.

The dwelling of such a King is never fixed: he has a number of villages to support his wives and families. In the village where I was, ... there were from forty to fifty grass huts close together in a circle, surrounded by hedges and groves of great trees, leaving but one or two gaps as entrances. Each hut has a yard divided off by hedges.... In this place Budomel had nine wives: and likewise in his other dwellings, according to his will and pleasure. Each of these wives has five or six young negro girls in attendance upon her, and it is as lawful for the lord to sleep with these attendants as with his wives, to whom this does not appear an injury, for it is customary.

These negroes, both men and women, are exceedingly lascivious: Budomel demanded of me importunately, having been given to understand that Christians knew how to do many things, whether by chance I could give him the means by which he could satisfy many women, for which he offered me a great reward.

This Budomel always has at least two hundred negroes with him, who constantly follow him.... [T]he nearer one approaches the apartment of Budomel, the greater is the dignity of those living in these courts, up to the door of Budomel.

This Budomel exhibits haughtiness, showing himself only for an hour in the morning, and for a short while towards evening.... Such lords as he, when granting audience to anyone, display much ceremony: however considerable he who seeks audience may be, or however high born, on entering the door of Budomel's courtyard he throws himself down on his knees, bows his head to the ground, and with both hands scatters sand upon his naked shoulders and head.... No man would be bold enough to come before him to parley, unless he had stripped himself naked save for the girdle of leather they wear.

All this appears to me to proceed from the great fear and dread in which these people hold their lord, since for the most trivial misdeed he seizes and sells their wives and children. Thus it appears to me that his power exacts obedience and fear from the people by selling their wives and children. In two ways they exercise the rights of lords, and display power, that is, in maintaining a train of followers, in allowing themselves to be seen rarely, and in being greatly reverenced by their subjects....

I was permitted to enter the mosque where they pray: arriving towards evening, and having called those of his ... Arabs (those who are learned in the laws of Muhammad), he entered with some of his chief lords into a certain place. There they prayed in this fashion: standing upright and frequently looking up to the sky, they took two paces forward, and recited some words in a low voice: then bowed down very often and kissed the earth.... And thus they continued for the space of half an hour. [*Note: Cadamosto witnessed the* salat, *the ritual prayer of Islam.*]

When he had finished, he asked me what I thought of it.... Finally I told him that his faith was false, and that those who had instructed him in such things were ignorant of the truth. On many grounds I proved his faith to be false and our faith to be true and holy, thus getting the better of his learned men in argument.... The lord laughed at this, saying that our faith appeared to him to be good: for it could be no other than God that had bestowed so many good and rich gifts and so much skill and knowledge upon us.... He was much pleased with the actions of the Christians, and I am certain it would have been easy to have converted him to the Christian faith, if he had not feared to lose his power.

Each of his wives sends him a certain number of dishes of food every day. All the negro lords and men of this land follow this fashion, their women supplying them with food. They eat on the ground, like animals, without manners. No one eats with these negro rulers, save those Moors [North African Muslims] who teach the law, and one or two of their chief men.

[After learning about a snake-charming ritual], I conclude that all these negroes are great magicians; and others could bear witness to the truth of this charming of the snakes....

I decided to go to see a market.... This was held in a field, on Mondays and Fridays. Men and women came to it from the neighbourhood country within a distance of four or five miles, for those who dwelt farther off attended other markets. In this market I perceived quite clearly that these people are exceedingly poor, judging from the wares they brought for sale: that is, cotton, but not in large quantities, cotton thread and cloth, vegetables, oil and millet, wooden bowls, palm leaf mats, and all the other articles they use in their daily life. Men as well as women came to sell, some of the men offering their weapons, and others a little gold, but not in any quantity. They sold everything, item by item, by barter, and not for money, for they have none. They do not use money of any kind, but barter only, one thing for another, two for one, three for two.

These negroes, men and women, crowded to see me as though I were a marvel. It seemed to be a new experience to them to see Christians, whom they had not previously seen. They marvelled no less at my clothing than at my white skin.... Some touched my hands and limbs, and rubbed me with their spittle to discover whether my whiteness was dye or flesh. Finding that it was flesh they were astounded.

Horses are highly prized in this country of the Blacks, because they are to be had only with great difficulty, for they are brought from our Barbary [North Africa] by the Arabs and ... cannot withstand the great heat. A horse with its trappings is sold for from nine to fourteen negro slaves, according to the condition and breeding of the horse. When a chief buys a horse, he sends for his horse-charmers, who have a great fire of certain herbs lighted after their fashion, which makes a great smoke. Into this they lead the horse by the bridle, muttering their spells.... Then they fasten to its neck charms [probably containing passages from the Quran].... They believe that with these they are safer in battle.

The women of this country are very pleasant and light-hearted, ready to sing and to dance, especially the young girls. They dance, however, only at night by the light of the moon. Their dances are very different from ours.

These negroes marvelled greatly at many of our possessions, particularly at our crossbows, and, above all, our mortars. Some came to the ship, and I had them shown the firing of a mortar, the noise of which frightened them exceedingly. I then told them that a mortar would slay more than a hundred men at one shot, at which they were astonished, saying that it was an invention of the devil's....

When I had despatched my business, and had acquired a certain number of slaves, I decided to continue beyond Capo Verde, to discover new lands, and to make good my venture.

Source: G. R. Crone, *The Voyages of Cadamosto and Other Documents on Western Africa* (Farnham, UK: Hakluyt Society, 1937), 35–52. Used by permission of the Hakluyt Society.

■ ■ ■

SOURCE 12.2 Vasco da Gama at Calicut, India

On May 20, 1498, the Portuguese marked a major milestone in more than eighty years of voyaging down the west coast of Africa, when Vasco da Gama led a small fleet of four ships around the Cape of Good Hope and across the Indian Ocean, arriving at the south Indian port city of Calicut. That event represented the first direct entry of Europeans into the long-established network of Indian Ocean commerce from which they had long obtained precious spices, gemstones, and other luxury goods, albeit only through Muslim intermediaries.

Now they were directly operating within this complex, international system of exchange, much of it dominated by Muslims. Commercial desires combined with an anti-Muslim crusading sensibility to fuel Portuguese entry into what was for them another "New World."

At the time when da Gama arrived, the coast of southwestern India hosted a number of small states, cities, and kingdoms—all of which were fierce rivals for the rich profits of trade in spices, and especially in pepper. Calicut, the most prominent of these states, was ruled by Hindus, but Arab Muslims were the most strongly established trading community operating in the city. Both economic interest and religious hostility to Christians ensured that they did not look favorably on the arrival of da Gama.

This initial encounter lasted about three months, much of it recorded in an official journal of da Gama's voyage compiled by an unknown author. Excerpts from the journal provide a flavor of that encounter, obviously from a Portuguese perspective, but "between the lines" we can perhaps discern other perspectives as well.

- How might you summarize the motivations and hopes that animated da Gama's voyage? To what extent were they fulfilled?
- How did da Gama explain the difficulties he faced in Calicut? Can you think of other possible explanations for these problems?
- The ruler of Calicut at times seems quite welcoming to da Gama and at other times suspicious and hostile. How might you explain this ambivalence?

A Journal of the First Voyage of Vasco da Gama | 1498

[*The first sustained interaction between da Gama and local people occurred in an encounter with two Arab Muslims from Tunis, who could speak Spanish and Italian.*]

The first greeting that he [da Gama] received was in these words: "May the Devil take thee! What brought you hither?" They asked what he sought so far away from home, and he told them that we came in search of Christians and of spices.... [One of the Muslims] said these words: "A lucky venture.... Plenty of rubies, plenty of emeralds! You owe great thanks to God, for having brought you to a country holding such riches!" We were greatly astonished to hear his talk, for we never expected to hear our language spoken so far away from Portugal....

[*A few days later, da Gama traveled inland for an audience with the ruler of Calicut. The journal notes that his party observed "many large ships," huge crowds of curious people, and an elaborate "church," most likely a Hindu temple. The Portuguese initially mistook Hindus for Christians, perhaps because they had heard rumors of a small Christian community, allegedly derived from the early missionary work of Saint Thomas, that did in fact live in southern India.*]

On landing, the captain-major [da Gama] was received by [an official], with whom were many men, armed and unarmed. The reception was friendly, as if the people were pleased to see us, though at first appearances looked threatening, for they carried naked swords in their hands. A palanquin [a covered chair carried on poles by four men] was provided for the captain-major, such as is used by men of distinction in that country....

Source 12.2 Vasco da Gama at Calicut, India

The king was in a small court, reclining upon a couch covered with a cloth of green velvet, above which was a good mattress, and upon this again a sheet of cotton stuff, very white and fine.... The king ... asked the captain-major what he wanted. And the captain-major told him he was the ambassador of a King of Portugal, who was Lord of many countries and the possessor of great wealth of every description, exceeding that of any king of these parts; that for a period of sixty years his ancestors had annually sent out vessels to make discoveries in the direction of India, as they knew that there were Christian kings there like themselves. This, he said, was the reason which induced them to order this country to be discovered, not because they sought for gold or silver, for of this they had such abundance that they needed not what was to be found in this country.

[*This visit seemed to go well, but the next day, when da Gama was preparing gifts for the king, several officials came to inspect the gifts.*]

They came, and when they saw the present they laughed at it, saying that it was not a thing to offer to a king, that the poorest merchant from Mecca, or any other part of India, gave more, and that if he wanted to make a present it should be in gold, as the king would not accept such things....

[*The following day, the king kept da Gama waiting for four hours and then belittled Portuguese goods.*]

The king then said that he [da Gama] had told him that he came from a very rich kingdom, and yet had brought him nothing.... The king then asked what it was he had come to discover: stones [gems] or men? If he came to discover men, as he said, why had he brought nothing? The king then asked what kind of merchandise was to be found in his country. The captain-major said there was much corn, cloth, iron, bronze, and many other things. The king asked whether he had any merchandise with him. The captain-major replied that he had a little of each sort, as samples, and that if permitted to return to the ships he would order it to be landed.... The king said no! He might take all his people with him, securely moor his ships, land his merchandise, and sell it to the best advantage [in the private market].... [But even in this private trading], we did not, however, effect these sales at the prices hoped for when we arrived..., for a very fine shirt which in Portugal fetches 300 reis, was worth here only 30 reis. And just as we sold shirts cheaply so we sold other things, in order to take some things away from this country, if only for samples. Those who visited the city bought there cloves, cinnamon, and precious stones.

[*The Portuguese had little doubt as to the source of this apparent hostility.*]

We also felt grieved that a Christian [actually a Hindu] king, to whom we had given of ours, should do us such an ill turn. At the same time we did not hold him as culpable as he seemed to be, for we were well aware that the Moors [Muslims] of the place, who were merchants from Mecca and elsewhere, could ill digest us. They had told the king that we were thieves, and that if once we navigated to his country, no more ships from Mecca, nor ... any other part, would visit him. They added that he would derive no profit from this [trade with Portugal] as we had nothing to give, but would rather take away, and that thus his country would be ruined. They, moreover, offered rich bribes to the king to capture and kill us, so that we should not return to Portugal.

[*What followed was a series of controversies about the unloading of da Gama's ships, the mutual seizure of hostages, the payment required before leaving Calicut, and more. Several minor naval engagements showed da Gama that even if his goods were not so appealing, his on-board artillery far surpassed anything available locally. When he arrived home, da Gama found a very pleased king of Portugal, who wrote with pleasure to the monarchs of Spain about da Gama's achievement.*]

[W]e learn that they did reach and discover India and other kingdoms and lordships bordering upon it; that they entered and navigated its sea, finding large cities, large edifices and rivers, and great populations, among whom is carried on all the trade in spices and precious stones, which are forwarded in ships ... to Mecca, and thence to Cairo, whence they are dispersed throughout the world. Of these [spices, etc.] they have brought a quantity, including cinnamon, cloves, ginger, nutmeg, and pepper as well as other kinds, together with the boughs and leaves of the same; also many fine stones of all sorts, such as rubies and others. And they also came to a country in which there are mines of gold. . . .

[W]hat we have learnt concerning the Christian people whom these explorers reached [is] that it will be possible, notwithstanding that they are not as yet strong in the faith or possessed of a thorough knowledge of it, to do much in the service of God and the exaltation of the Holy Faith, once they shall have been converted and fully fortified (confirmed) in it. And when they shall have thus been fortified in the faith there will be an opportunity for destroying the Moors of those parts. Moreover we hope, with the help of God that the great trade which now enriches the Moors of those parts ... shall, in consequence of our regulations, be diverted to the natives and ships of our own kingdom.

Source: E. G. Ravenstein, trans., *A Journal of the First Voyage of Vasco da Gama, 1497–1499* (London, UK: Hakluyt Society, 1898), https://openlibrary.org/books/OL6912713M/A_journal_of_the_first_voyage_of_Vasco_da_Gama_1497-1499.

■ ■ ■

SOURCE 12.3 Celebrating da Gama's Arrival in Calicut ▶

The extraordinary feats of navigation accomplished by Portuguese sailors gave their kingdom a new prominence on the European stage. Portuguese rulers publicized their accomplishments by displaying the exotic products from the East to a European public that was hungry for information about distant lands. Perhaps no single item brought back from India created a greater stir than the live rhinoceros that arrived in 1515. Crowds flocked in amazement to view a beast that had not been seen in Europe for more than 1,000 years and was known only through an account by the ancient Roman scholar Pliny.

The most systematic effort to associate the Portuguese monarchy with the opening of the East took the form of a twenty-six-panel series of tapestries commemorating da Gama's 1498 voyage to Calicut. Commissioned by King Manuel in 1504, these expensive woven works of art were intended to hang in the great hall of the royal palace where official business was conducted. The scenes incorporate a wide variety of exotica, including dark-skinned people dressed in elaborate, if often inaccurate, costumes and

Source 12.3 Celebrating da Gama's Arrival in Calicut

rare or mythical animals. Woven in the Low Countries (modern-day Belgium and the Netherlands) by artisans who had never seen their subjects, the tapestries feature many scenes containing fanciful elements, while other scenes draw on more familiar topics, including classical accounts of Alexander the Great's conquests in the East. Nevertheless, these tapestries proved influential in shaping European conceptions of India, as the same artisans produced many copies and variations on these panels for other European elites fascinated by the Portuguese discoveries.

The panel reproduced here depicts the arrival of da Gama at Calicut. This scene includes accurate renderings of Portuguese vessels anchored in the port; in contrast, the buildings and town gates of Calicut are more fanciful, constructed out of distinctly European — rather than Indian — architectural elements. In the foreground to the left, da Gama presents a letter from his monarch to the ruler of Calicut. In the center of the scene, the Portuguese are in the process of unloading from their vessels exotic animals, including ostriches, wild cats, and even a unicorn. To the right, a great crowd dressed in garments reminiscent of European styles gathers to view these curiosities, very much like the Europeans who gathered to view the Indian rhinoceros unloaded in Lisbon harbor in 1515.

- In what ways does this image reflect the written account in Source 12.2? In what ways does it differ?
- How does this tapestry serve the purposes of King Manuel of Portugal, who commissioned it?
- What can you discern about European knowledge of India from this image?

Tapestry Depicting the Arrival of da Gama at Calicut | **Early sixteenth century**

(Alfredo Dagli Orti / Art Resource, NY)

SOURCE 12.4 Columbus in the Caribbean

Even apart from its horrific long-term consequences, Columbus's arrival in the Caribbean region in October 1492 retains a distinctive significance. Europeans were at least aware of Asian and African societies and had experienced some interactions, often indirect, with them. In contrast, except for the brief and unremembered incursions of the Vikings, no one from the Afro-Eurasian hemisphere had set foot in the Americas since the last migrants from Siberia had crossed the Bering Strait perhaps 15,000 years earlier. Clearly, the arrival of Columbus in this region was an extraordinary encounter.

Columbus's voyage, sponsored by the monarchs of Spain, found dense settlements of an agricultural people, known as the Taino, on the islands now called Cuba, Jamaica, Puerto Rico, and Hispaniola (modern Haiti and Dominican Republic). Organized into substantial village communities governed by a hierarchy of chiefs (*cacique*), Taino society featured modest class distinctions. An elite group of chiefs, warriors, artists, and religious specialists enjoyed a higher status than did commoners, who worked the fields, fished, and hunted.

On the voyage back to Europe in early 1493, Columbus penned a letter to Lord Raphael Sanchez, a prominent official in the government of his patrons, King Ferdinand and Queen Isabella of Spain. In it he summarized his initial impressions and his hopes for the future for both Sanchez and his royal patrons.

- What can you infer from the letter about Columbus's expectations for his journey and what he wanted from his Spanish patrons?
- Scholars have noted a number of omissions from Columbus's letter: that one of his ships had been lost; that some of his men had abused local women; that he had had at least one violent encounter with local people; that his ability to communicate with the Taino was minimal. Why might he have omitted these incidents?
- How might you summarize Columbus's posture toward the people he met on this first voyage? Can you see ways in which he was trying to "spin" his description of these people? Did he have preconceptions that may have colored his understanding of them?

CHRISTOPHER COLUMBUS | *Letter to Ferdinand and Isabella* | 1493

Thirty-three days after my departure from Cadiz [in Spain] I reached the Indian [Caribbean] sea, where I discovered many islands, thickly peopled, of which I took possession without resistance in the name of our most illustrious Monarch, by public proclamation and with unfurled banners ...; to each of these I also gave a name, ordering that one should be called Santa Maria de la Concepcion, another Fernandina, the third Isabella, the fourth Juana, and so with all the rest respectively.

As soon as we arrived at Juana, I proceeded along its coast a short distance.... I could not suppose it to be an island, but the continental province of Cathay [China]. Seeing, however, no towns or populous places on the sea coast, but only a few detached houses and cottages, with whose inhabitants I was unable to communicate, because they fled as soon as they saw us, I went further on, thinking that in my progress I should certainly find some city or village.... I afterwards dispatched two of our men to ascertain whether there were a king or any cities in that province. These men reconnoitered the country for three days, and found a most numerous population, and great numbers of houses, though small, and built without any regard to order....

The inhabitants of both sexes in this island, and in all the others which I have seen, go always naked as they were born, with the exception of some of the women, who use the covering of a leaf, or small bough, or an apron of cotton.... None of them ... are possessed of any iron, neither have they weapons, being unacquainted with, and indeed incompetent to use them, not from any deformity of body (for they are well-formed), but because they are timid and full of fear.... This timidity did not arise from any loss or injury that they had received from us; for, on the contrary, I gave to all I approached whatever articles I had about me, such as cloth and many other things, taking nothing of theirs in return.... As soon however as they see that they are safe, and have laid aside all fear, they are very simple and honest, and exceedingly liberal with all they have; none of them refusing anything he may possess when he is asked for it, but on the contrary inviting us to ask them. They exhibit great love towards all others in preference to themselves: they also give objects of great value for trifles....

Thus they bartered, like idiots, cotton and gold for fragments of bows, glasses, bottles, and jars; which I forbade as being unjust, and myself gave them many beautiful and acceptable articles which I had brought with me, taking nothing from them in return; I did this in order that I might the more easily conciliate them, that they might be led to become Christians, and be inclined to entertain a regard for the King and Queen, our Princes, and all Spaniards, and that I might induce them to take an interest in seeking out, and collecting, and delivering to us such things as they possessed in abundance, but which we greatly needed.

They practice no kind of idolatry, but have a firm belief that all strength and power, and indeed all good things, are in heaven, and that I had descended from thence with these ships and sailors, and under this impression was I received after they had thrown aside their fears. Nor are they slow or stupid, but of very clear understanding; and those men who have crossed to the neighbouring islands give an admirable description of everything they observed; but they never saw any people clothed, nor any ships like ours.

On my arrival at that sea, I had taken some Indians by force from the first island that I came to, in order that they might learn our language, and communicate to us what they knew respecting the country; which plan succeeded excellently, and was a great advantage to us, for in a short time, either by gestures and signs, or by words, we were enabled to understand each other.

Each of these islands has a great number of canoes, built of solid wood, narrow.... These canoes are of various sizes, but the greater number are constructed with eighteen banks of oars, and with these they cross to the other islands.... I took possession of all these islands in the name of our invincible King, yet there was one large town in Espanola of which especially I took possession, situated ... in every way convenient for the purposes of gain and commerce.

To this town I gave the name of Navidad del Senor, and ordered a fortress to be built there, I also ... engaged the favor and friendship of the King of the island ..., for these people are so amiable and friendly that even the King took a pride in calling me his brother.... [T]hose who hold the said fortress, can easily keep the whole island in check, without any pressing danger to themselves....

As far as I have learned, every man throughout these islands is united to but one wife, with the exception of the kings and princes, who are allowed to have twenty: the women seem to work more than the men. I could not clearly understand whether the people possess any private property, for I observed that one man had the charge of distributing various things to the rest, but especially meat and provisions and the like....

[I]n a certain island called Charis ... dwell a people who are considered by the neighbouring islanders as most ferocious: and these feed upon human flesh. The same people have many kinds of canoes, in which they cross to all the surrounding islands and rob and plunder wherever they can.... These are the men who form unions with certain women, who dwell alone in the island Matenin, which lies next to Espanola on the side towards India; these latter [women] employ themselves in no labour suitable to their own sex, for they use bows and javelins as I have already described their paramours as doing....

I promise, that with a little assistance afforded me by our most invincible sovereigns, I will procure them as much gold as they need, as great a quantity of spices, of cotton, and of mastic ..., and as many men [slaves] for the service of the navy as their Majesties may require. I promise also rhubarb and other sorts of drugs.... Although all I have related may appear to be wonderful and unheard of, yet the results of my voyage would have been more astonishing if I had had at my disposal such ships as I required. But these great and marvellous results are not to be attributed to any merit of mine, but to the holy Christian faith, and to the piety and religion of our Sovereigns.... Thus it has happened to me in the present instance, who have accomplished a task to which the powers of mortal men had never hitherto attained.

Source: Christopher Columbus, letter to Lord Raphael Sanchez (treasurer to Ferdinand and Isabella), 14 March 1493, The Internet Modern History Sourcebook, Fordham University, accessed June 1, 2015, http://www2.fiu.edu/~harveyb/colum.html.

■ ■ ■

SOURCE 12.5 Columbus Engraved

Precisely one century after Columbus first arrived in the Americas, the Flemish artist Theodore de Bry depicted his landing in an engraving that has become an iconic image of that event. While some elements of the engraving are accurate, including the ships, the raising of a cross, and the dress of Columbus's men, others are fanciful, like the jewelry, ornate vessels, and chests, all made of gold and in European Renaissance styles, that the Taino offer Columbus.

- How does de Bry portray Columbus's assertion of authority in a land so far from his own?
- How does the artist differentiate between the Europeans and the Taino?
- How would you summarize the "message" of this image?

Columbus Arriving on Hispaniola | 1594

(bpk, Bildagentur/Art Resource, NY)

DOING HISTORY

1. **Comparing first encounters:** How would you compare the first impressions that these three encounters generated for the Europeans involved? What surprised them? What offended their sensibilities? How did they describe or portray cultural differences? How open to these differences did they seem to be?

2. **Establishing political ties:** What political relationship with the host society did each of the European explorers have? What were they seeking from those societies? To what extent did these factors shape their posture toward those they were meeting for the first time?

3. **Reading between the lines:** Although these sources all derive from Europeans, what might we infer, reading between the lines, about how the West African, Indian, and Native American figures may have understood these encounters?

4. **Foreshadowing future encounters:** In what ways did these encounters bear the seeds of future developments, although unknown to everyone at the time?

HISTORIANS' VOICES

Assessing Christopher Columbus and His Legacy

Christopher Columbus's first voyage to the Americas was a crucial moment in the creation of the globally connected world in which we live today. But how Columbus and the legacy of his "discovery" should be understood has sparked considerable debate among modern historians. The two selections that follow summarize and assess contrasting current interpretations. In Voice 12.1, Zvi Dor-Ner, who produced a PBS television series on Columbus at the time of the 500th anniversary of his first voyage in 1992, examines several contrasting assessments of Columbus's legacy. In Voice 12.2, Charles Mann explores how Christopher Columbus has been memorialized and judged through time.

- What do these two assessments of Columbus share? How do they differ?

- In Voice 12.2, how does Mann grapple with the problem of assessing historical figures using modern criteria?

- **Integrating primary and secondary sources:** How do these two Voices shape your interpretation of Sources 12.4 and 12.5?

VOICE 12.1

Zvi Dor-Ner on Christopher Columbus's Legacy | 1991

Christopher Columbus changed the world. He took his world . . . and set it on its way to becoming the place that we inhabit today. Though his acts were forceful and deliberate, their results were unintended. . . . And yet the forces he set in motion wrought a profound transformation of the European sphere into which he had been born, of the Americas and Africa, and of the Asia whose riches he sought by sailing west. . . . Columbus's bold venture likewise heralded a new emphasis on the empirical method in global exploration, and—despite the Discoverer's own devout Catholicism—made final the separation of religion from science and cosmography. . . .

Columbus has become a symbol, a powerful mythic figure: the very model for the explorer. His first voyage is still the world's most powerful metaphor of discovery, and of the courage and conviction that discovery requires. His very name signifies the essence of qualities that we revere—risk taking, entrepreneurship, perseverance—and so we name cities, countries, and space vehicles after him. . . .

To some, however, especially in Latin America, Columbus represents the double-edged nature of much of human achievement. His legacy is mixed, for his deeds had a price. Because of the European discovery of the New World, entire peoples were decimated in the Americas as alien diseases, culture shock, and sheer rapacity took their toll. Others were subjugated and enslaved. To them Columbus's acts amount not to discovery but to invasion: He is the archetype of the alien conqueror, the oppressor. And part of the Old World was drawn against its will into the global exchange, as millions of Africans were brought to the discovered lands to toil as slaves.

Source: Zvi Dor-Ner, *Columbus and the Age of Discovery* (New York, NY: William Morrow and Company, 1991), 1–2.

VOICE 12.2

Charles Mann on Remembering Columbus | 2012

Like a medieval church, the [Columbus] lighthouse [in the Dominican Republic] is laid out as a cross.... At the central intersection, inside a crystal security box, is an ornate golden sarcophagus said to contain the admiral's bones.... Beyond the sarcophagus are a series of exhibits from many nations ... most focused on the hemisphere's original inhabitants, depicting them as the passive or even grateful recipients of European largesse, cultural and technological.

Unsurprisingly, native people rarely endorse this view of their history, and Colón's [Columbus's] part in it. An army of activists and scholars has bombarded the public with condemnations of the man and his works. They have called him brutal (he was, by today's standards) and racist (he wasn't strictly speaking—modern concepts of race had not yet been invented); incompetent as an administrator (he was) and as a seaman (he wasn't); a religious fanatic (he surely was, from a secular point of view); and a greedy monomaniac (a charge, the admiral's supporters would say, that could be leveled against all ambitious souls). Colón, his detractors charge, never understood what he had found.

How different it was in 1852, when Antonio del Monte y Tejada, a celebrated Dominican *literateur*, closed the first of four volumes of his history of Santo Domingo by extoling Colón's "great, generous, memorable and eternal" career. The admiral's every action "breathes greatness and elevation," del Monte y Tejada wrote. Do not "all nations ... owe him eternal gratitude"?

Source: Charles C. Mann, *1493: Uncovering the New World Columbus Created* (New York, NY: Vintage, 2012), 15–16.

CHAPTER 13

Thinking through Sources

The Spanish and the Aztecs: From Encounter to Conquest (1519–1521)

Among the sagas of early modern empire building, few have been more dramatic, more tragic, or better documented than the Spanish conquest of the Aztec Empire during the early sixteenth century. In recounting this story, historians are fortunate in having considerable evidence from both the Spanish and the Aztec sides of the encounter.

SOURCE 13.1 The Meeting of Cortés and Moctezuma: A Spanish View

In February 1519, twenty-seven years after Columbus first claimed the New World for Spain, Hernán Cortés, accompanied by some 350 Spanish soldiers, set off from Cuba with a fleet of eleven ships. He stopped at several places along the Gulf of Mexico before proceeding to march inland toward Tenochtitlán (te-nawch-tee-TLAHN), the capital of the Aztec Empire. Along the way, Cortés learned something about the fabulous wealth of this empire and about the fragility of its political structure. He also received various emissaries from the Aztec ruler Moctezuma, bearing rich gifts and warm greetings. Through a combination of force and astute diplomacy, Cortés was able to negotiate alliances with a number of the Aztecs' restive subject peoples and with the Aztecs' many rivals or enemies, especially the Tlaxcalans. With his modest forces thus greatly reinforced, Cortés arrived on November 8, 1519, in Tenochtitlán, where his famous meeting with Moctezuma took place. Bernal Díaz, a Spanish soldier who took part in the expedition, recounted his recollection of this encounter some thirty years later.

- How would you describe the Spanish posture toward the Aztecs? What amazed the Spaniards, and what appalled them?
- Does the account by Díaz confirm or challenge the controversial notion that the Aztecs viewed the Spanish as divine beings of some kind?
- What differences in religious understanding emerged in the conversations between the two leaders? Were there any areas of agreement?

BERNAL DÍAZ | *The True History of the Conquest of New Spain* | Mid-sixteenth century

We proceeded along the Causeway which ... runs straight to the City of Mexico. It was so crowded with people that there was hardly room for them all. They had never before seen horses or men such as we are.

Gazing on such wonderful sights, we did not know what to say, ... for on one side, on the land, there were great cities, and in the lake ever so many more, and the lake itself was crowded with canoes, and in the Causeway were many bridges at intervals, and in front of us stood the great City of Mexico, and we,—we did not even number four hundred soldiers!

When we arrived, ... many more chieftains and Caciques approached clad in very rich mantles. The Great Moctezuma had sent these great Caciques in advance to receive us, and when they came before Cortés they bade us welcome in their language, and as a sign of peace, they touched their hands against the ground, and kissed the ground with the hand.

When we arrived near to Mexico, the Great Moctezuma got down from his litter, and those great Caciques supported him with their arms beneath a marvellously rich canopy of green coloured feathers with much gold and silver embroidery and with pearls suspended from a sort of bordering, which was wonderful to look at. Besides these four Chieftains, there were four other great Caciques, who supported the canopy over their heads, and many other Lords who walked before the Great Moctezuma, sweeping the ground where he would tread and spreading cloths on it, so that he should not tread on the earth. Not one of these chieftains dared even to think of looking him in the face, but kept their eyes lowered with great reverence, except those four relations, his nephews, who supported him with their arms.

When Cortés was told that the Great Moctezuma was approaching, he dismounted from his horse, and when he was near Moctezuma, they simultaneously paid great reverence to one another. Moctezuma bade him welcome, and our Cortés replied through Doña Marina wishing him very good health. And it seems to me that Cortés, through Doña Marina, offered him his right hand, and Moctezuma did not wish to take it, but he did give his hand to Cortés and Cortés brought out a necklace which he had ready at hand, made of glass stones, ... and he placed it round the neck of the Great Moctezuma and when he had so placed it he was going to embrace him, and those great Princes who accompanied Moctezuma held back Cortés by the arm so that he should not embrace him, for they considered it an indignity.

Then Cortés through the mouth of Doña Marina told him that now his heart rejoiced at having seen such a great Prince, and that he took it as a great honour that he had come in person to meet him and had frequently shown him such favour. Then Moctezuma spoke other words of politeness to him, and told two of his nephews ... to go with us and show us to our quarters. ... They took us to lodge in some large houses, where there were apartments for all of us. ... They took us to lodge in that house,

Source 13.1 The Meeting of Cortés and Moctezuma: A Spanish View

because they called us Teules [the Spanish took this word to mean "gods"], and took us for such, so that we should be with the Idols or Teules which were kept there....

[*After a "sumptuous dinner" and more "polite speech," everyone retired for the night. The next day Cortés and Moctezuma met again and exchanged views on religion. After Cortés outlined the basics of the Christian faith, he invited Moctezuma to embrace it.*]

[Cortés told] how such a brother as our great Emperor, grieving for the perdition of so many souls, such as those which their idols were leading to Hell, where they burn in living flames, had sent us, so that after what he [Moctezuma] had now heard he would put a stop to it and they would no longer adore these Idols or sacrifice Indian men and women to them, for we were all brethren, nor should they commit sodomy or thefts.... At present we merely came to give them due warning, and so he prayed him to do what he was asked and carry it into effect.

Moctezuma replied—"Señor Malinche, I have understood your words and arguments very well before now, from what you said to my servants....We have not made any answer to it because here throughout all time we have worshipped our own gods, and thought they were good, as no doubt yours are, so do not trouble to speak to us any more about them at present. Regarding the creation of the world, we have held the same belief for ages past, and for this reason we take it for certain that you are those whom our ancestors predicted would come from the direction of the sunrise. As for your great King, I feel that I am indebted to him, and I will give him of what I possess...."

And Moctezuma said, laughing, for he was very merry in his princely way of speaking: "Malinche, I know very well that these people of Tlaxcala with whom you are such good friends have told you that I am a sort of God or Teul, and that everything in my houses is made of gold and silver and precious stones, I know well enough that you are wise and did not believe it but took it as a joke. Behold now, Señor Malinche, my body is of flesh and bone like yours, my houses and palaces of stone and wood and lime; that I am a great king and inherit the riches of my ancestors is true, but not all the nonsense and lies that they have told you about me, although of course you treated it as a joke, as I did your thunder and lightning."

[*A few days later Cortés asked Moctezuma to "show us your gods and Teules." On a visit to the main temple, Díaz described the many grotesquely carved "idols" and recalled evidence of recent human sacrifices.*]

They had offered to this Idol five hearts from that day's sacrifices.... Everything was covered with blood, both walls and altar, and the stench was such that we could hardly wait the moment to get out of it.

Our Captain said to Moctezuma through our interpreter, half laughing: "Señor Moctezuma, I do not understand how such a great Prince and wise man as you are has not come to the conclusion, in your mind, that these idols of yours are not gods, but evil things that are called devils, and so that you may know it and all your priests may see it clearly, do me the favour to approve of my placing a cross ... [and] divide off a space where we can set up an image of Our Lady."

Moctezuma replied half angrily (and the two priests who were with him showed great annoyance), and said: "Señor Malinche, if I had known that you would have said such defamatory things I would not have shown you my gods, we consider them to be very good, for they give us health and rains and good seed times and seasons and as many victories as we desire, and we are obliged to worship them and make sacrifices, and I pray you not to say another word to their dishonour."

When our Captain heard that and noted the angry looks he did not refer again to the subject, but said with a cheerful manner: "It is time for your Excellency and for us to return." And Moctezuma replied that it was well, but that he had to pray and offer certain sacrifices on account of the great tatacul, that is to say sin, which he had committed in allowing us to ascend his great Cue [temple], and being the cause of our being permitted to see his gods, and of our dishonouring them by speaking evil of them, so that before he left he must pray and worship.

Then Cortés said "I ask your pardon if it be so. . . ." After our Captain and all of us were tired of walking about and seeing such a diversity of Idols and their sacrifices, we returned to our quarters.

Source: Bernal Díaz, *The True History of the Conquest of New Spain* (London, UK: Hakluyt Society, 1908). Excerpt taken from Bedford series book Stuart B. Schwartz, *Victors and Vanquished* (Boston, MA: Bedford/St. Martin's, 2000), 133–55.

■ ■ ■

SOURCE 13.2 The Meeting of Cortés and Moctezuma: An Aztec Account

Another account of this initial encounter comes from *The Florentine Codex*, a compilation of text and images collected under the leadership of Fray Bernardino de Sahagún, a Franciscan missionary who believed that an understanding of Aztec culture was essential to the task of conversion. Because Sahagún relied on Aztec informants and artists, many scholars believe that *The Florentine Codex* and other codices represent indigenous understandings of the conquest. Even so, these sources require a critical reading, because they date from several decades after the events they describe. At that point, many contributors to the codices had been influenced by the Christian and European culture of their missionary mentors, and they were writing or painting in a society thoroughly dominated by Spanish colonial rule. Furthermore, the codices reflect the ethnic and regional diversity of Mesoamerica rather than a single Aztec perspective. Despite such limitations, these codices represent a unique window into Mesoamerican understandings of the conquest.

- How does this account differ from that of Díaz (Source 13.1)? In what ways does it overlap with or supplement Díaz's understanding?
- What, in particular, did the author of this report notice about the Spanish?
- This text and that of Díaz were composed some thirty years or so after the events they describe. How might this fact affect our understanding of these documents?

Source 13.2 The Meeting of Cortés and Moctezuma: An Aztec Account

FRAY BERNARDINO DE SAHAGÚN | *The Florentine Codex* | Mid-sixteenth century

Then they [the Spaniards] set out in this direction, about to enter Mexico [the city of Tenochtitlán] here. Then they all dressed and equipped themselves for war. They girded themselves, tying their battle gear lightly on themselves and then on their horses. Then they arranged themselves in rows, files, ranks. . . . They kept turning about as they went, facing people, looking this way and that, looking sideways, gazing everywhere between the houses, examining things, looking up at the roofs.

By himself came marching ahead, all alone, the one who bore the standard [flag] on his shoulder. . . . Following him came those with iron swords. Their iron swords came bare and gleaming.

The second contingent and file were horses carrying people, each with his cotton cuirass [armor], his leather shield, his iron lance, and his iron sword hanging down from the horse's neck. They came with bells on, jingling or rattling. The deer [horses] neighed, there was much neighing. . . . Their hooves made holes, they dug holes in the ground wherever they placed them. . . .

The third file were those with iron crossbows. As they came, the iron crossbows lay in their arms. They came along testing them out, brandishing them, (aiming them). . . .

The fourth file were likewise [horsemen].

The fifth group were those with harquebuses [crude guns]. . . . And when they went into the great palace, the residence of the ruler, they repeatedly shot off their harquebuses. They exploded, sputtered, discharged, thundered. Smoke spread. . . . The fetid smell made people dizzy and faint.

And last, bringing up the rear, went the war leader, thought to be the ruler and director in battle. . . . Gathered and massed about him, going at his side, accompanying him, enclosing him were his warriors, the strong and valiant ones of the altepetl [a region or city].

Then all those from the various altepetl on the other side of the mountains, the Tlaxcalans, the people of Tliliuhquitepec, of Huexotzinco, came following behind. They came outfitted for war. . . . Some bore burdens and provisions on their backs. . . . Some dragged the large cannons, which went resting on wooden wheels, making a clamor as they came.

And when they [the Spaniards] had come as far as Xoloco, when they had stopped there, Moctezuma dressed and prepared himself for a meeting, along with other great rulers and high nobles, his rulers and nobles. Then they went to the meeting. On gourd bases they set out different precious flowers. . . . And they carried golden necklaces, necklaces with pendants, wide necklaces.

And when Moctezuma went out to meet them, thereupon he gave various things to the war leader [Cortés]; he gave him flowers, he put necklaces on him, he put flower necklaces on him, he girded him with flowers, he put flower wreaths on his head. Then he laid before him the golden necklaces, all the different things for greeting people.

Then [Cortés] said in reply to Moctezuma "Is it not you? Is it not you then? Moctezuma?"

Moctezuma said, "Yes, it is me." Thereupon he stood up straight, he stood up with their faces meeting. He bowed down deeply to him. He stretched as far as he could, standing stiffly. Addressing him, he said to him:

"O our lord, be doubly welcomed on your arrival in this land; you have come to satisfy your curiosity about your altepetl of Mexico, you have come to sit on your seat of authority, which I have kept a while for you.... For a time I have been concerned, looking toward the mysterious place from which you have come, among clouds and mist. It is so that the [former] rulers on departing said that you would come in order to acquaint yourself with your altepetl and sit upon your seat of authority. And now it has come true, you have come."

[*Then Cortés responded:*]

"Let Moctezuma be at ease, let him not be afraid, for we greatly esteem him. Now we are truly satisfied to see him in person and hear him, for until now we have greatly desired to see him and look upon his face. Well, now we have seen him, we have come to his homeland of Mexico. Bit by bit he will hear what we have to say."

Thereupon [the Spaniards] took [Moctezuma] by the hand. They came along with him, stroking his hair to show their good feeling. And the Spaniards looked at him, each of them giving him a close look. They would start along walking, then mount, then dismount again in order to see him.

Source: James Lockhart, ed. and trans., *We People Here: Nahuatl Accounts of the Conquest of Mexico* (Los Angeles, CA: University of California Press, 1993), 108–18. Copyright 1993 by the Regents of the University of California. Reprinted by permission.

■ ■ ■

SOURCE 13.3 Images of Encounter ▶

Source 13.3A presents another Mesoamerican view of the first epic encounter between Cortés and Moctezuma, drawn from the Lienzo de Tlaxcala, a series of paintings completed by 1560. Created by Tlaxcalan artists, who had absorbed some elements of European styles, these paintings highlighted the role of the Tlaxcalan people as valued allies of the Spanish.

- How does this painting present the relationship between Cortés and Moctezuma? Are they meeting as equals, as enemies, as allies, or as ruler and subject? Notice that both sit on European-style chairs, which had come to suggest authority in the decades following Spanish conquest. Is it significant that Cortés is seated on a platform?

Source 13.3 Images of Encounter

- Does this image support or challenge the perception that the Aztecs viewed the Spanish newcomers, at least initially, in religious terms as gods?
- What does this painting add to the written accounts of this initial encounter in Sources 13.1 and 13.2?

SOURCE 13.3A
Moctezuma and Cortés | 1560

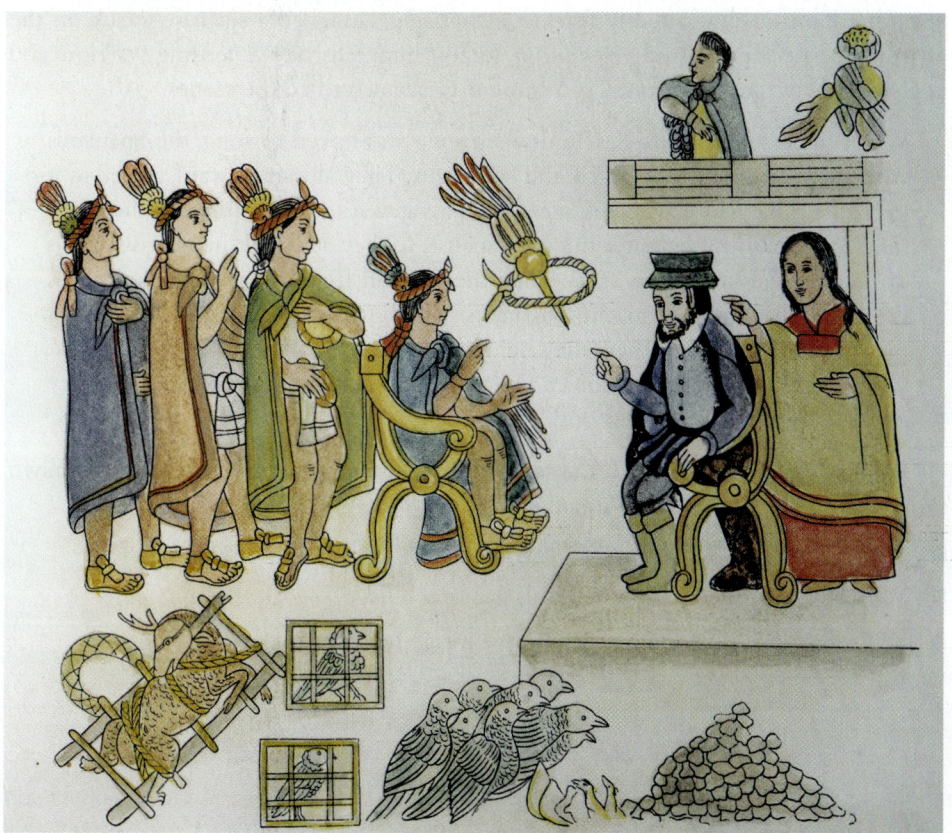

(Granger, NYC–All rights reserved.)

Whatever the character of their initial meeting, the relationship of the Spanish and Aztecs soon deteriorated amid mutual suspicion. Within a week, Cortés had seized Moctezuma, holding him under a kind of house arrest in his own palaces. For reasons not entirely clear, this hostile act did not immediately trigger a violent Aztec response. Perhaps Aztec authorities were concerned for the life of their ruler, or possibly their factional divisions inhibited coordinated resistance.

But in May 1520, while Cortés was temporarily away at the coast, an incident occurred that set in motion the most violent phase of the encounter. During a religious ceremony in honor of Huitzilopochtli, the Aztec patron deity of Tenochtitlán, the local Spanish commander, apparently fearing an uprising, launched a surprise attack on the unarmed participants in the celebration, killing hundreds of the leading warriors and nobles. An Aztec account from *The Florentine Codex* described the scene:

> When the dance was loveliest and when song was linked to song, the Spaniards were seized with an urge to kill the celebrants. They all ran forward, armed as if for battle. They closed the entrances and passageways ... then [they] rushed into the Sacred Patio to slaughter the inhabitants.... They attacked the man who was drumming and cut off his arms. Then they cut off his head, and it rolled across the floor. They attacked all the celebrants stabbing them, spearing them, striking them with swords.... Others they beheaded ... or split their heads to pieces.... The blood of the warriors flowed like water and gathered into pools.... [T]hey invaded every room, hunting and killing."[1]

Source 13.3B shows a vivid Aztec depiction of this "massacre of the nobles," drawn from the *Codex Duran*, first published in 1581.

- What elements of the preceding description are reflected in this painting?
- What image of the Spanish does this painting reflect?
- What do the drums in the center of the image represent?

SOURCE 13.3B
The Massacre of the Nobles | 1581

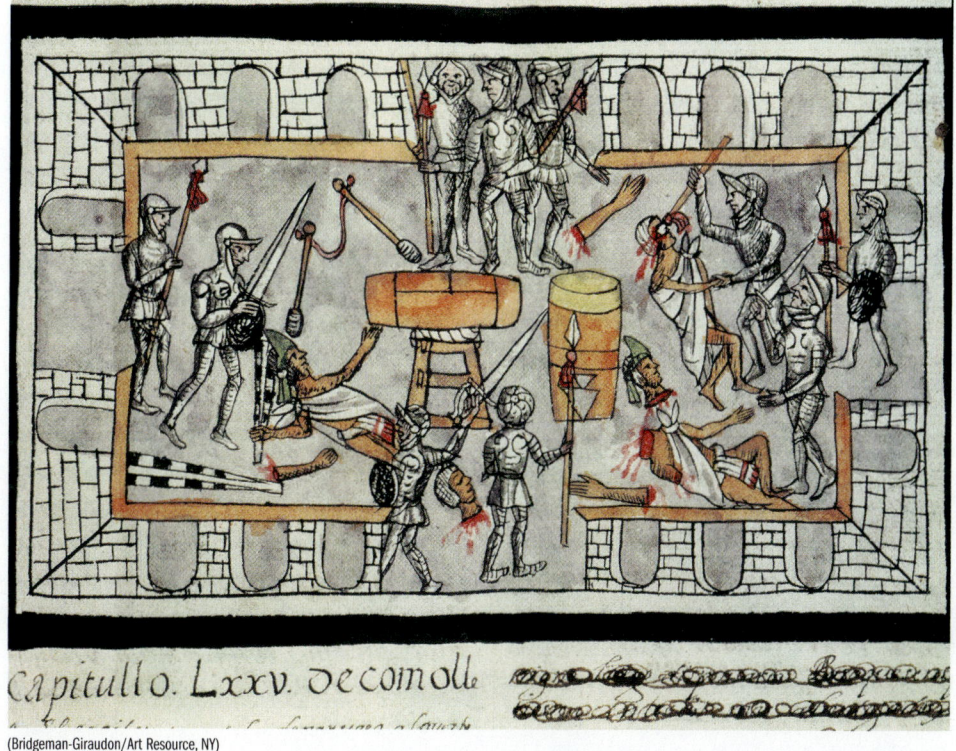

(Bridgeman-Giraudon/Art Resource, NY)

SOURCE 13.4 Conquest and Victory: The Fall of Tenochtitlán from a Spanish Perspective

The massacre of the nobles prompted a citywide uprising against the hated Spanish, who were forced to flee Tenochtitlán on June 30, 1520, across a causeway in Lake Texcoco amid ferocious fighting. Some six hundred Spaniards and several thousand of their Tlaxcalan allies perished in the escape, many of them laden with gold they had collected in Tenochtitlán. For the Spaniards, it was La Noche Triste (the night of sorrow); for the Aztecs, it was no doubt a fitting revenge and a great triumph.

While the Aztecs may have thought themselves permanently rid of the Spanish, La Noche Triste offered only a temporary respite from the European invaders. Cortés and his now-diminished forces found refuge among their Tlaxcalan allies, where they regrouped and planned for yet another assault on Tenochtitlán. In mid-1521, Cortés returned, strengthened with yet more Mesoamerican allies, and laid siege to the Aztec capital. Bitter fighting ensued for several months, often in the form of house-to-house combat, ending with the surrender of the last Aztec emperor on August 13, 1521.

A Spanish account of this event comes from Francisco de Aguilar, a conquistador who took part in the siege of Tenochtitlán, though he subsequently regretted his action and became a priest. Much later in life, around 1560, he wrote an account of his experiences, including this description of the final battle of the Spanish conquest.

- How does Aguilar account for the Spanish victory?
- How does he portray the Spanish and their Aztec adversaries?

FRANCISCO DE AGUILAR | *Brief Record of the Conquest of New Spain* | ca. 1560

[W]ith [Spanish] forces encircling the city and with the brigantines [warships], which were a great help on the lake, the city [Tenochtitlán] began to be battered by land and water. In addition great trouble was taken to cut off the fresh water from the springs, which reached the city by conduits....

The Christians wounded some of the Indians, and great numbers of Indians were killed in the assaults on horseback and by the guns, harquebuses and crossbows. In spite of all this, they put up their strong barricades, and opened causeways and canals and defended themselves courageously.... They also killed some of the Spaniards and captured alive one of them called Guzman, who was Cortés's aide.

The war was sustained fiercely by both sides, since on our side we had the help of many Tlaxcalan warriors, while the Mexicans [had the advantage of] their rooftops and high buildings from which they battered us.... As soon as the Spaniards took any of the houses, which were all on the water, they had the Tlaxcalan Indians demolish and level them, for this gave more freedom to maneuver.

Source 13.4 Conquest and Victory: The Fall of Tenochtitlán from a Spanish Perspective

When some of the Indian lords inside the city began to see the danger they were in ..., they decided to escape by night ... [and] came over to our side.... In addition to this, when the Christians were exhausted from the war, God saw fit to send the Indians smallpox and there was a great pestilence in the city, because there were so many people there, especially women, and they had nothing more to eat.... Also for these reasons they began to slacken in their fighting.

The Mexicans, almost vanquished, withdrew to their fortresses on the water, and since a great number of women were left among them, they armed them all and stationed them on the rooftops. The Spaniards were alarmed at seeing so many of the enemy again, whooping and shouting at them, and when they began killing them and saw they were women, there was dismay on both sides.

[*Twice the last Aztec ruler, Cuauhtemoc, refused Spanish offers to surrender in return for a "pardon and many privileges." He was finally captured.*]

This done, the Spaniards seized the house that had been Cuauhtemoc's stronghold, where they found a great quantity of gold and jewels and other plunder. The Tlaxcalans, who were assisting us in the war ..., knew [the city's] ins and outs, so that when they went home again, they were rich with the spoils they took.

Source: From *The Conquistadors: First-Person Accounts of the Conquest of Mexico*, edited by Patricia de Fuentes, translated by Patricia de Fuentes, translation copyright © 1963 by Penguin Random House LLC, 158–60. Used by permission of Viking Books, an imprint of Penguin Publishing Group, a division of Penguin Random House LLC.

■ ■ ■

SOURCE 13.5 Defeat: The Fall of Tenochtitlán from an Aztec Perspective

From *The Florentine Codex* (see Source 13.2) comes an Aztec account of what was, to the Aztecs, a devastating defeat.

- To what extent does this document confirm, contradict, or supplement Aguilar's account of the fall of Tenochtitlán?
- How does this account explain the terrible defeat?
- What posture toward the Spanish does this document reflect?

FRAY BERNARDINO DE SAHAGÚN | *The Florentine Codex* | Mid-sixteenth century

Before the Spaniards appeared to us, first an epidemic broke out, a sickness of pustules.... Large bumps spread on people; some were entirely covered.... [The disease] brought great desolation.... They could no longer walk about, but lay in their dwellings and sleeping places, no longer able to move or stir.... Very many people died of them;... starvation reigned, and no one took care of others any longer.... The Mexica warriors were greatly weakened by it.

And when things were in this state, the Spaniards came.... The warriors fought in boats; the war-boat people shot at the Spaniards, and their arrows sprinkled down on them.... Many times they skirmished, and the Mexica went out to face them....

When [the Spanish finished adjusting the guns], they shot at the wall. The wall then ripped and broke open. The second time it was hit, the wall went to the ground; it was knocked down in places, perforated, holes were blown in it.... [T]he warriors who had been lying at the wall dispersed and came fleeing; everyone escaped in fear. And then all the different people [who were on the side of the Spaniards] quickly went filling in the canals.... And when the canals were stopped up, some horse[men] came.... And the Spaniards did not move at all; when they fired the cannon, it grew very dark, and smoke spread....

[In the fighting, the Aztecs captured fifty-three Spaniards and many of their allies.] Then [the Aztecs] took the captives.... Some went weeping, some singing, some went shouting while hitting their hands against their mouths. When they got to Yacacolco, they lined them all up. Each one went to the altar platform, where the sacrifice was performed. The Spaniards went first, going in the lead.... And when the sacrifice was over, they strung the Spaniards' heads on poles; they also strung up the horses' heads....

And the common people suffered greatly. There was famine; many died of hunger. They no longer drank good, pure water, but the water they drank was salty. Many people died of it, and because of it many got dysentery and died. Everything was eaten: lizards, swallows, maize straw, grass that grows on salt flats. And they chewed at ... wood, glue flowers, plaster, leather, and deerskin, which they roasted, baked and toasted so that they could eat them, and they ground up medicinal herbs and adobe bricks. There had never been the like of such suffering.

Along every stretch of road, the Spaniards took things from people by force. They were looking for gold; they cared nothing for green stone, feathers, or turquoise. They looked everywhere with the women, on their abdomens, under their skirts. And they looked everywhere with the men, under their loincloths and in their mouths. And [the Spaniards] took, picked out the beautiful women, with yellow bodies. And some of the women covered their faces with mud..., clothing themselves in rags....

And when the weapons were laid down and we collapsed, the year was Three House and the day count was One Serpent.

Source: James Lockhart, ed. and trans., *We People Here: Nahuatl Accounts of the Conquest of Mexico* (Los Angeles, CA: University of California Press, 1993), 180–84, 192–94; 216–18, 248. Copyright 1993 by the Regents of the University of California. Reprinted by permission.

■ ■ ■

SOURCE 13.6 Depicting the Seizure of the Aztec Capital ▶

The seizure of Tenochtitlán was a formative event in the creation of colonial Mexico and represented the starting point for the profound transformations of Mexican society that accompanied the conquest. In the centuries that followed, the drama of this event attracted the interest of artists, writers, and others in this new society. One particularly impressive late seventeenth-century effort to depict the siege was painted by an unknown artist in Mexico on a large folding screen, which was most likely given by a local member of the Spanish elite to the new viceroy, Conde de Galve. On one side, the conquest of the city in 1521 unfolds in a series of scenes from the top left—where Cortés, bathed in sunshine, lands in Mexico and meets Moctezuma—to the bottom right—where in darker tones the Spanish are driven from the city on the "sad night" and Native American refugees flee into the surrounding forests to escape the violence. In between, scenes depicting critical moments in the conquest take place in different parts of an imagined cityscape. While key elements of the conquest story are present, the overall scene is most striking for its depiction of what one critic has called the "motley banquet of violence," which contrasts sharply with the serene, peaceful, and idealized cityscape of seventeenth-century Mexico City depicted on the other side of the screen.[2]

The scene reproduced here chronicles a dramatic moment from a central panel in the screen, in which Aztecs battle the Spanish near the Temple Mayor in the central plaza of Tenochtitlán. The building labeled D is the temple itself, depicted here as a hollowed-out octagon rather than in its true form, a towering pyramid. While violent scenes of battle swirl around the temple, in the background one can see the remains of ritually sacrificed Spanish soldiers and those of a horse, which had also been sacrificed.

- What elements of the struggle described in Sources 13.4 and 13.5 can you identify?
- Does this painting have a point of view? Was it created more from a European or an indigenous perspective?
- Why might the artist have included the gruesome depiction of the executed Spaniards in this painting?

The Conquest of Tenochtitlán | Seventeenth century

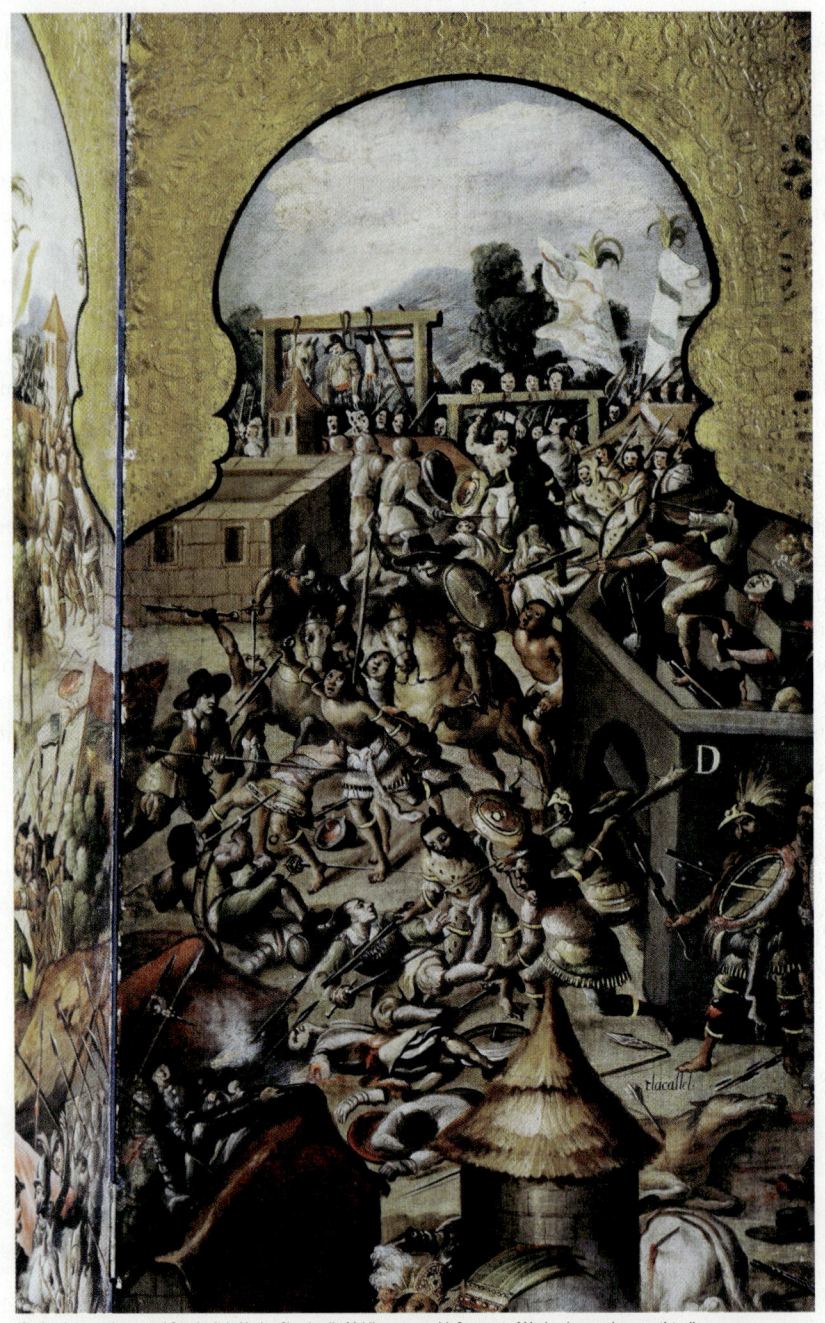

(Clashes between Aztecs and Spaniards in Mexico City, detail of folding screen with Conquest of Mexico, by an unknown artist, oil on canvas, 16th century/DE AGOSTINI EDITORE/Bridgeman Images)

SOURCE 13.7 Lamentation: The Aftermath of Defeat

In the aftermath of their agonizing defeat by Cortés and his men, the Aztec survivors composed a number of songs or poems, lamenting their terrible loss. These selections are part of a larger collection of Aztec poetry known as the *Cantares Mexicanos* (Songs of the Aztecs), compiled in the late sixteenth century.

- What do the poems of lamentation suggest about Aztec efforts to come to terms with their enormous loss?
- To what extent do these lamentations represent universal expressions of loss and defeat? In what ways might they be considered uniquely and distinctly Aztec?

Cantares Mexicanos | Late sixteenth century

The Fall of Tenochtitlán

Our cries of grief rise up / and our tears rain down, / for Tlatelolco [an Aztec city] is lost.
The Aztecs are fleeing across the lake; / they are running away like women.
How can we save our homes, my people? / The Aztecs are deserting the city: the city is in flames, and all / is darkness and destruction . . .
Weep, my people: / know that with these disasters / we have lost the Mexican nation.
The water has turned bitter, / our food is bitter! / These are the acts of the Giver of Life . . .
The Aztecs are besieged in the city; / the Tlatelolcas are besieged in the city!
The walls are black, / the air is black with smoke, / the guns flash in the darkness.
They have captured Cuauhtemoc; / they have captured the princes of Mexico . . . /
The kings are prisoners now. / They are bound with chains.

Flowers and Songs of Sorrow

Nothing but flowers and songs of sorrow / are left in Mexico and Tlatelolco,
where once we saw warriors and wise men.
We know it is true / that we must perish, / for we are mortal men.
You, the Giver of Life, / you have ordained it.
We wander here / and there in our desolate poverty. / We are mortal men.
We have seen bloodshed and pain / where once we saw beauty and valor.
We are crushed to the ground; / we lie in ruins.
There is nothing but grief and suffering / In Mexico and Tlatelolco, /
where once we saw beauty and valor.
Have you grown weary of your servants? / Are you angry with your servants, / O Giver of Life?

Source: From *The Broken Spears* by Miguel León-Portilla, 146–49. Copyright © 1962, 1990 by Miguel León-Portilla. Expanded and updated edition Copyright © 1992 by Miguel León-Portilla. Reprinted by permission of Beacon Press, Boston.

DOING HISTORY

1. **Evaluating evidence and objectivity:** Based on these sources, how might a historian compose a history of the conquest of Mexico, seeking to be as objective as possible? What information from these sources might be reliably used, and what might be discarded? Is it actually possible to be wholly objective about these events? How would such an account differ if it were written from a distinctly Aztec or Spanish point of view?
2. **Considering morality:** What moral or ethical issues arose for the participants in these events? Should historians take a position on such questions? Is it possible to avoid doing so?
3. **Considering outcomes:** Was Spanish victory inevitable? Under what circumstances might the outcome have been different?
4. **Assessing perspective:** What differences in outlook can you identify between the Spanish and the Aztec sources?

HISTORIANS' VOICES

Conquest, Disease, and Demographic Collapse in the Aztec Empire

Historians agree that diseases endemic in Africa and Eurasia but new to the Americas played a significant role in the demographic collapse of the Native American population in central Mexico. However, the relative importance of new pandemic diseases as opposed to other factors in both the initial conquest of the Aztecs by the Spanish and the "Great Dying" that followed this event has sparked considerable scholarly debate, which is reflected in the two selections that follow. In Voice 13.1, the historian Alfred Crosby, who coined the term "Columbian Exchange," makes the case that disease played an important role both at the time of conquest and over the longer term. In Voice 13.2, Philip Hoffman, an historian and economist, offers a skeptical view of the relative importance of new epidemic diseases in the conquest and the demographic collapse that followed.

- Do Crosby and Hoffman offer opposing interpretations, or can you find some common ground between them?
- How does Hoffman's longer time frame, which incorporates the post-conquest period, affect his account?
- **Integrating primary and secondary sources:** How might you construct an account of the role of disease in the Spanish conquest of the Aztecs that integrates both primary and secondary sources?

VOICE 13.1

Alfred Crosby on the Impact of Disease on the Conquest of the Aztec Empire | 1972

The melodrama of Cortés and the conquest of Mexico needs no retelling. After occupying Tenochtitlán . . . he and his troops had to fight their way out of the city to sanctuary. . . . Even as the Spanish withdrew, an ally more formidable than the Tlacala [a Native American group allied with the Spanish] appeared. Years later Francisco de Aguillar, a former follower of Cortés. . . . recalled the terrible retreat. . . . "When the Christians were exhausted from war, God saw fit to send the Indians smallpox, and there was a great pestilence in the city." . . .

The sixty days during which the epidemic lasted in the city . . . gave Cortés and his troops desperately needed respite to reorganize and prepare a counterattack. When the epidemic subsided, the siege of the Aztec capital began. Had there been no epidemic, the Aztecs. . . . could have pursued the Spaniards. . . . Clearly the epidemic sapped the endurance of Tenochtitlán. . . .

The impact of the smallpox pandemic on the Aztec [Empire] . . . is easy for the twentieth-century reader to underestimate. We have so long been hypnotized by the daring of the conquistador that we have overlooked the importance of biological allies. Because of the achievements of modern medical science we find it hard to accept statements from the conquest period that the pandemics killed one-third to one-half of the populations struck by it. . . . The proportion may be exaggerated but perhaps not by as much as we might think. The Mexicans had no resistance to the disease at all. Other diseases were probably operating quietly and efficiently behind the screen of smallpox. Add the factors of food shortage and the lack of even minimal care for the sick. . . .

Source: Alfred Crosby, *The Columbian Exchange: Biological and Cultural Consequences of 1492* (Westport, CT: Greenwood, 1972), 48–49, 52–53.

VOICE 13.2

Philip Hoffman on the Roles of Disease, Social Disruption, and Technology in the Conquest of the Aztecs | 2015

The trouble, though, is that the demographic catastrophe in the Aztec and Inca Empires had multiple causes—and not just smallpox and measles—for otherwise the native population would have recovered even if the epidemics returned repeatedly. That at least is the conclusion of a demographic analysis that takes into account how populations react after being ravaged by new diseases like smallpox. And what kept the Native American population from recovering was the conquest itself, by wreaking havoc with their domestic life. Indians fled from warfare, and survivors were forced to work for the Europeans, often away from home, so that they could not provide their families with food. Indian women were also drawn into the conquerors' households often as their sexual partners. In short, it became much harder for the Native Americans to have children, making much of the population decline the result, not of disease, but of brutal conquest itself. . . .

How could the Europeans triumph against such numbers? As an answer disease alone fails. . . . For some military historians, the answer is clear: the Europeans simply had better technology. Epidemics and divisions among the natives helped in the Americas . . . but technology gave the Europeans the edge, particularly against the centralized empires of the Aztecs and Incas.

Source: Philip T. Hoffman, *Why Did Europe Conquer the World* (Princeton, NJ: Princeton University Press, 2015), 5–7.

NOTES

1. Stuart B. Schwartz, *Victors and Vanquished* (Boston, MA: Bedford/St. Martin's, 2000), 164.

2. Much of this interpretation is taken from Anna More, *Baroque Sovereignty: Carlos de Sigüenza y Góngora and the Creole Archive of Colonial Mexico* (Philadelphia, PA: University of Pennsylvania Press, 2012).

CHAPTER 14

Thinking through Sources

Voices from the Slave Trade

By any measure, the Atlantic slave trade was an enormous enterprise and enormously significant in modern world history. Its geographical scope encompassed four continents; it endured for almost four centuries; its victims numbered in the many millions; its commercial operation was global, complex, and highly competitive; and its consequences echo still in both public and private life. The sources that follow allow us to hear several individual voices from this vast historical process and to sample the evidence available to historians as they seek to chart this painful chapter of the human story.

SOURCE 14.1 The Journey to Slavery

We begin with the voice of an individual victim of the slave trade—Olaudah Equiano. Born in what is now the Igbo-speaking region of southern Nigeria around 1745, Equiano was seized from his home at the age of eleven and sold into the Atlantic slave trade at the high point of that infamous commerce. In service to three different owners, his experience as a slave in the Americas was quite unusual. He learned to read and write, traveled extensively as a seaman aboard one of his masters' ships, and was allowed to buy his freedom in 1766. Settling in England, he became a prominent voice in the emerging abolitionist movement of the late eighteenth century and wrote a widely read account of his life, addressed largely to European Christians: "O, ye nominal Christians! Might not an African ask you, Learned you this from your God, who says unto you, Do unto all men as you would men should do unto you?" His book was published in 1789 as abolitionism was gaining wider acceptance.

Despite some controversy about his birthplace and birth date, most historians accept Equiano's autobiography as broadly accurate. Source 14.1 presents Equiano's account of his capture, his journey to the coast, his experience on a slave ship, and

211

his arrival in the Americas. It was a journey forcibly undertaken by millions of others as well.

- How does Equiano describe the kind of slavery he knew in Africa? How does it compare with the plantation slavery of the Americas?
- What part did Africans play in the slave trade, according to this account?
- What aspects of the shipboard experience contributed to the slaves' despair?

OLAUDAH EQUIANO | *The Interesting Narrative of the Life of Olaudah Equiano* | 1789

As we live in a country where nature is prodigal of her favours, our wants are few and easily supplied; of course we have few manufactures. They consist for the most part of calicoes, earthen ware, ornaments, and instruments of war and husbandry.... We have also markets, at which I have been frequently with my mother. These are sometimes visited by stout mahogany-coloured men from the south west of us:... They generally bring us fire-arms, gunpowder, hats, beads, and dried fish.... They always carry slaves through our land;... Sometimes indeed we sold slaves to them, but they were only prisoners of war, or such among us as had been convicted of kidnapping or adultery, and some other crimes, which we esteemed heinous....

My father, besides many slaves, had a numerous family, of which seven lived to grow up, including myself and a sister, who was the only daughter.... I was trained up from my earliest years in the art of war; my daily exercise was shooting and throwing javelins; and my mother adorned me with emblems, after the manner of our greatest warriors. In this way I grew up till I was turned the age of eleven, when an end was put to my happiness in the following manner....

One day, when all our people were gone out to their works as usual, and only I and my dear sister were left to mind the house, two men and a woman got over our walls and in a moment seized us both, and, without giving us time to cry out, or make resistance, they stopped our mouths, and ran off with us into the nearest wood. Here they tied our hands, and continued to carry us as far as they could, till night came on.... The next morning we left the house, and continued travelling all the day. For a long time we had kept [to] the woods, but at last we came into a road which I believed I knew. I had now some hopes of being delivered; for we had advanced but a little way before I discovered some people at a distance, on which I began to cry out for their assistance: but my cries had no other effect than to make them tie me faster and stop my mouth, and then they put me into a large sack....

The next day proved a day of greater sorrow than I had yet experienced; for my sister and I were then separated, while we lay clasped in each other's arms. It was in vain that we besought them not to part us; she was torn from me, and immediately carried away....

At length, after many days traveling, during which I had often changed masters, I got into the hands of a chieftain, in a very pleasant country. This man had two wives and some children, and they all used me extremely well, and did all they could to comfort me; particularly the first wife, who was something like my mother. Although I was a great many days journey from my father's house, yet these people spoke exactly the same language with us....

[After about a month], I was again sold.... The people I was sold to used to carry me very often, when I was tired, either on their shoulders or on their backs. I saw many convenient well-built sheds along the roads, at proper distances, to accommodate the merchants and travelers, who lay in those buildings along with their wives, who often accompany them; and they always go well armed.

I was again sold, and carried through a number of places, till, after traveling a considerable time, I came to a town called Tinmah, in the most beautiful country I had yet seen in Africa.... Their money consisted of little white shells, the size of the finger nail. I was sold here for one hundred and seventy-two of them by a merchant who lived and brought me there. I had been about two or three days at his house, when a wealthy widow, a neighbor of his, came there one evening, and brought with her an only son, a young gentleman about my own age and size. Here they saw me; and, having taken a fancy to me, I was bought of the merchant, and went home with them.... The next day I was washed and perfumed, and when meal-time came I was led into the presence of my mistress, and ate and drank before her with her son. This filled me with astonishment; and I could scarce help expressing my surprise that the young gentleman should suffer me, who was bound, to eat with him who was free; and not only so, but that he would not at any time either eat or drink till I had taken first, because I was the eldest, which was agreeable to our custom. Indeed everything here, and all their treatment of me, made me forget that I was a slave. The language of these people resembled ours so nearly, that we understood each other perfectly.... In this resemblance to my former happy state I passed about two months; and I now began to think I was to be adopted into the family, and was beginning to be reconciled to my situation, and to forget by degrees my misfortunes when all at once the delusion vanished; for, without the least previous knowledge, one morning early, while my dear master and companion was still asleep, I was wakened out of my reverie to fresh sorrow, and hurried away....

Thus I continued to travel, sometimes by land, sometimes by water, through different countries and various nations, till, at the end of six or seven months after I had been kidnapped, I arrived at the sea coast.... The first object which saluted my eyes when I arrived on the coast was the sea, and a slave ship, which was then riding at anchor, and waiting for its cargo. These filled me with astonishment, which was soon converted into terror when I was carried on board. I was immediately handled and tossed up to see if I were sound by some of the crew; and I was now persuaded that I had gotten into a world of bad spirits, and that they were going to kill me. Their complexions too differing so much from ours, their long hair, and the language they spoke ... united to confirm me in this belief.... When I looked round the ship too and saw a large furnace or copper boiling, and a multitude of black people of every description chained together, every one of their countenances expressing dejection and sorrow, I no longer doubted of my fate; and quite overpowered with horror and anguish, I fell motionless on the deck and fainted....

I was soon put down under the decks, and there I received such a salutation in my nostrils as I had never experienced in my life: so that, with the loathsomeness of the stench and crying together, I became so sick and low that I was not able to eat, nor had I the least desire to taste anything. I now wished for the last friend, death, to relieve me; but soon, to my grief, two of the white men offered me eatables; and on my refusing to eat, one of them held me fast by the hands, and laid me across I think the windlass and tied my feet, while the other flogged me severely....

I had never seen among any people such instances of brutal cruelty; and this not only shewn towards us blacks, but also to some of the whites themselves. One white man in particular I saw, when we were permitted to be on deck, flogged so unmercifully with a large rope near the foremast that he died in consequence of it; and they tossed him over the side as they would have done a brute....

The closeness of the place, and the heat of the climate, added to the number in the ship, which was so crowded that each had scarcely room to turn himself, almost suffocated us. This produced copious perspirations, so that the air soon became unfit for respiration, from a variety of loathsome smells, and brought on a sickness among the slaves, of which many died, thus falling victims to the improvident avarice, as I may call it, of their purchasers. This wretched situation was again aggravated by the galling of the chains, now become insupportable; and the filth of the necessary tubs, into which the children often fell, and were almost suffocated. The shrieks of the women, and the groans of the dying, rendered the whole a scene of horror almost inconceivable....

At last we came in sight of the island of Barbados, at which the whites on board gave a great shout, and made many signs of joy to us.... Many merchants and planters now came on board, though it was in the evening. They put us in separate parcels, and examined us attentively. They also made us jump, and pointed to the land, signifying we were to go there. We thought by this we should be eaten by those ugly men, as they appeared to us;... at last the white people got some old slaves from the land to pacify us. They told us we were not to be eaten, but to work, and were soon to go on land, where we should see many of our country people. This report eased us much; and sure enough, soon after we were landed, there came to us Africans of all languages. We were conducted immediately to the merchant's yard, where we were all pent up together like so many sheep in a fold, without regard to sex or age.

Source: Olaudah Equiano, *The Interesting Narrative of the Life of Olaudah Equiano, or Gustavus Vassa, the African*, vol. 1 (London, 1789), chaps. 1, 2.

■ ■ ■

SOURCE 14.2 The Business of the Slave Trade

For its African victims like Equiano, the slave trade was a horror beyond imagination; for kings and merchants—both European and African—it was a business. Source 14.2 explains how that business was conducted. This account comes from the journal of an

English merchant, Thomas Phillips, who undertook a voyage to the kingdom of Whydah in what is now the West African country of Benin in 1693–1694.

- How would you describe the economic transactions described in the document? To what extent were they conducted between equal parties? Who, if anyone, held the upper hand in these dealings?
- How might an African merchant have described the same transaction? How might Equiano have described it?
- Notice the outcomes of Phillips's voyage to Barbados in the last two paragraphs. What does this tell you about European preferences for slaves, about the Middle Passage, and about the profitability of the enterprise?

THOMAS PHILLIPS | *A Journal of a Voyage Made in the Hannibal of London* | 1694

As soon as the king understood of our landing, he sent two of his cappasheirs, or noblemen, to compliment us at our factory, where we design'd to continue that night, and pay our [respects] to his majesty next day ... whereupon he sent two more of his grandees to invite us there that night, saying he waited for us, and that all former captains used to attend him the first night: whereupon being unwilling to infringe the custom, or give his majesty any offence, we took our hamocks, and Mr. Peirson, myself, Capt. Clay, our surgeons, pursers, and about 12 men, arm'd for our guard, were carry'd to the king's town, which contains about 50 houses....

We returned him thanks by his interpreter, and assur'd him how great affection our masters, the royal African company of England, bore to him, for his civility and fair and just dealings with their captains; and that notwithstanding there were many other places, more plenty of negro slaves that begg'd their custom, yet they had rejected all the advantageous offers made them out of their good will to him, and therefore had sent us to trade with him, to support his country with necessaries, and that we hop'd he would endeavour to continue their favour by his kind usage and fair dealing with us in our trade, that we may have our slaves with all expedition.... He answer'd that we should be fairly dealt with, and not impos'd upon; But he did not prove as good as his word ... so after having examin'd us about our cargoe, what sort of goods we had, and what quantity of slaves we wanted, etc., we took our leaves and return'd to the factory....

According to promise we attended his majesty with samples of our goods, and made our agreement about the prices, tho' not without much difficulty; ... next day we paid our customs to the king and cappasheirs, ... then the bell was order'd to go about to give notice to all people to bring their slaves to the trunk to sell us....

Capt. Clay and I had agreed to go to the trunk to buy the slaves by turns, each his day, that we might have no distractions or disagreement in our trade, as often happens when there are here more ships than one, and ... their disagreements create animosities, underminings, and out-bidding each other, whereby they enhance the prices to their general loss and detriment, the blacks well knowing how to make the best use of such opportunities, and as we found make it their business, and endeavour to create and foment misunderstandings and jealousies between commanders, it turning to their great account in the disposal of their slaves.

When we were at the trunk, the king's slaves, if he had any, were the first offer'd to sale, ... and we must not refuse them, tho' as I observ'd they were generally the worst slaves in the trunk, and we paid more for them than any others, which we could not remedy, it being one of his majesty's prerogatives: then the cappasheirs each brought out his slaves according to his degree and quality, the greatest first, etc. and our surgeon examin'd them well in all kinds, to see that they were sound wind and limb, making them jump, stretch out their arms swiftly, looking in their mouths to judge of their age; for the cappasheirs are so cunning, that they shave them all close before we see them, so that let them be never so old we can see no grey hairs in their heads or beards; and then having liquor'd them well and sleek with palm oil, 'tis no easy matter to know an old one from a middle-age one....

When we had selected from the rest such as we liked, we agreed in what goods to pay for them, the prices being already stated before the king, how much of each sort of merchandize we were to give for a man, woman, and child, which gave us much ease, and saved abundance of disputes and wranglings.... [T]hen we mark'd the slaves we had bought in the breast, or shoulder, with a hot iron, having the letter of the ship's name on it, the place being before anointed with a little palm oil, which caus'd but little pain, the mark being usually well in four or five days, appearing very plain and white after....

After we are come to an agreement for the prices of our slaves, ... we are oblig'd to pay our customs to the king and cappasheirs for leave to trade, protection and justice; which for every ship are as follow, viz.

To the king six slaves value in cowries, or what other goods we can perswade him to take, but cowries are most esteem'd and desir'd; all which are measur'd in his presence, and he would wrangle with us stoutly about heaping up the measure.

To the cappasheirs in all two slaves value, as above....

The best goods to purchase slaves here are cowries, the smaller the more esteem'd....

The next in demand are brass neptunes or basons, very large, thin, and flat; for after they have bought them they cut them in pieces to make ... bracelets, and collars for their arms legs and necks....

[I]f they can discover that you have good store of cowries and brass aboard, then no other goods will serve their turn, till they have got as much as you have; and after, for the rest of the goods they will be indifferent, and make you come to their own terms, or else lie a long time for your slaves, so that those you have on board are dying while you are buying others ashore....

Having bought my compliment of 700 slaves, viz. 480 men and 220 women, and finish'd all my business at Whidaw, I took my leave of the old king, and his cappasheirs, and parted, with many affectionate expressions on both sides, being forced to promise him that I would return again the next year, with several things he desired me to bring him from England; and having sign'd bills of lading . . . for the negroes aboard, I set sail the 27th of July in the morning. . . .

I deliver'd alive at Barbadoes to the company's factors 372, which being sold, came out at about nineteen pounds per head.

Source: Thomas Phillips, "A Journal of a Voyage Made in the *Hannibal* of London in 1694," in *Documents Illustrative of the History of the Slave Trade to America*, edited by Elizabeth Donnan (Washington, DC: Carnegie Institute, 1930), 399–405, 408, 410.

■ ■ ■

SOURCE 14.3 The Slave Trade and the Kingdom of Kongo

While African elites often eagerly facilitated the traffic in slaves and benefited from doing so, in one well-known case, quite early in the slave-trade era, an African ruler sought to curtail it. This effort occurred in the Kingdom of Kongo, in what is now Angola. That state had welcomed Portuguese traders as early as the 1480s, as its rulers imagined that an alliance with Portugal could strengthen their regime. The royal family converted to Christianity and encouraged the importation of European guns, cattle, and horses. Several Kongolese were sent to Portugal for education, while Portuguese priests, artisans, merchants, and soldiers found a place in the kingdom. This relationship did not work out as planned, however, and by the early sixteenth century, Kongo was in disarray and the authority of its ruler greatly undermined. This was the context in which its monarch Nzinga Mbemba, whose Christian name was Affonso I, wrote a series of letters to King João of Portugal in 1526, extracts of which are presented here.

- What did Affonso seek from Portugal? What kind of relationship did he envisage with the Portuguese?
- To what extent did Affonso seek the end of the slave trade? What was the basis for his opposition to it? Do you think he was opposed to slavery itself?
- How did the operation of the slave trade in Kongo differ from that of Whydah as described in Source 14.2? How did the rulers of these two states differ in their relationship to Europeans?

KING AFFONSO I | Letters to King João of Portugal | 1526

Sir, Your Highness [of Portugal] should know how our Kingdom is being lost in so many ways that it is convenient to provide for the necessary remedy, since this is caused by the excessive freedom given by your factors and officials to the men and merchants who are allowed to come to this Kingdom to set up shops with goods and many things which have been prohibited by us, and which they spread throughout our Kingdoms and Domains in such an abundance that many of our vassals, whom we had in obedience, do not comply because they have the things in greater abundance than we ourselves; and it was with these things that we had them content and subjected under our vassalage and jurisdiction, so it is doing a great harm not only to the service of God, but to the security and peace of our Kingdoms and State as well.

And we cannot reckon how great the damage is, since the mentioned merchants are taking every day our natives, sons of the land and the sons of our noblemen and vassals and our relatives, because the thieves and men of bad conscience grab them wishing to have the things and wares of this Kingdom which they are ambitious of; they grab them and get them to be sold; and so great, Sir, is the corruption and licentiousness that our country is being completely depopulated, and Your Highness should not agree with this nor accept it as in your service. And to avoid it we need from those [your] Kingdoms no more than some priests and a few people to teach in schools, and no other goods except wine and flour for the holy sacrament. That is why we beg of Your Highness to help and assist us in this matter, commanding your factors that they should not send here either merchants or wares, because it is our will that in these Kingdoms there should not be any trade of slaves nor outlet for them. Concerning what is referred above, again we beg of Your Highness to agree with it, since otherwise we cannot remedy such an obvious damage....

Moreover, Sir, in our Kingdoms there is another great inconvenience which is of little service to God, and this is that many of our people, keenly desirous as they are of the wares and things of your Kingdoms, which are brought here by your people, and in order to satisfy their voracious appetite, seize many of our people, freed and exempt men; and very often it happens that they kidnap even noblemen and the sons of noblemen, and our relatives, and take them to be sold to the white men who are in our Kingdoms; and for this purpose they have concealed them; and others are brought during the night so that they might not be recognized.

And as soon as they are taken by the white men they are immediately ironed and branded with fire, and when they are carried to be embarked, if they are caught by our guards' men the whites allege that they have bought them but they cannot say from whom, so that it is our duty to do justice and to restore to the freemen their freedom, but it cannot be done if your subjects feel offended, as they claim to be.

And to avoid such a great evil we passed a law so that any white man living in our Kingdoms and wanting to purchase goods in any way should first inform three of our noblemen and officials of our court ... who should investigate if the mentioned goods are captives or free men, and if cleared by them there will be no further doubt nor embargo for them to be taken and embarked. But if the white men do not comply with it they will lose the aforementioned goods....

Sir, Your Highness has been kind enough to write to us saying that we should ask in our letters for anything we need, and that we shall be provided with everything, and as the peace and the health of our Kingdom depend on us, and as there are among us old folks and people who have lived for many days, it happens that we have continuously many and different diseases which put us very often in such a weakness that we reach almost the last extreme; and the same happens to our children, relatives, and natives owing to the lack in this country of physicians and surgeons who might know how to cure properly such diseases. And as we have got neither dispensaries nor drugs which might help us in this forlornness, many of those who had been already confirmed and instructed in the holy faith of Our Lord Jesus Christ perish and die; and the rest of the people in their majority cure themselves with herbs and breads and other ancient methods, so that they put all their faith in the mentioned herbs and ceremonies if they live, and believe that they are saved if they die; and this is not much in the service of God.

And to avoid such a great error and inconvenience, since it is from God in the first place and then from your Kingdoms and from Your Highness that all the goods and drugs and medicines have come to save us, we beg of you to be agreeable and kind enough to send us two physicians and two apothecaries and one surgeon, so that they may come with their drugstores and all the necessary things to stay in our kingdoms, because we are in extreme need of them all and each of them.

Source: Basil Davidson, *The African Past* (Boston, MA: Little, Brown, 1964), 191–94.

■ ■ ■

SOURCE 14.4 The Slave Trade and the Kingdom of Asante

The slave trade did not always have such politically destabilizing effects as it did in Kongo. In the region known as the Gold Coast (now the modern state of Ghana), the Kingdom of Asante (uh-SAWN-tay) arose in the eighteenth century, occupying perhaps 100,000 square miles and encompassing some 3 million people. It was a powerful conquest state, heavily invested in the slave trade, from which much of its wealth derived. Many slaves from Asante's wars of expansion and from the tribute of its subject people were funneled into Atlantic commerce, while still others were used as labor in the goldmines and on the plantations within Asante itself. No wonder, then, that the ruler (or Asantehene) Osei Bonsu was dismayed in the early nineteenth century when, in reaction to the expanding abolitionist movement, the British stopped buying slaves. A conversation between Osei Bonsu and a British diplomat in 1820 highlights the role of the slave trade in Asante and in the thinking of its monarch.

- How did Osei Bonsu understand the slave trade and its significance for his kingdom?
- Some scholars have argued that the slave trade increased the incidence of warfare in West Africa, as various states deliberately sought captives whom they could exchange for desired goods from Europe. How might Osei Bonsu respond to that idea? What was his understanding of the relationship between war and the slave trade?
- In what ways did Osei Bonsu compare Muslim traders from the north with European merchants from the sea?

OSEI BONSU | Conversation with Joseph Dupuis | 1820

"Now," said the king, after a pause, "I have another palaver, and you must help me to talk it. A long time ago the great king [of England] liked plenty of trade, more than now; then many ships came, and they bought ivory, gold, and slaves; but now he will not let the ships come as before, and the people buy gold and ivory only. This is what I have in my head, so now tell me truly, like a friend, why does the king do so?" "His majesty's question," I replied, "was connected with a great palaver, which my instructions did not authorise me to discuss. I had nothing to say regarding the slave trade." "I know that too," retorted the king; "because, if my master liked that trade, you would have told me so before. I only want to hear what you think as a friend: this is not like the other palavers." I was confessedly at a loss for an argument that might pass as a satisfactory reason, and the sequel proved that my doubts were not groundless. The king did not deem it plausible, that this obnoxious traffic should have been abolished from motives of humanity alone; neither would he admit that it lessened the number either of domestic or foreign wars.

Taking up one of my observations, he remarked, "[T]he white men who go to council with your master, and pray to the great God for him, do not understand my country, or they would not say the slave trade was bad. But if they think it bad now, why did they think it good before? Is not your law an old law, the same as the Crammo [Muslim] law? Do you not both serve the same God, only you have different fashions and customs? Crammos are strong people in fetische [magical powers], and they say the law is good, because the great God made the book [Quran]; so they buy slaves, and teach them good things, which they knew not before. This makes everybody love the Crammos, and they go everywhere up and down, and the people give them food when they want it. Then these men come all the way from the great water [Niger River], and from Manding, and Dagomba, and Killinga; they stop and trade for slaves, and then go home. If the great king would like to restore this trade, it would be good for the white men and for me too, because Ashantee is a country for war, and the people are strong; so if you talk that palaver for me properly, in the white country, if you go there, I will give you plenty of gold, and I will make you richer than all the white men."

I urged the impossibility of the king's request, promising, however, to record his sentiments faithfully. "Well then," said the king, "you must put down in my master's book all I shall say, and then he will look to it, now he is my friend. And when he sees what is true, he will surely restore that trade. I cannot make war to catch slaves in the bush, like a thief. My ancestors never did so. But if I fight a king, and kill him when he is insolent, then certainly I must have his gold, and his slaves, and the people are mine too. Do not the white kings act like this? Because I hear the old men say, that before I conquered Fantee and killed the Braffoes and the kings, that white men came in great ships, and fought and killed many people; and then they took the gold and slaves to the white country: and sometimes they fought together. That is all the same as these black countries. The great God and the fetische made war for strong men every where, because then they can pay plenty of gold and proper sacrifice. When I fought Gaman, I did not make war for slaves, but because Dinkera (the king) sent me an arrogant message and killed my people, and refused to pay me gold as his father did. Then my fetische made me strong like my ancestors, and I killed Dinkera, and took his gold, and brought more than 20,000 slaves to Coomassy. Some of these people being bad men, I washed my stool in their blood for the fetische. But then some were good people, and these I sold or gave to my captains: many, moreover, died, because this country does not grow too much corn like Sarem, and what can I do? Unless I kill or sell them, they will grow strong and kill my people. Now you must tell my master that these slaves can work for him, and if he wants 10,000 he can have them. And if he wants fine handsome girls and women to give his captains, I can send him great numbers."

Source: Joseph Dupuis, *Journal of a Residence in Ashantee* (London, UK: Henry Colburn, 1824), 162–64.

SOURCE 14.5 Images of the Slave Trade ▶

Images of the slave trade abound, offering another perspective on the journey from freedom to slavery. Source 14.5A, a French engraving published in 1796 as part of an encyclopedic travel book, shows the sale of slaves at Gorée, a major slave-trading port in what is now Dakar, Senegal. A European merchant and an African slave trader negotiate the arrangement, while the shackled victims wait for their fate to be decided. Based on an early photograph, Source 14.5B is an engraving published in the popular American periodical *Harper's Weekly* in 1860. It illustrates the Middle Passage by recording the enormously crowded conditions aboard a slave ship, which was captured before it could land its human cargo in Cuba. Source 14.5C, a handbill advertising a slave auction in South Carolina in 1769, indicates what lay ahead for those who survived the Middle Passage.

- What aspects of the documents in Sources 14.1 through 14.4 do these images illustrate?
- In what ways do images such as these provide an understanding of the slave trade beyond what written sources can convey? What are their limitations as sources useful to historians?

SOURCE 14.5A
Sale of Slaves in West Africa | 1796

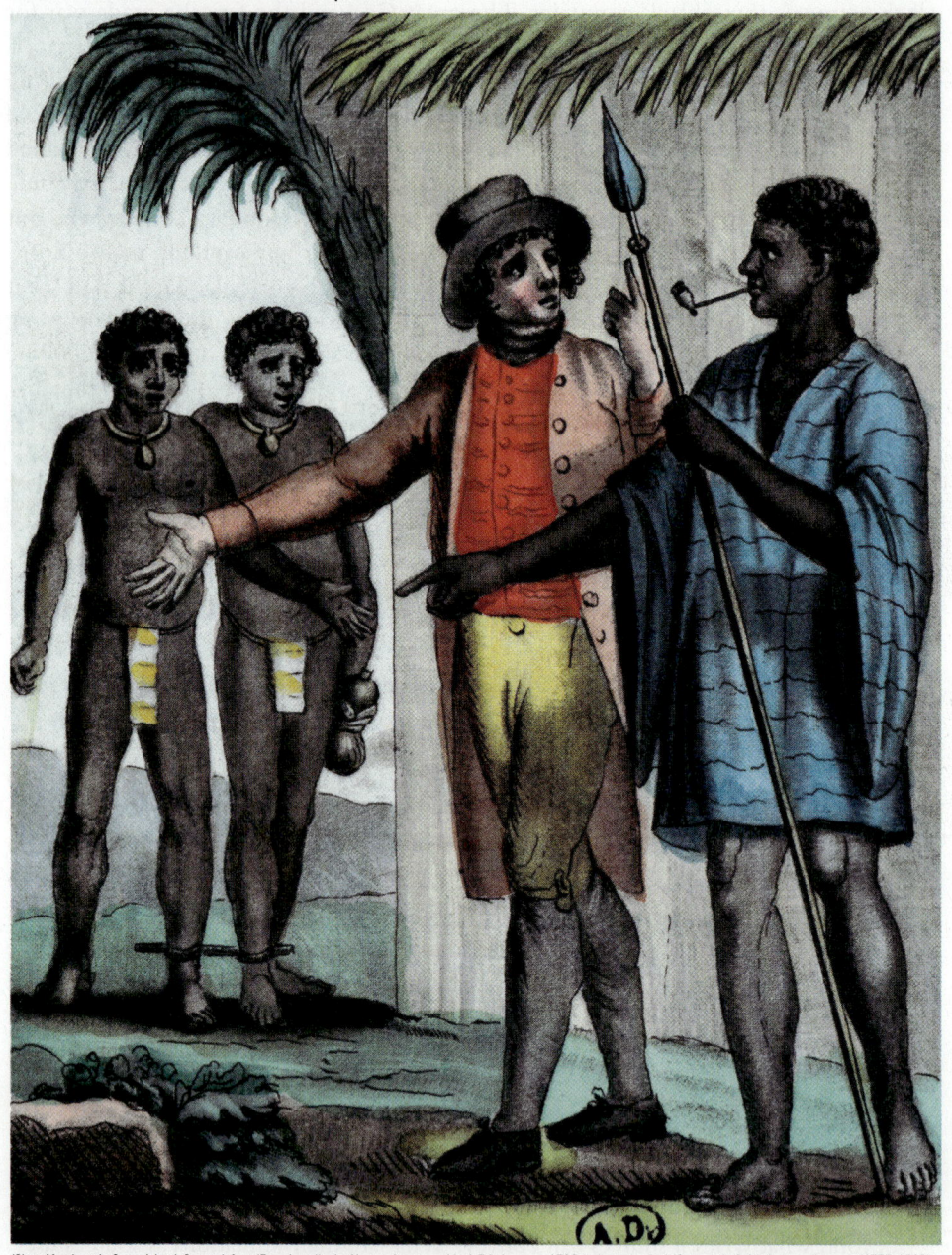

(Slave Merchant in Goree Island, Senegal, from 'Encyclopedie des Voyages', engraved by L.F. Labrousse, 1796 (color engraving)/Grasset de Saint-Sauveur, Jacques (1757–1810) (after)/INDIVISION CHARMET/Bibliotheque des Arts Decoratifs, Paris, France/Bridgeman Images)

Source 14.5 Images of the Slave Trade

SOURCE 14.5B

The Slave Ship Wildfire | 1860

THE SLAVE DECK OF THE BARK "WILDFIRE," BROUGHT INTO KEY WEST ON APRIL 30, 1860.—[FROM A DAGUERREOTYPE.]

(The Slave Deck of the Bark *Wildfire*, Brought into Key West on April 30, 1860, illustration from *Harper's Weekly*, June 2 1860 (engraving from a daguerreotype) (b&w photo)/ American School, (19th century)/Private Collection/Bridgeman Images)

SOURCE 14.5C
Advertisement for a Slave Auction in Charleston, South Carolina | 1769

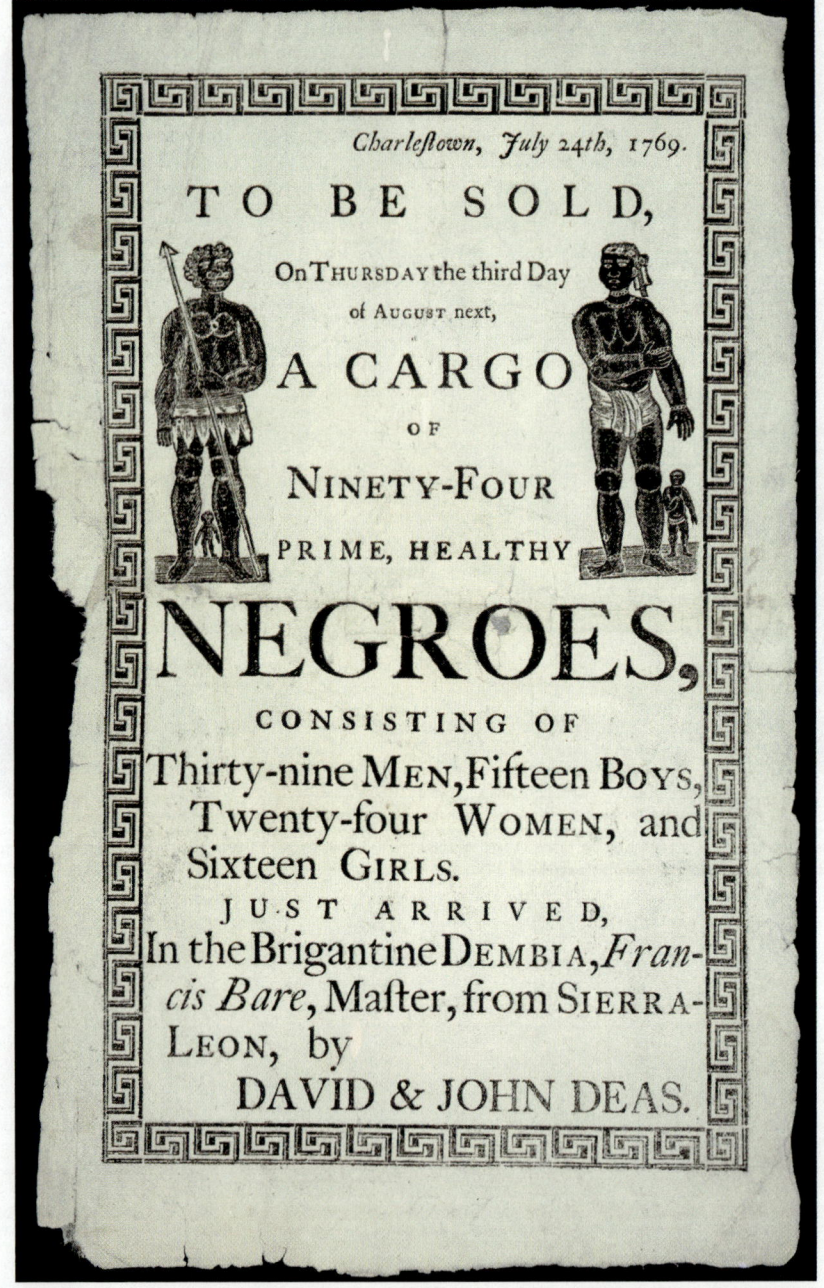

> Charlestown, July 24th, 1769.
>
> TO BE SOLD,
>
> On THURSDAY the third Day of AUGUST next,
>
> A CARGO
>
> OF
>
> NINETY-FOUR
>
> PRIME, HEALTHY
>
> NEGROES,
>
> CONSISTING OF
> Thirty-nine MEN, Fifteen BOYS, Twenty-four WOMEN, and Sixteen GIRLS.
> JUST ARRIVED,
> In the Brigantine DEMBIA, *Francis Bare*, Master, from SIERRA-LEON, by
> DAVID & JOHN DEAS.

(Broadside from Charlestown, South Carolina advertising the sale of a new shipment of slaves, 24th July, 1769 (print)/American School, (18th century)/AMERICAN ANTIQUARIAN SOCIETY/American Antiquarian Society, Worcester, Massachusetts, USA/Bridgeman Images)

SOURCE 14.6 Data: Patterns of the Slave Trade

Numbers, or quantitative data, may not convey the same immediacy or emotional impact that images or first-person accounts often carry. Nevertheless, they have an important role in informing historians' efforts to understand the slave trade. Here are two tables and an aggregate statistic that provide information on various aspects of the slave trade. They are derived from the Trans-Atlantic Slave Trade Database (slavevoyages.org), a huge collection of searchable information culled from almost 35,000 individual slave voyages.

- What kind of understandings can be obtained from data such as this that are not available from the other sources in this feature? What are the limitations of this information?
- In what ways did the slave trade change over time, according to this data? How might you account for these changes?
- What might you find surprising in this data?

SOURCE 14.6A
Voyages and Slave Rebellion: An Aggregate Statistic

Overall percentage of voyages (1501–1866) that experienced a major slave rebellion: 10 percent

SOURCE 14.6B
Changing Patterns of the Slave Trade

Century	Total Taken from Africa	Total Landed at Destination	% Died During Middle Passage	Avg. Days in Middle Passage	Avg. % Slaves = Children	Avg. % Slaves = Male
1501–1600	227,506	199,285	12.0	—	0	58
1601–1700	1,875,631	1,522,677	23.3	76.1	11.6	58.4
1701–1800	6,494,619	5,609,869	11.9	70	18.4	64.2
1801–1866	3,873,580	3,370,825	10.3	45.9	29.4	67.6
Total or Average	12,521,336 (Total)	10,702,656 (Total)	11.9 (Avg.)	60 (Avg.)	20.9 (Avg.)	64.7 (Avg.)

Source: *Voyages: The Trans-Atlantic Slave Trade Database*, 2009, http://www.slavevoyages.org (accessed June 8, 2015).

SOURCE 14.6C
Percentage of Slave Arrivals by Destination

Century	Europe	North America	Caribbean	Spanish American Mainland	Brazil	Africa	Other
1501–1600	1.1	—	8	66.7	1.9	0.3	22
1601–1700	0.6	1.5	56.4	22.7	17	0.1	1.6
1701–1800	0.1	5.2	64.4	1.2	29	0.1	0.1
1801–1866	—	2.0	31.9	0.9	60	4.8	0
Average of Total	0.1	3.8	51.9	3.3	38.9	1.8	0.3

Source: *Voyages: The Trans-Atlantic Slave Trade Database*, 2009, http://www.slavevoyages.org (accessed June 8, 2015).

DOING HISTORY

1. **Noticing what is missing:** What perspectives are missing that might add other dimensions to our understanding of this trade in people?

2. **Understanding the operation of the transatlantic slave system:** To what extent was that system based on conquest and coercion? In what ways was it a negotiated arrangement?

3. **Assessing historical responsibility:** What light do these sources shed on the much-debated question about who should be held responsible for the tragedy of the Atlantic slave trade?

HISTORIANS' VOICES

Describing the Middle Passage

The sources used and questions asked by historians can lead to accounts of the same event or process that differ significantly in tone or emphasis. This is the case with the two Voices that follow, both of which describe the Middle Passage — the harrowing sea journey across the Atlantic taken by millions of slaves. In Voice 14.1, Lisa Lindsay, a specialist in West African history, draws upon eyewitness accounts of the voyages to describe the conditions on board slave ships during Middle Passage. Note in particular Lindsay's use of a passage from Equiano that is reproduced in Source 14.1. In Voice 14.2, Johannes Postma, a specialist in the Atlantic slave trade, summarizes the recent scholarship on mortality rates during the Middle Passage, which draws heavily on slave-ship logbooks.

- How do the two accounts differ in tone and coverage?
- What does each voice add to your understanding of the Middle Passage?
- **Integrating primary and secondary sources:** Write a description of the Middle Passage using both the primary sources and historians' voices in this feature.

VOICE 14.1

Lisa Lindsay on Conditions Above and Below Deck during the Middle Passage | 2008

Between the large numbers of people crammed into unventilated spaces and the intestinal diseases that ravaged them, the holds of slave vessels became filthy cesspools. "The closeness of the place, and the heat of the climate," Equiano wrote, "added to the number in the ship, which was so crowded that each had scarcely room to turn himself, almost suffocated us. This produced copious perspirations, so that the air soon became unfit for respiration, from a variety of loathsome smells, and brought on a sickness among the slaves, of which many died." The French slave trader Jean Barbot noted that sometimes the heat and lack of oxygen on the lower decks of slave ships were so intense that the surgeons would faint away and the candles would not burn." . . . Below decks, the muck and stench from blood, sweat, urine, feces, and vomit overwhelmed any attempts at cleanliness. Crews were ordered to mop up the mess, scrub down the ship, and clear the air below decks with vinegar, whitewash or tar. . . .

Women and children frequently were allowed to move freely on deck, but slave traders brought out adult men only at specific times, including for exercise. With the prodding of a whip and occasionally a drum, accordion, or fiddle for accompaniment, they forced slaves to "dance": on deck. . . . Sometimes ships' crews took sadistic delight in such spectacles. In 1792, for instance, Capitan John Kimber was tried in the British Court of Admiralty over the death of a 15-year-old female slave. . . . According to the prosecution, Kimber tortured the young woman to death because she had refused to dance naked on the deck of his ship. He was ultimately acquitted. . . .

Source: Lisa A. Lindsay, *Captives as Commodities: The Transatlantic Slave Trade* (Upper Saddle River, NJ: Pearson/Prentice Hall, 2008), 91–92.

VOICE 14.2

Johannes Postma on Mortality during the Middle Passage | 2003

One of the much debated issues concerning the Atlantic slave trade is the death rate for slaves during the Middle Passage.... Abolitionists cited extremely high mortality figures for slaves and sailors, and used them to denounce the slave trade as both immoral and wasteful. Because slaves were valuable investment property, ship captains kept careful records in logbooks and mortality lists of the dates and causes of death, as well as the gender and age of the deceased. These records survive for about one-fifth of the documented slave voyages and are now accessible through the Cambridge University Press Database. They show that on average 12 percent of the enslaved did not survive the ocean crossing, though there was considerable variation from one transport to another. Before 1700, death rates tended to be higher, averaging more than 22 percent. They decreased to about 10 percent by the end of the eighteenth century, but rose again to nearly 12 percent during the years of illegal trading in the mid-nineteenth century....

High mortality rates during the Middle Passage were usually blamed on conditions aboard the slave ships, and there is no doubt that crowding spread contagious diseases quickly. Intestinal disorders such as dysentery were the most common killers, often appearing in epidemic proportions. These ailments, along with tropical diseases such as malaria and yellow fever were responsible for about 70 percent of the casualties. Smallpox and scurvy also killed slaves, particularly before the mid-eighteenth century. Respiratory illnesses, heart attacks, suicide (jumping overboard or refusing to eat), revolts, storms, shipwrecks, attacks by pirates, and fights among slaves were also listed as causes of death.

Source: Johannes Postma, *The Atlantic Slave Trade* (Westport, CT: Greenwood Press, 2003), 43–45.

CHAPTER 15

Thinking through Sources

Renewal and Reform in the Early Modern World

Cultural and religious traditions change over time in various ways and for various reasons. Some of these changes occur as a result of internal tensions or criticisms within these traditions or in response to social and economic transformations in the larger society. The Protestant Reformation, for example, grew out of deep dissatisfaction with the prevailing teachings and practices of the Roman Catholic Church and drew support from a growing middle class and a disaffected peasantry. At other times, cultural change has occurred by incorporating or reacting against new ideas drawn from contact with outsiders. Chinese Confucianism took on a distinctive tone and flavor as it drew on the insights of Buddhism, and a new South Asian religion called Sikhism sought to combine elements of Hindu and Muslim beliefs. Whatever the stimulus for cultural change, departures from accepted ways of thinking have sometimes been expressed as a return to a purer and more authentic past, even if that past is largely imaginary. In other cases, however, change was presented as a necessary break from an outmoded past, even if many elements from earlier times were retained.

All across the Eurasian world of the early modern era—in Western Europe, India, and the Middle East—significant protests against established ways of thinking were brewing. In each of the sources that follow, we are listening in on just one side of extended debates or controversies, focusing on those seeking change. To what extent were these changes moving in the same direction? How did they differ? What were the sources of these changes, and how were they expressed? How might those who opposed these changes respond?

SOURCE 15.1 Luther's Protest

Europe was home to perhaps the most substantial cultural transformations during the early modern centuries. In that region, the Protestant Reformation sharply challenged both the doctrines and the authority of the Roman Catholic Church, ending the near monopoly on religion that the church had exercised in Western Europe for many centuries and introducing a bitter and often-violent divide into the religious and political life of the region. Later, the practitioners of the Scientific Revolution, and the Enlightenment that followed from it, introduced a revolutionary new understanding of both the physical world and human society while urging novel means of obtaining knowledge.

The Protestant Reformation and the Scientific Revolution/Enlightenment shared a common hostility to established authority, and both represented a clear departure from previous patterns of thought and behavior. But they differed sharply in how they represented the changes they sought. Reformation leaders looked to the past, seeking to restore or renew what they believed was an earlier and more authentic version of Christianity. Leaders of the Scientific Revolution and the Enlightenment, by contrast, foresaw and embraced an altogether new world in the making. They were the "moderns" combating the "ancients."

The most prominent figure in the Protestant Reformation was Martin Luther (1483–1546), a German monk, priest, and theologian. A prolific scholar and writer, Luther translated the Bible into German and composed many theological treatises and hymns. The excerpts in Source 15.1, however, come from conversations with his students, friends, and colleagues, which they carefully recorded. After Luther's death, these recollections of the reformer's thoughts were compiled and published under the title *Table Talk*.

- Based on this source, what issues drove the Protestant Reformation?
- What theological questions are addressed in these excerpts? How does Luther understand the concepts of law, good works, grace, and faith?
- In what ways is Luther critical of the papacy, monks, and the monastic orders of the Catholic Church? What do you make of the tone of Luther's remarks?

MARTIN LUTHER | *Table Talk* | Early sixteenth century

On the Bible

No greater mischief can happen to a Christian people, than to have God's Word taken from them, or falsified, so that they no longer have it pure and clear. The ungodly papists prefer the authority of the church far above God's Word; a blasphemy abominable and not to be endured; wherewith, void of all shame and piety, they spit in God's face.

Pope, cardinals, bishops, not a soul of them has read the Bible; 'tis a book unknown to them. They are a pack of guzzling, stuffing wretches, rich, wallowing in wealth and laziness, resting secure in their power, and never, for a moment, thinking of accomplishing God's will.

On Salvation

He that goes from the gospel to the law, thinking to be saved by good works, falls as uneasily as he who falls from the true service of God to idolatry; for, without Christ, all is idolatry and fictitious imaginings of God, whether of the Turkish Koran [Quran], of the pope's decrees, or Moses' law.

The Gospel preaches nothing of the merit of works; he that says the Gospel requires works for salvation, I say, flat and plain, is a liar. Nothing that is properly good proceeds out of the works of the law, unless grace be present; for what we are forced to do, goes not from the heart, nor is acceptable.

But a true Christian says: I am justified and saved only by faith in Christ, without any works or merits of my own....

Prayer in popedom is mere tongue-threshing...; not prayer but a work of obedience.

On the Pope and the Church Hierarchy

The great prelates, the puffed-up saints, the rich usurers, the ox drovers that seek unconscionable gain, etc., these are not God's servants....

Our dealing and proceeding against the pope is altogether excommunication, which is simply the public declaration that a person is disobedient to Christ's Word. Now we affirm in public, that the pope and his retinue believe not; therefore we conclude that he shall not be saved, but be damned....

Antichrist is the pope and the Turk together; a beast full of life must have a body and soul; the spirit or soul of antichrist is the pope, his flesh or body the Turk.... Kings and princes coin money only out of metals, but the pope coins money out of every thing—indulgences, ceremonies, dispensations, pardons; 'tis all fish comes to his net....

The pope and his crew are mere worshippers of idols, and servants of the devil.... He pretends great holiness, under color of the outward service of God, for he has instituted orders with hoods, with shavings, fasting, eating of fish, saying mass, and such like.... [F]or his doctrine he gets money and wealth, honor and power, and is so great a monarch, that he can bring emperors under his girdle.

The chief cause that I fell out with the pope was this: the pope boasted that he was the head of the church, and condemned all that would not be under his power and authority....

The fasting of the friars is more easy to them than our eating to us. For one day of fasting there are three of feasting. Every friar for his supper has two quarts of beer, a quart of wine, and spice-cakes, or bread prepared with spice and salt, the better to relish their drink. Thus go on these poor fasting brethren; getting so pale and wan, they are like the fiery angels.

The state of celibacy is great hypocrisy and wickedness.... Christ with one sentence confutes all their arguments: God created them male and female.... Now eating, drinking, marrying, etc., are of God's making, therefore they are good....

A Christian's worshipping is not the external, hypocritical mask that our spiritual friars wear, when they chastise their bodies, torment and make themselves faint, with ostentatious fasting, watching, singing, wearing hair shirts, scourging themselves, etc. Such worshipping God desires not.

Source: William Hazlitt, ed. and trans., *The Table Talk of Martin Luther* (London: H. G. Bohn, 1857).

■ ■ ■

SOURCE 15.2 Calvinism and Catholicism ▶

Protestant opposition to Roman Catholic practice was not limited to matters of theology, liturgy, and church corruption, but came to include the physical appearance of churches as well. Martin Luther was suspicious of the many sculptures and paintings that served as objects of devotion to the Catholic faithful, but John Calvin, the prominent French-born Protestant theologian, went even further, declaring that "God forbade . . . the making of any images representing him."

Perhaps the most dramatic expression of these ideas took place in regions of Europe where Protestants took over formerly Roman Catholic churches for their new forms of worship. During the 1560s, waves of Protestant image smashing, sometimes called the Iconoclastic Fury, took place in England, France, Switzerland, the Netherlands, and elsewhere. This engraving, produced in 1566 at the height of these religious conflicts, depicts Protestants "cleansing" a Catholic church in Antwerp, in what is now Belgium, of what they viewed as idolatrous decorations but Catholics revered as objects of devotion.

An English Catholic observer described this event and others like it with horror: "These fresh followers of this new preaching [Protestantism] threw down the graven and defaced the painted images. . . . They tore the curtains, dashed in pieces the carved work of brass and stone, . . . pulled up the brass of the gravestones. . . . [T]he Blessed Sacrament of the altar . . . they trod under their feet and (horrible it is to say!) shed their stinking piss upon it. . . . [T]hese false brethren burned and rent not only all kind of Church books, but, moreover, destroyed whole libraries of books of all sciences and tongues, yea the Holy Scriptures and the ancient fathers, and tore in pieces the maps and charts of the descriptions of countries."[1]

These often-dramatic attacks on churches served a practical purpose in preparing the site for Protestant worship. But they also reflected the new beliefs of the Protestants, or, as one scholar has put it, expressed "theology in stone." These churches were stripped of visual distractions and altars where the miracle of the mass took place. Instead there emerged a church, frequently without any images or other diversions like organs or other musical instruments, whose main focal point was the pulpit where the word of God was preached.

- What elements of the Catholic description of this attack can you identify in the image? What other acts of destruction can you notice?
- What differences in religious understanding lay behind such attacks?
- What accounts for the passion displayed in these attacks? Is this kind of religious violence a thing of the past or does it have contemporary counterparts today?

Source 15.2 Calvinism and Catholicism

Engraving of Calvinists Destroying Statues in a Catholic Church | 1566

SOURCE 15.3 Progress and Enlightenment

If the Protestant Reformation represented a major change within the framework of the Christian faith, the Scientific Revolution and the European Enlightenment came to be seen by many as a challenge to all Christian understandings of the world. After all, these two movements celebrated the powers of human reason to unlock the mysteries of the universe and proclaimed the possibility of a new human society shaped by human reason. Among the most prominent spokesmen for the Enlightenment was the Marquis de Condorcet (1743–1794), a French mathematician, philosopher, and active participant in the French Revolution. In his *Sketch of the Progress of the Human Mind*, Condorcet described ten stages of human development. Source 15.3 contains excerpts from "The Ninth Epoch," whose title refers to the era in which Condorcet was living, and "The Tenth Epoch," referring to the age to come. Condorcet's optimism about that future was not borne out in his own life, for he fell afoul of the radicalism of the French Revolution and died in prison in 1794.

- What is Condorcet's view of the relationship between the Scientific Revolution and the Enlightenment?
- How, precisely, does Condorcet imagine the future of humankind?
- How might Martin Luther respond to Condorcet's vision of the future? How do their understandings of human potential differ?

MARQUIS DE CONDORCET | *Sketch of the Progress of the Human Mind* | 1793–1794

The Ninth Epoch: From Descartes to the Formation of the French Republic

[T]he progress of philosophy ... destroyed within the general mass of people the prejudices that have afflicted and corrupted the human race for so long a time.

Humanity was finally permitted to boldly proclaim the long ignored right to submit every opinion to reason, that is to utilize the only instrument given to us for grasping and recognizing the truth. Each human learned with a sort of pride that nature had never destined him to believe the word of others. The superstitions of antiquity and the abasement of reason before the madness of supernatural religion disappeared from society just as they had disappeared from philosophy....

If we were to limit ourselves to showing the benefits derived from the immediate applications of the sciences, or in their applications to man-made devices for the well-being of individuals and the prosperity of nations, we would be making known only a slim part of their benefits. The most important, perhaps, is having destroyed prejudices, and reestablished human intelligence, which until then had been forced to bend down to false instructions instilled in it by absurd beliefs passed on to the children of each generation by the terrors of superstition and the fear of tyranny....

The advances of scientific knowledge are all the more deadly to these errors because they destroy them without appearing to attack them, while lavishing on those who stubbornly defend them the degrading taunt of ignorance....

Finally this progress of scientific knowledge...results in a belief that not birth, professional status, or social standing gives anyone the right to judge something he does not understand. This unstoppable progress cannot be observed without having enlightened men search unceasingly for ways to make the other branches of learning follow the same path....

The Tenth Epoch: The Future Progress of the Human Mind

Our hopes for the future of the human species may be reduced to three important points: the destruction of inequality among nations; the progress of equality within nations themselves; and finally, the real improvement of humanity. Should not all the nations of the world approach one day the state of civilization reached by the most enlightened peoples such as the French and the Anglo-Americans? Will not the slavery of nations subjected to kings, the barbarity of African tribes, and the ignorance of savages gradually disappear?...

If we cast an eye at the existing state of the globe, we will see right away that in Europe the principles of the French constitution are already those of all enlightened men. We will see that they are too widely disseminated and too openly professed for the efforts of tyrants and priests to prevent them from penetrating into the hovels of their slaves....

Can it be doubted that either wisdom or the senseless feuds of the European nations themselves, working with the slow but certain effects of progress in their colonies, will not soon produce the independence of the new world; and that then the European population, spreading rapidly across that immense land, must either civilize or make disappear the savage peoples that now inhabit these vast continents?...

Thus the day will come when the sun will shine only on free men born knowing no other master but their reason; where tyrants and their slaves, priests and their ignorant, hypocritical writings will exist only in the history books and theaters.... If we consider the human creations based on scientific theories, we shall see that their progress can have no limits;...that new tools, machines, and looms will add every day to the capabilities and skill of humans; they will improve and perfect the precision of their products while decreasing the amount of time and labor needed to produce them....

A smaller piece of land will be able to produce commodities of greater usefulness and value than before; greater benefits will be obtained with less waste; the production of the same industrial product will result in less destruction of raw materials and greater durability.... [E]ach individual will work less but more productively and will be able to better satisfy his needs....

Among the advances of the human mind we should reckon as most important for the general welfare is the complete destruction of those prejudices that have established an inequality of rights between the sexes, an inequality damaging even to the party it favors....

The most enlightened people ... will slowly come to perceive war as the deadliest plague and the most monstrous of crimes.... They will understand that they cannot become conquerors without losing their liberty; that perpetual alliances are the only way to preserve independence; and that they should seek their security, not power....

We may conclude then that the perfectibility of humanity is indefinite.

Finally, can we not also extend the same hopes to the intellectual and moral faculties? ... Is it not also probable that education, while perfecting these qualities, will also influence, modify, and improve that bodily nature itself? ...

Source: Marquis de Condorcet, *Sketch of the Progress of the Human Mind* (Paris: Firmin Didot Frères, 1847), Epoch 9 and Epoch 10.

■ ■ ■

SOURCE 15.4 Art and Enlightenment ▶

Public lectures on scientific topics became widespread in Europe during the eighteenth century, serving to spread the new knowledge and to bring "enlightenment" to a wider circle of people. The following painting, titled *A Philosopher Giving a Lecture on the Orrery*, by English artist Joseph Wright (1734–1797), illustrates such a presentation. The central figure in a red robe — modeled, some suggest, on the famous scientist Isaac Newton — is demonstrating the movements of the planets around the sun, using an "orrery," a mechanical device that shows their orbits and their relationship to one another. His captivated audience includes three men, two small boys, and two girls or young women. The light source is an oil lamp, which represents the sun at the center of the solar system.

- The kind of fascination or awe that characterizes the spectators had previously been reserved largely for witnesses to religious events. What is stimulating that sense of wonderment in this painting? Is there something quasi-religious about the scene?

- What metaphorical or symbolic meaning might be attached to the illuminated faces, which contrast sharply with the surrounding darkness?

- In what ways does this painting illustrate Condorcet's vision of the role that science and reason will play in the coming age of progress and enlightenment?

Source 15.4 Art and Enlightenment

JOSEPH WRIGHT | *A Philosopher Giving a Lecture on the Orrery* | ca. 1766

('The Orrery', c.1766 (oil on canvas), Wright of Derby, Joseph (1734–97) / Derby Museum and Art Gallery, UK / Bridgeman Images)

■ ■ ■

SOURCE 15.5 The Wahhabi Perspective on Islam

Within the Islamic world, the major cultural movements of the early modern era were those of religious renewal. Such movements sought to eliminate the "deviations" that had crept into Islamic practice over the centuries and to return to a purer version of the faith that presumably had prevailed during the foundational period of the religion. The most influential of these movements was associated with Muhammad Ibn Abd al-Wahhab, whose revivalist movement spread widely in Arabia during the second half of the eighteenth century. Source 15.5, written by the grandson of al-Wahhab shortly after the capture of Mecca in 1803, provides a window into the outlook of Wahhabi Islam.

- What specific objections did the Wahhabis have to the prevailing practice of Islam in eighteenth-century Arabia?
- How did the Wahhabis put their ideas into practice once they had seized control of Mecca?
- What similarities do you see between the outlook of the Wahhabis and that of Martin Luther? What differences can you identify?

ABDULLAH WAHHAB | *History and Doctrines of the Wahhabis* | 1803

Now I was engaged in the holy war . . . , when God, praised be He, graciously permitted us to enter Mecca. . . . Now, though we were more numerous, better armed and disciplined than the people of Mecca, yet we did not cut down their trees, neither did we hunt, nor shed any blood except the blood of victims, and of those four-footed beasts which the Lord has made lawful by his commands.

When our pilgrimage was over . . . our leader, whom the Lord saves, explained to the divines what we required of the people, . . . namely, a pure belief in the Unity of God Almighty. He pointed out to them that there was no dispute between us and them except on two points, and that one of these was a sincere belief in the Unity of God, and a knowledge of the different kinds of prayer. . . .

They then acknowledged our belief, and there was not one among them who doubted. . . . And they swore a binding oath, although we had not asked them, that their hearts had been opened and their doubts removed, and that they were convinced whoever said, "Oh prophet of God!" or "Oh Ibn 'Abbes!" or "Oh 'Abdul Qadir!" or called on any other created being, thus entreating him to turn away evil or grant what is good (where the power belongs to God alone), such as recovery from sickness, or victory over enemies, or protection from temptation, etc.; he is a Mushrik, guilty of the most heinous form of shirk [unbelief], his blood shall be shed and property confiscated. . . . Again, the tombs which had been erected over the remains of the pious, had become in these times as it were idols where the people went to pray for what they required; they humbled themselves before them, and called upon those lying in them, in their distress, just as did those who were in darkness before the coming of Muhammad. . . .

Source 15.5 The Wahhabi Perspective on Islam

We razed all the large tombs in the city which the people generally worshipped and believed in, and by which they hoped to obtain benefits or ward off evil, so that there did not remain an idol to be adored in that pure city, for which God be praised. Then the taxes and customs we abolished, all the different kinds of instruments for using tobacco we destroyed, and tobacco itself we proclaimed forbidden. Next we burned the dwellings of those selling hashish, and living in open wickedness, and issued a proclamation, directing the people to constantly exercise themselves in prayer. They were not to pray in separate groups . . . , but all were directed to arrange themselves at each time of prayer behind any Imam who is a follower of any of the four Imams [founders of major schools of Islamic law]. . . . For in this way the Lord would be worshiped by as it were one voice, the faithful of all sects would become friendly disposed towards each other, and all dissensions would cease. . . .

[W]e do not reject anyone who follows any of the four Imams, as do the Shias. . . . We do not claim to exercise our reason in all matters of religion, and of our faith, save that we follow our judgment where a point is clearly demonstrated to us in either the Quran or the Sunnah [traditions of Muhammad's actions]. . . . We do not command the destruction of any writings except such as tend to cast people into infidelity to injure their faith, such as those on Logic, which have been prohibited by all Divines. But we are not very exacting with regard to books or documents of this nature; if they appear to assist our opponents, we destroy them. . . . We do not consider it proper to make Arabs prisoners of war, nor have we done so, neither do we fight with other nations. Finally, we do not consider it lawful to kill women or children. . . .

We consider pilgrimage is supported by legal custom, but it should not be undertaken except to a mosque, and for the purpose of praying in it. Therefore, whoever performs pilgrimage for this purpose, is not wrong, and doubtless those who spend the precious moments of their existence in invoking the Prophet, shall . . . obtain happiness in this world and the next. . . . We do not deny miraculous powers to the saints, but on the contrary allow them. . . . But whether alive or dead, they must not be made the object of any form of worship. . . .

We prohibit those forms of Bidah [innovation or heresy] that affect religion or pious works. Thus drinking coffee, reciting poetry, praising kings, do not affect religion or pious works and are not prohibited. . . .

All games are lawful. Our prophet allowed play in his mosque. So it is lawful to chide and punish persons in various ways; to train them in the use of different weapons; or to use anything which tends to encourage warriors in battle, such as a war-drum. But it must not be accompanied with musical instruments. These are forbidden, and indeed the difference between them and a war drum is clear.

Source: J. O'Kinealy, "Translation of an Arabic Pamphlet on the History and Doctrines of the Wahhabis," *Journal of the Asiatic Society of Bengal* 43 (1874): 68–82.

SOURCE 15.6 The Poetry of Kabir

Early modern India was a place of much religious creativity and the interaction of various traditions. The majority of India's people practiced one or another of the many forms of Hinduism, while its Mughal rulers and perhaps 20 percent of the population were Muslims. And a new religion—Sikhism—took shape in the sixteenth century as well. Certainly there was tension and sometimes conflict among these religious communities, but not all was hostility across religious boundaries. In the writings of Kabir (1440–1518), perhaps India's most beloved poet, the sectarian differences among these religions dissolved into a mystical and transcendent love of the Divine in all of its many forms. Born into a family of Muslim weavers, Kabir as a young man became a student of a famous Hindu ascetic, Ramananda. Kabir's own poetry was and remains revered among Hindus, Muslims, and Sikhs alike. Source 15.6 contains selections from his poetry, translated by the famous Indian writer Rabindranath Tagore in the early twentieth century.

- In what ways was Kabir critical of conventional religious practice—both Muslim and Hindu?
- How would you describe Kabir's religious vision?
- How might more orthodox Hindus and Muslims respond to Kabir? How would the Wahhabis, in particular, take issue with Kabir's religious outlook?

KABIR | *Poetry* | ca. late fifteenth century

O servant, where dost thou seek Me? Lo! I am beside thee.

I am neither in temple nor in mosque: I am neither in Kaaba [central shrine of Islam] nor in Kailash [a mountain sacred to Hindus]
Neither am I in rites and ceremonies, nor in Yoga and renunciation.
If thou art a true seeker, thou shalt at once see Me: . . . Kabir says, "O Sadhu! [a Hindu ascetic seeker] God is the breath of all breath."

It is needless to ask of a saint the caste to which he belongs;
For the priest, the warrior, the tradesman, and all the thirty-six castes, alike are seeking for God.
 The barber has sought God, the washerwoman, and the carpenter—
Even Raidas [a low-caste poet] was a seeker after God.
The Rishi Swapacha was a tanner by caste [an untouchable].
Hindus and Moslems alike have achieved that End, where remains no mark of distinction.

Within this earthen vessel [the human body] are bowers and groves, and within it is the Creator:
Within this vessel are the seven oceans and the unnumbered stars.

The touchstone and the jewel-appraiser are within;
And within this vessel the Eternal soundeth, and the spring wells up.
Kabir says: "Listen to me, my Friend! My beloved Lord is within."

Your Lord is near: yet you are climbing the palm-tree to seek Him.
The Brâhman priest goes from house to house and initiates people into faith:
Alas! the true fountain of life is beside you, and you have set up a stone to worship.
Kabir says: "I may never express how sweet my Lord is.
Yoga and the telling of beads, virtue and vice—these are naught to Him."

I do not ring the temple bell:
I do not set the idol on its throne:
I do not worship the image with flowers.
It is not the austerities that mortify the flesh which are pleasing to the Lord,
When you leave off your clothes and kill your senses, you do not please the Lord.
The man who is kind and who practices righteousness, who remains passive amidst the affairs of the world, who considers all creatures on earth as his own self,
He attains the Immortal Being, the true God is ever with him.

There is nothing but water at the holy bathing places;
And I know that they are useless, for I have bathed in them.
The images are all lifeless, they cannot speak; I know, for I have cried aloud to them.
The Purana [Hindu religious texts] and the Koran [Quran] are mere words; lifting up the curtain, I have seen.

Kabir gives utterance to the words of experience; and he knows very well that all other things are untrue.

Source: Rabindranath Tagore, trans., *The Songs of Kabir* (New York, NY: Macmillan, 1915).

■ ■ ■

SOURCE 15.7 Religious Syncretism in Indian Art ▶

Another site of religious blending in early modern India took shape at the court of the Mughal emperor. There, Akbar presided over what we might now call interfaith gatherings and created a blended religious cult for Mughal elites. European-style religious art, painted by Mughal artists, appeared prominently at court, featuring scenes including Jesus, Mary, and various Christian saints.

The Muslim rulers of the Mughal Empire were also taking a growing interest in the ancient Hindu mind–body practice known as yoga. Some of the sultans seemed persuaded that such postures and practices conveyed great power that might well benefit themselves. Around 1550, a Muslim Sufi master closely connected to the Mughal court, Muhammad Gwaliyari, compiled systematic descriptions of twenty-two yoga postures, hoping to incorporate them into Sufi spiritual practice. Somewhat later, the Muslim prince Salim, who subsequently became the emperor Jahangir, commissioned a Hindu artist to illustrate this text, known as *The Ocean of Life*. In some of these illustrations, such as the one reproduced here, the yogi's face is painted to resemble that of Jesus, as depicted in the European religious literature then circulating in the Mughal court. Such images represented a remarkable cultural blending of Islamic patrons, Hindu practice, and Christian traditions.

- Why might Muslim rulers and Sufi masters want to incorporate Hindu-based yoga techniques into their own practices?
- What does the painting of a yogi with the face of Christ suggest about Indian views of Jesus?

Source 15.7 Religious Syncretism in Indian Art

Kumbhaka (breathing exercises) | ca. 1600

(© The Trustees of the Chester Beatty Library, Dublin)

DOING HISTORY

1. **Comparing views of human potential:** What different understandings of human potential might you infer from these sources? What do the people who created them believe is necessary to realize or fulfill that potential?

2. **Comparing religious reformers:** Consider the religious outlooks of Luther, al-Wahhab, and Kabir. What similarities and differences can you identify?

3. **Imagining a conversation:** Construct an imaginary debate or conversation between Condorcet and one or more of the religious or spiritually inclined authors of these sources.

HISTORIANS' VOICES

Reform and Renewal in the Christian and Islamic Worlds

Both the Christian and Islamic worlds experienced vibrant reform movements in the early modern period that were expressed through commitments to do away with human corruptions of the faith that had accrued over centuries and to return to the "pure" and uncorrupted original message of each faith's holy text. The two selections that follow offer an opportunity to compare the goals and principles of two of the most prominent movements of the period—the Protestant Reformation in Christian Europe and Wahhabism in Islamic Arabia. Voice 15.1 is that of Robert W. Scribner, a leading British historian of the early Protestant Reformation in Germany, while Voice 15.2 belongs to Natana Delong-Bas, a theologian and historian based in Canada who has written extensively on the founder of the Wahhabi movement.

- For Scribner in Voice 15.1, what were the positive and negative elements of the Protestant Reform agenda, and what does he mean by "positive" and "negative"?
- In what ways are the reform agendas of German Protestants and al-Wahhab similar?
- **Integrating primary and secondary sources:** Using these two Voices and Sources 15.1, 15.2, and 15.5, compare and contrast the agendas of the Protestant Reformation and the Wahhabi movement.

VOICE 15.1

R. W. Scribner on the Evangelical Agenda in Protestant Germany | 1986

For some time now it has been common for scholars of the Reformation to speak of it as an 'evangelical movement'. The term captures the tone of the upsurge of religious enthusiasm that swept through Germany in the early 1520s. In its broadest manifestations, it was a movement of biblical renewal. Many felt that the genuine Christian message, the 'pure word of God' as it was recorded in the Bible, had been rediscovered after it had lain hidden or obscured for many generations. . . .

Beyond its catchwords, what was the message of this movement? It is traditional to associate it with the doctrines of Luther, and these certainly played a prominent role. . . . However, the evangelical message was far more complex than the ideas of one man. It had both positive and negative elements. The negative elements drew on an endemic anticlericalism, the product of a long disillusionment with the clergy. . . . Priests and monks were stigmatised as 'enemies of the Gospel'. . . . who were likely to lead people to damnation rather than to salvation.

The positive message stood in counterpoint to the negative: the laity no longer needed the clergy for salvation, since each Christian was free to find salvation through a direct encounter with God in the Bible. This encounter occurred in two ways: through reading the Bible, and through hearing the Word preached. . . . The Word was seen not just as a way to salvation, but as a guide for life in the world.

Source: R. W. Scribner, *The German Reformation* (Basingstoke, UK: Macmillan, 1986), 17–18.

VOICE 15.2

Natana DeLong-Bas on the Teachings of Ibn Abd al-Wahhab | 2004

Ibn Abd al-Wahhab's dissatisfaction with and ultimate rejection of adherence to past interpretations of Islam (*taqlid*) grew out of his encounter with *hadith* criticism [the writings of earlier scholars on the *hadith*, sayings traditionally attributed to Muhammad]. Recognizing the importance of returning directly to scripture rather than relying on secondhand interpretations, led him to call for the rejuvenation of the practice of independent reasoning (*ijtihad*). His rejuvenation of *ijtihad* involved the clear and unequivocal assertion of the Quran and *hadith* alone as authoritative sources of revelation, taking precedence over human interpretation....

His rejection of *taqlid*, therefore, was not so much a matter of rejecting the past as it was a desire to break away from a mentality insisting that only people who had lived in the past were capable of correct interpretation of the scripture.... [H]e sought to push Muslims into their own personal encounters with God by direct reading and interpretation of scripture.

Source: Natana J. DeLong-Bas, *Wahhabi Islam: From Revival and Reform to Global Jihad* (Oxford, UK: Oxford University Press, 2004), 282.

NOTE

1. Robert S. Miola, ed., *Early Modern Catholicism: An Anthology of Primary Sources* (Oxford: Oxford University Press, 2007), 59.

CHAPTER 16

Thinking through Sources

Claiming Rights

In the discourse of the age of Atlantic revolutions, no idea had a more enduring resonance than that of "rights"—natural rights, political and civic rights, and "the rights of man," or, in a more recent expression, "human rights." However these rights were defined, they were understood as both natural and universal. They were considered inherent in the human condition, rather than granted by some authority, and they were envisioned as being the same for everyone rather than depending on a person's birth, rank, or status in society. Growing out of the European Enlightenment, this understanding of "rights" was genuinely revolutionary, challenging almost all notions of government and society prior to the late eighteenth century. But even among supporters, the idea of human rights was highly controversial. What precisely were these rights? Did they support or contradict one another? Did they apply equally to women and slaves? How should they be established and maintained? Such questions were central to this age of revolution and have informed much of the world's political history ever since.

SOURCE 16.1 The French Revolution and the "Rights of Man"

The most prominent example of the language of rights found expression during the French Revolution in the Declaration of the Rights of Man and Citizen. This document was hammered out in the French National Assembly early in that revolutionary upheaval and adopted at the end of August 1789. It has long been viewed as the philosophical core of the French Revolution. Later it became the preamble of the 1791 French Constitution.

The French document bore clear similarities to the language of the U.S. Declaration of Independence, as both drew on the ideas of the European Enlightenment. Furthermore, Thomas Jefferson, who largely wrote the U.S. Declaration, served as the ambassador to France at this time and was in close contact with Marquis de Lafayette, the principal author of the French Declaration. Lafayette, in turn, had earlier served with the American revolutionary forces seeking independence from England.

- What purposes did the writers of the Declaration expect it to fulfill?
- What specific rights are spelled out in this document? What rights does it omit?
- What was revolutionary about the Declaration? What grievances against the old regime did the Declaration reflect?

The Declaration of the Rights of Man and Citizen | 1789

The representatives of the French people, constituted as a National Assembly, and considering that ignorance, neglect, or contempt of the rights of man are the sole causes of public misfortunes and governmental corruption, have resolved to set forth in a solemn declaration the natural, inalienable and sacred rights of man....

1. Men are born and remain free and equal in rights. Social distinctions may be based only on common utility.

2. The purpose of all political association is the preservation of the natural and imprescriptible rights of man. These rights are liberty, property, security, and resistance to oppression.

3. The principle of all sovereignty rests essentially in the nation. No body and no individual may exercise authority which does not emanate expressly from the nation.

4. Liberty consists in the ability to do whatever does not harm another; hence the exercise of the natural rights of each man has no other limits than those which assure to other members of society the enjoyment of the same rights. These limits can only be determined by the law.

5. The law only has the right to prohibit those actions which are injurious to society. No hindrance should be put in the way of anything not prohibited by the law, nor may any one be forced to do what the law does not require.

6. The law is the expression of the general will. All citizens have the right to take part, in person or by their representatives, in its formation. It must be the same for everyone whether it protects or penalizes. All citizens being equal in its eyes are equally admissible to all public dignities, offices, and employments, according to their ability, and with no other distinction than that of their virtues and talents.

7. No man may be indicted, arrested, or detained except in cases determined by the law and according to the forms which it has prescribed....

9. Every man being presumed innocent until judged guilty, if it is deemed indispensable to arrest him, all rigor unnecessary to securing his person should be severely repressed by the law.

10. No one should be disturbed for his opinions, even in religion, provided that their manifestation does not trouble public order as established by law.

11. The free communication of thoughts and opinions is one of the most precious of the rights of man. Every citizen may therefore speak, write, and print freely, if he accepts his own responsibility for any abuse of this liberty in the cases set by the law.

12. The safeguard of the rights of man and the citizen requires public powers. These powers are therefore instituted for the advantage of all, and not for the private benefit of those to whom they are entrusted.

13. For maintenance of public authority and for expenses of administration, common taxation is indispensable. It should be apportioned equally among all the citizens according to their capacity to pay....

17. Property being an inviolable and sacred right, no one may be deprived of it except when public necessity, certified by law, obviously requires it, and on the condition of a just compensation in advance.

Source: From *The French Revolution and Human Rights: A Brief Documentary History*. Edited, translated, and with an Introduction by Lynn Hunt. Copyright © 1996 by Bedford/St. Martin's. Used by permission of the publisher.

■ ■ ■

SOURCE 16.2 Representing the Declaration ▶

In the months that followed the drafting of the Declaration of the Rights of Man and Citizen, the new authorities worked to spread the Declaration's revolutionary ideas among the French population. Perhaps the most iconic representation of the Declaration to appear in the months following its promulgation was a painting created by Jean-Jacques Le Barbier (1738–1826). Like many other artists who have sought to publicize and assert the legitimacy of radically new ideas, he drew heavily on older, established symbols and artistic conventions to convey his message. Thus, Le Barbier reproduced the text of the Declaration on tablets similar to those used in religious paintings to represent the Ten Commandments brought down by Moses from Mount Sinai. The two easily identifiable symbolic female figures — the winged allegorical figure representing Fame and the other personifying France — conveyed the virtue of and the audience for the Declaration's articles. Throughout the painting, Le Barbier used common classical symbols to provide visual cues to help his audience interpret its message, such as the snake biting its tail, representing eternity; the broken chains in the hands of France, representing victory over oppression; and the laurel bunting, long associated with glory, draped over the tablets. One symbol in particular, the red bonnet or "Phrygian," would have resonated with Le Barbier's audience. It was of ancient Greek origin but had become a popular symbol of the new French nation. Engravings of Le Barbier's painting were printed in large numbers and circulated across the kingdom, spreading the Declaration's ideas and Le Barbier's visual tribute to them to a broad audience.

- Why do you think that Le Barbier used well-known figures, symbols, and imagery in his painting? Why did the artist adorn the image with only female figures?
- What message is conveyed by placing the Declaration of the Rights of Man and Citizen on tablets evoking the Ten Commandments?
- The whole composition is overseen by the eye of God the Creator radiating from a triangle that by the late eighteenth century had both biblical and Masonic connotations. What does this symbol add to the composition?

JEAN-JACQUES LE BARBIER | *Declaration of the Rights of Man and Citizen (Painting)* | ca. 1789

SOURCE 16.3 Rights and National Independence

If the "rights of man" could be mobilized on behalf of individuals against an oppressive class system as in France, those rights also came to be applied to oppressed peoples, nations, and colonial subjects, as in the United States, Haiti, Latin America, and later all across Asia and Africa. In a well-known letter written in 1815, Simón Bolívar, a prominent political and military leader in the struggle against Spanish rule in Latin America, made the case for the independence of his continent, arguing that Latin Americans' collective "rights," derived from Europe itself, had been massively violated.

- What understanding of "rights" informed Bolívar's demand for independence? Why did he feel that the situation of his people was so "extraordinary and involved"?
- What were Bolívar's chief objections to Spanish rule?
- What difficulties did Bolívar foresee in achieving the kind of stable and unified independence that he so much desired?

SIMÓN BOLÍVAR | The Jamaica Letter | 1815

Success will crown our efforts, because the destiny of [Latin] America has been irrevocably decided; the tie that bound her to Spain has been severed.... The hatred that the Peninsula has inspired in us is greater than the ocean between us. It would be easier to have the two continents meet than to reconcile the spirits of the two countries. The habit of obedience; a community of interest, of understanding, of religion; mutual goodwill; a tender regard for the birthplace and good name of our forefathers; in short, all that gave rise to our hopes, came to us from Spain.... At present the contrary attitude persists: we are threatened with the fear of death, dishonor, and every harm; there is nothing we have not suffered at the hands of that unnatural stepmother—Spain. The veil has been torn asunder.... For this reason America fights desperately....

We are, moreover, neither Indian nor European, but a species midway between the legitimate proprietors of this country and the Spanish usurpers. In short, though Americans by birth we derive our rights from Europe, and we have to assert these rights against the rights of the natives, and at the same time we must defend ourselves against the invaders. This places us in a most extraordinary and involved situation....

The role of the inhabitants of the American hemisphere has for centuries been purely passive. Politically they were nonexistent. We are still in a position lower than slavery, and therefore it is more difficult for us to rise to the enjoyment of freedom.... We have been harassed by a conduct which has not only deprived us of our rights but has kept us in a sort of permanent infancy with regard to public affairs.

Americans today ... occupy a position in society no better than that of serfs destined for labor, or at best they have no more status than that of mere consumers. Yet even this status is surrounded with galling restrictions, such as being forbidden to grow

European crops, or to store products which are royal monopolies, or to establish factories of a type the Peninsula itself does not possess. To this add the exclusive trading privileges, even in articles of prime necessity, and the barriers between American provinces, designed to prevent all exchange of trade, traffic, and understanding. In short, do you wish to know what our future held?—simply the cultivation of the fields of indigo, grain, coffee, sugar cane, cacao, and cotton; cattle raising on the broad plains; hunting wild game in the jungles; digging in the earth to mine its gold—but even these limitations could never satisfy the greed of Spain.... Is it not an outrage and a violation of human rights to expect a land so splendidly endowed, so vast, rich, and populous, to remain merely passive? ...

We were cut off and, as it were, removed from the world in relation to the science of government and administration of the state. We were never viceroys or governors, save in the rarest of instances; seldom archbishops and bishops; diplomats never; as military men, only subordinates; as nobles, without royal privileges. In brief, we were neither magistrates nor financiers and seldom merchants....

These laws favor, almost exclusively, the natives of the country who are of Spanish extraction. Thus ... those born in America have been despoiled of their constitutional rights....

The American provinces are fighting for their freedom, and they will ultimately succeed.... It is a grandiose idea to think of consolidating the New World into a single nation, united by pacts into a single bond. It is reasoned that, as these parts have a common origin, language, customs, and religion, they ought to have a single government to permit the newly formed states to unite in a confederation. But this is not possible. Actually, America is separated by climatic differences, geographic diversity, conflicting interests, and dissimilar characteristics.... This type of organization may come to pass in some happier period of our regeneration....

As soon as we are strong and under the guidance of a liberal nation which will lend us her protection, we will achieve accord in cultivating the virtues and talents that lead to glory. Then will we march majestically toward that great prosperity for which South America is destined. Then will those sciences and arts which, born in the East, have enlightened Europe, wing their way to a free Colombia, which will cordially bid them welcome.

Source: Francisco Javier Yanes y Cristóbal Mendoza Montilla: *Colección de documentos relativos a la vida pública del Libertador de Colombia y del Perú Simón Bolívar para servir a la historia de la independencia de Suramérica*, Caracas, 1833, T. XXII, pp. 207–29. Translated by Suzanne Sturn. Used by permission of Suzanne Sturn.

■ ■ ■

SOURCE 16.4 Rights and Slavery: Picturing "Reason and Nature" ▶

The language of "rights," derived from the French Revolution, had implications for race relations and the long-established practice of slavery, as well as for colonial rule. France legally abolished slavery in its colonies in 1794, though this practice was restored by Napoleon in 1802. The contradictions among the "rights of man," racial inequality, and slavery were addressed in an engraving produced in 1793, the year before slavery was abolished, titled "All Mortals Are Equal, It Is Not Birth But Virtue That Makes the Difference." The allegorical figure at the center of the image is Reason, with the sacred flame of "love of the fatherland" emerging from her head. She places a level on a white man and a man of color, behind whom is a cornucopia of abundance. The man of color holds in one hand the Declaration of the Rights of Man and Citizen (1789) and in the other the Decree of May 15, 1791, which granted free blacks and mulattoes political rights. Reason is pushed by the allegorical figure of Nature, who is seated on a sack, out of which flee the demons labeled Aristocracy, Selfishness, Injustice, and Insurrection. While this image celebrates political rights granted to free blacks and mulattoes, it could also be read as advocating the same rights for slaves at a time when France was edging toward emancipation legislation.

- What roles do the allegorical figures of Reason and Nature play in this scene?
- What does the level symbolize in this image? What meaning might you derive from the fact that the man of color is depicted in a loincloth, while the white man is fully clothed?
- How might a supporter of slave emancipation interpret this scene? How might an opponent?

All Mortals Are Equal, It Is Not Birth But Virtue That Makes the Difference | 1793

('All Mortals are Equal, it is not Birth but Virtue that Makes the Difference', 1793 (coloured engraving)/French School, (18th century)/Bibliotheque Nationale, Paris, France/Bridgeman Images)

SOURCE 16.5 Rights and Slavery: An African American Voice

In the United States, the language of the Declaration of Independence, with its affirmation that "all men are created equal," stood in glaring contrast to the brutal realities of slavery. In a famous speech, Frederick Douglass forcefully highlighted that great contradiction in the new American nation. Born a slave in 1818, Douglass had escaped from bondage to become a leading abolitionist, writer, newspaper publisher, and African American spokesperson. The extract that follows is drawn from his address to an antislavery meeting in Rochester, New York, on July 4, 1852.

- On what basis does Douglass demand the end of slavery? How do his arguments relate to the ideology of the American Revolution?
- How would you describe the rhetorical strategy of his speech?
- Why, in the end, can Douglass claim, "I do not despair of this country"? What are the "forces in operation, which must inevitably work the downfall of slavery"?

FREDERICK DOUGLASS | *What to the Slave Is the Fourth of July?* | 1852

Fellow-citizens, pardon me, allow me to ask, why am I called upon to speak here to-day? What have I, or those I represent, to do with your national independence? Are the great principles of political freedom and of natural justice, embodied in that Declaration of Independence, extended to us? and am I, therefore, called upon to bring our humble offering to the national altar, and to confess the benefits and express devout gratitude for the blessings resulting from your independence to us?

Would to God, both for your sakes and ours, that an affirmative answer could be truthfully returned to these questions! . . .

But, such is not the state of the case. I say it with a sad sense of the disparity between us. I am not included within the pale of this glorious anniversary! Your high independence only reveals the immeasurable distance between us. . . . This Fourth [of] July is yours, not mine. . . . You may rejoice, I must mourn.

I shall see, this day . . . from the slave's point of view. . . . I do not hesitate to declare, with all my soul, that the character and conduct of this nation never looked blacker to me than on this 4th of July! . . . Standing with God and the crushed and bleeding slave on this occasion, I will . . . dare to call in question and to denounce, with all the emphasis I can command, everything that serves to perpetuate slavery—the great sin and shame of America!

For the present, it is enough to affirm the equal manhood of the Negro race. Is it not astonishing that . . . while we are engaged in all manner of enterprises common to other men . . . , we are called upon to prove that we are men!

Would you have me argue that man is entitled to liberty? that he is the rightful owner of his own body? You have already declared it. Must I argue the wrongfulness of slavery? Is that a question for Republicans? ...

At a time like this, scorching irony, not convincing argument, is needed.... For it is not light that is needed, but fire.... [T]he conscience of the nation must be roused; ... the hypocrisy of the nation must be exposed; and its crimes against God and man must be proclaimed and denounced.

What, to the American slave, is your 4th of July? I answer: a day that reveals to him, more than all other days in the year, the gross injustice and cruelty to which he is the constant victim. To him, your celebration is a sham; your boasted liberty, an unholy license; your national greatness, swelling vanity; your sounds of rejoicing are empty and heartless; your denunciations of tyrants, brass-fronted impudence; your shouts of liberty and equality, hollow mockery; your prayers and hymns, your sermons and thanksgivings, with all your religious parade, and solemnity, are, to him, mere bombast, fraud, deception, impiety, and hypocrisy — a thin veil to cover up crimes which would disgrace a nation of savages. There is not a nation on the earth guilty of practices, more shocking and bloody, than are the people of these United States, at this very hour. ...

Fellow-citizens! I will not enlarge further on your national inconsistencies. The existence of slavery in this country brands your republicanism as a sham, your humanity as a base pretence, and your Christianity as a lie. It destroys your moral power abroad; it corrupts your politicians at home. It saps the foundation of religion; it makes your name a hissing, and a byword to a mocking earth. It is the antagonistic force in your government, the only thing that seriously disturbs and endangers your Union. It fetters your progress; it is the enemy of improvement, the deadly foe of education; it fosters pride; it breeds insolence; it promotes vice; it shelters crime; it is a curse to the earth that supports it; and yet, you cling to it, as if it were the sheet anchor of all your hopes. Oh! be warned! be warned! a horrible reptile is coiled up in your nation's bosom; the venomous creature is nursing at the tender breast of your youthful republic; for the love of God, tear away, and fling from you the hideous monster, and let the weight of twenty millions crush and destroy it forever! ...

Allow me to say, in conclusion ..., I do not despair of this country. There are forces in operation, which must inevitably work the downfall of slavery.... While drawing encouragement from the Declaration of Independence, the great principles it contains, and the genius of American Institutions, my spirit is also cheered by the obvious tendencies of the age. Nations do not now stand in the same relation to each other that they did ages ago. No nation can now shut itself up from the surrounding world, and trot round in the same old path of its fathers without interference.... But a change has now come over the affairs of mankind. Walled cities and empires have become unfashionable. The arm of commerce has borne away the gates of the strong city. Intelligence is penetrating the darkest corners of the globe. It makes its pathway over and under the sea, as well as on the earth. Wind, steam, and lightning are its chartered agents. Oceans no longer divide, but link nations together. From Boston to London is now a holiday excursion. Space is comparatively annihilated. Thoughts expressed on one side of the Atlantic are distinctly heard on the other. The far off and almost fabulous Pacific rolls in grandeur at our feet. The Celestial Empire, the mystery of ages, is being solved. The fiat of the Almighty, "Let there be Light," has not yet spent its force.

Source: Frederick Douglass, "What to the Slave Is the Fourth of July?," July 5, 1852, *Africans in America*, PBS Online, http://www.pbs.org/wgbh/aia/part4/4h2927t.html.

■ ■ ■

SOURCE 16.6 The Rights of Women: Depicting a Revolutionary Woman ▶

Did the "rights of man" include women? During the French Revolution, the question of women's rights was sharply debated. As the revolution unfolded, many women became actively involved, taking part in street demonstrations, establishing dozens of women's clubs, and petitioning legislative bodies on behalf of women. Nevertheless, most men—even ardent revolutionaries—agreed with the French lawyer Jean-Denis Lanjuinais that "the physique of women, their goal in life [marriage and motherhood], and their position distance them from the exercise of a great number of political rights and duties."[1] In late 1793, all women's clubs were officially prohibited. But in the same year, the posture of these increasingly assertive women found expression in an anonymous engraving titled "Frenchwomen Freed." The woman's cap displays the tricolor cockade that came to symbolize the revolution; she carries a pike inscribed with the slogan "liberty or death"; the medal on her waistband reads: "Liberty, armed with a pike, is victorious, July 14 [Bastille Day]." The prayer to the Roman goddess of war Bellona below the image extols the martial prowess of French women:

> And we [women], too, know how to fight and conquer. We know how to handle other weapons than the needle and the spindle. O Bellona! companion of Mars [the Roman god of war], to your example, all women should they not march in front and with a step equal with the men? Goddess of strength and courage! at least you will no longer have to blush for these French women.

- How would you read the overall message of this engraving?
- How does the woman's physical stance and facial expression contribute to this message?
- What might attract such women to the cause of the revolution?

Frenchwomen Freed | 1793

FRANÇAISES DEVENUES LIBRES.

.... Et nous aussi, nous savons combattre et vaincre. Nous savons manier d'autres armes que l'aiguille et le fuseau. O Bellone! compagne de Mars, a ton exemple, toutes les femmes ne devroient-elles pas marcher de front et d'un pas égal avec les hommes? Déesse de la force et du courage! du moins tu n'auras point à rougir des *FRANÇAISES*.

Extrait d'une Priere des Amazones à Bellone

De la Collection Générale des Caricatures sur la Révolution Française de 1789.

Paris chez **Villeneuve** *Graveur, rue Zacharie, S.ᵗ Severin Maison du Passage N.º 21.*

(Musée Carnavalet/Roger-Viollet/The Image Works)

SOURCE 16.7 The Rights of Women: An American Feminist Voice

Throughout the nineteenth century, debates about the rights of women echoed loudly across Europe, North America, and beyond. Among the most well-known and eloquent appeals for these rights came from the American feminist leader Elizabeth Cady Stanton (1815–1902) in an 1892 address to a U.S. congressional committee. Stanton was urging then, as she had for decades, an amendment to the Constitution giving women the right to vote. That effort was finally successful in 1920, almost two decades after Stanton died.

- What kind of rights was Stanton seeking for women? Do you think she was advocating a reform of gender relations or a more revolutionary transformation?
- How might you summarize in your own words Stanton's argument as to why women should have such rights?
- How might women and men with other points of view have argued with Stanton?

ELIZABETH CADY STANTON | *The Solitude of Self* | 1892

The point I wish plainly to bring before you on this occasion is the individuality of each human soul.... In discussing the rights of woman, we are to consider, first, what belongs to her as an individual, in a world of her own....

The strongest reason for giving woman all the opportunities for higher education, for the full development of her faculties...; for giving her the most enlarged freedom of thought and action; a complete emancipation from all forms of bondage, of custom, dependence, superstition; from all the crippling influences of fear, is the solitude and personal responsibility of her own individual life. The strongest reason why we ask for woman a voice in the government under which she lives; in the religion she is asked to believe; equality in social life, where she is the chief factor; a place in the trades and professions, where she may earn her bread, is because of her birthright to self-sovereignty; because, as an individual, she must rely on herself. No matter how much women prefer to lean, to be protected and supported, nor how much men desire to have them do so, they must make the voyage of life alone.... It matters not whether the solitary voyager is man or woman.... Alike amid the greatest triumphs and darkest tragedies of life we walk alone....

In [old] age, when the pleasures of youth are passed, children grown up, married and gone, the hurry and hustle of life in a measure over, when the hands are weary of active service, when the old armchair and the fireside are the chosen resorts, then men and women alike must fall back on their own resources....

If from a lifelong participation in public affairs a woman feels responsible for the laws regulating our system of education, the discipline of our jails and prisons, the sanitary conditions of our private homes, public buildings, and thoroughfares, an interest in commerce, finance, our foreign relations, in any or all of these questions, her solitude will at least be respectable....

Seeing then that the responsibilities of life rests equally on man and woman, that their destiny is the same, they need the same preparation for time and eternity. The talk of sheltering woman from the fierce storms of life is the sheerest mockery, for they beat on her from every point of the compass, just as they do on man, and with more fatal results, for he has been trained to protect himself, to resist, to conquer.... Whatever the theories may be of woman's dependence on man, in the supreme moments of her life he cannot bear her burdens....

[T]here is a solitude, which each and every one of us has always carried with him, more inaccessible than the ice-cold mountains, more profound than the midnight sea; the solitude of self. Our inner being, which we call ourself, no eye nor touch of man or angel has ever pierced.... Who, I ask you, can take, dare take, on himself the rights, the duties, the responsibilities of another human soul?

Source: Elizabeth Cady Stanton, "The Solitude of Self," address delivered before the Committee of the Judiciary of the United States Congress, January 18, 1892. The Library of Congress.

DOING HISTORY

1. **Considering ideas and circumstances:** Historians frequently debate the relative importance of ideas in shaping historical events. How did the ideas about rights expressed in these documents influence the historical development of the Atlantic world and beyond? What specific historical contexts or conditions shaped the understanding of "rights" expressed in each of these sources?

2. **Making comparisons:** Which sources speak more about individual rights, and which focus attention on collective rights? What common understandings can you identify?

3. **Imagining a conversation:** How might the creators of these sources have responded to one another? What points of agreement might they share? What differences might arise in a conversation among them?

4. **Defining a common origin:** In what respects did each of these sources derive from the French Revolution?

HISTORIANS' VOICES

Origins and Echoes of the American Revolution

Many historians, including the two Voices that follow, have sought to contextualize the American Revolution by examining its intellectual, social and cultural origins and its long-term echoes in such developments as abolitionism, nationalism, feminism, and European imperialism. In Voice 16.1, Dorinda Outram, who specializes in the European Enlightenment, explores the impact of that movement's ideas on the American Revolution. In Voice 16.2, Carl Guarneri, a specialist in American history, explores how the American Revolution redirected British imperial ambitions on three continents.

- In what ways did the American Revolution reveal contradictions in Enlightenment thinking?
- According to Guarneri, what impact did defeat by the American revolutionaries have on the British Empire?
- **Integrating primary and secondary sources:** Assess the legacy of the American Revolution using Voice 16.2 and Sources 16.5 and 16.7.

VOICE 16.1

Dorinda Outram on Enlightenment Ideas in the American Revolution | 1995

[T]he American Revolution has often been seen as the place where Enlightenment ideas and a violent change of government can best be seen in conjunction. . . .

But the ideology that filled this conflict had many different sources. Puritan religious ideas of man's essential sinfulness sat uneasily with Enlightenment ideas of progress, optimism and faith in man's rationality. . . . Other elements in American ideology also antedated the Enlightenment, especially the Republicanism which originated with classical Greco-Roman models. . . . The American interpretation of Republicanism emphasized the virtue of a simple society of autonomous citizens committed to the common good and emphasized the independence of each individual. . . . However, Americans also believed that citizen and government should be united by contract, an idea very strong in John Locke's *Two Treatises of Civil Government*. . . . This idea of contract itself ran into several difficulties in the American situation. . . . Locke's idea of contract presupposed a society whose members were equal. Could it really be applied in the American colonies, which were underpinned by the labor of slaves? . . . Maybe in the end the American revolutionaries found themselves faced with the same problem as was to face the French twenty years later, which was the impossibility of constructing a political order based on equality of rights without recasting the unequal social order. . . . This contradiction between support for supposedly universal rights, and the actual exclusion of large numbers of human beings from the enjoyment of those rights is central to, and characteristic of Enlightenment thought.

Source: Dorinda Outram, *The Enlightenment* (Cambridge, UK: Cambridge University Press, 1995), 121–22.

VOICE 16.2

Carl Guarneri on British Expansion Redirected | 2007

Some historians have called the American Revolution "England's Vietnam." Faced with a popular revolt in a distant land where unfamiliar terrain and irregular warfare made conquest impossible, the British, like the Americans 200 years later in southeast Asia, were forced to withdraw. But if the analogy is meant to imply imperial decline, it is off the mark. The British were galled by the colonists' victory, but prompt settlement of new territories compensated for their loss.

The American Revolution indirectly helped to develop three British colonies that eventually became new nations. Thousands of loyalist families fled the thirteen colonies for Canada, where the provinces of New Brunswick and Upper Canada (later Ontario) were organized to accommodate the influx and which their descendants transformed into a thriving British colony. Britain's West African colony of Sierra Leone was another indirect product of the American revolt. Four hundred African American refugees who had been freed and sent to London were settled there in 1787 ... and were joined by 1200 black loyalists from the Nova Scotia settlement. Finally, when Georgia and other American colonies no longer accepted prisoners sentenced to exile for crimes committed in England, British officials turned to Australia, which Captain James Cook had claimed for the Crown in 1770, as their dumping ground. Far from dampening British ambitions, the American Revolution stimulated British expansion elsewhere. Casting about for additional trade and territory in Africa, Asia, the Pacific, and the Middle East, Britain continued to build its empire. Its heyday was still a century ahead.

Source: Carl Guarneri, *America in the World: The United States in Global Context* (Boston, MA: McGraw-Hill, 2007), 103.

NOTE

1. Jean-Denis Lanjuinais, "Discussion of Citizenship under the Proposed New Constitution," in Hunt, *The French Revolution and Human Rights*, 133.

CHAPTER 17

Thinking through Sources

Experiencing the Early Industrial Revolution

The immense economic and social changes of the Industrial Revolution left almost no one untouched in the societies that experienced it most fully. Especially in its early phases (roughly 1780–1875), that immense transformation generated a traumatic upheaval in ways of living for many people. For others, it brought new opportunities, wealth, and comfort. In seeking to understand how individuals experienced this unprecedented revolutionary process, historians have at their disposal a wealth of evidence, both documentary and visual. Each of the sources that follow provides just a glimpse into what living through those early decades of the Industrial Revolution may have meant to those who experienced it, mostly in England where it all began.

SOURCE 17.1 The Experience of an English Factory Worker

The early Industrial Revolution represented not only a technological breakthrough of epic proportions, but also a transformation in the organization of work, expressed most fully in the factory. Unlike the artisan's workshop, which it increasingly replaced, the factory concentrated human labor in a single space and separated workers from the final product by assigning them highly specialized and repetitive tasks. In the name of efficiency and productivity, owners and managers imposed strict discipline in their factories and regulated workers' lives according to clock time. Finally, workers were wage earners, dependent for their economic survival on a very modest income and highly uncertain employment, both of which were subject to the vagaries of the market.

One such worker was Elizabeth Bentley, who had worked in a factory since the age of six. In 1831, when she was twenty-three years old, Bentley testified before a British parliamentary committee investigating conditions in textile mills. A subsequent inquiry elicited testimony from William Harter, a mill owner. As a result of these investigations, legislation in 1833 limited the hours of employment for women and children.

- Child labor was nothing new, as children had long worked in the fields and workshops of preindustrial Europe. What was different about the conditions under which children worked in early industrial factories?
- Why do you think the investigator queried Elizabeth Bentley specifically about the treatment of girls?
- How does William Harter's testimony explain the willingness of factory owners to impose these conditions on their workers? How might he respond to Elizabeth Bentley's testimony?

SOURCE 17.1A

ELIZABETH BENTLEY, FACTORY WORKER | Testimony | 1831

What age are you?—Twenty-three.

Where do you live?—At Leeds.

What time did you begin to work at a factory?—When I was six years old.

What kind of mill is it?—Flax-mill.

What was your business in that mill?—I was a little doffer [cleaner of the machines].

What were your hours of labour in that mill?—From 5 in the morning till 9 at night, when they were thronged [busy].

For how long a time together have you worked that excessive length of time?—For about half a year.

What were your usual hours when you were not so thronged?—From 6 in the morning till 7 at night.

What time was allowed for your meals?—Forty minutes at noon.

Had you any time to get your breakfast or drinking?—No, we got it as we could.

Explain what it is you had to do?—When the frames are full, they have to stop the frames, and take the flyers off, and take the full bobbins off, and carry them to the roller; and then put empty ones on, and set the frame going again.

Does that keep you constantly on your feet?—Yes, there are so many frames, and they run so quick.

Suppose you flagged a little, or were too late, what would they do?—Strap us.

Are they in the habit of strapping those who are last in doffing?—Yes.

Constantly?—Yes.

Girls as well as boys?—Yes.

Have you ever been strapped?—Yes.

Severely?—Yes.

Were the girls struck so as to leave marks upon their skin?—Yes, they have had black marks many times, and their parents dare not come to him about it, they were afraid of losing their work.

Could you eat your food well in that factory?—No, indeed I had not much to eat, and the little I had I could not eat it, my appetite was so poor, and being covered with dust; and it was no use to take it home, I could not eat it, and the overlooker took it, and gave it to the pigs.

How far had you to go for dinner?—We could not go home to dinner.

Where did you dine?—In the mill.

Did you live far from the mill?—Yes, two miles.

Supposing you had not been in time enough in the morning at these mills, what would have been the consequence?—We should have been quartered. If we were a quarter of an hour too late, they would take off half an hour; we only got a penny an hour, and they would take a halfpenny more.

Were you also beaten for being too late?—No, I was never beaten myself, I have seen the boys beaten for being too late.

Were you generally there in time?—Yes; my mother had been up at 4 o'clock in the morning, and at 2 o'clock in the morning; the colliers used to go to their work about 3 or 4 o'clock, and when she heard them stirring she has got up out of her warm bed, and gone out and asked them the time; and I have sometimes been at Hunslet Car at 2 o'clock in the morning, when it was streaming down with rain, and we have had to stay until the mill was opened.

SOURCE 17.1B

WILLIAM HARTER, MILL OWNER | *Testimony* | 1832

What effect would it have on your manufacture to reduce the hours of labor to ten?—It would instantly much reduce the value of my mill and machinery, and consequently far prejudice my manufacture.... To produce the same quantity of work under a ten-hours bill will require an additional outlay of 3,000 or 4,000 pounds; therefore a ten-hours bill would impose upon me the necessity of this additional outlay in such perishable property as buildings and machinery, or I must be content to relinquish one-sixth portion of my business.

Source: *British Sessional Papers*, vol. 15 (London, 1832), 195196; vol. 21, pt. D-3 (London, 1833), 2628.

■ ■ ■

SOURCE 17.2 Urban Living Conditions

If factory working conditions were deplorable in the early decades of the English Industrial Revolution, the urban living conditions for many of those workers were no less horrific. In a classic description of industrial Manchester in the early 1840s, a twenty-four-year-old

Friedrich Engels, who later became a close collaborator with Karl Marx, provided a vivid portrait of urban working-class life in England's premier industrial city. By the time his German-language account was translated into English in 1886, Engels acknowledged that "the most crying abuses described in this book have either disappeared or have been made less conspicuous." He added, however, that broadly similar conditions were prevalent in later-industrializing countries such as France, Germany, and the United States.

- How does Engels describe working-class life in Manchester in the early 1840s?
- What implied contrasts does Engels make with the earlier rural life of poor peasants?
- To what does he attribute these conditions?

FRIEDRICH ENGELS | *The Condition of the Working Class in England* | 1844

Manchester contains about four hundred thousand inhabitants.... The town itself is peculiarly built, so that a person may live in it for years, and go in and out daily without coming into contact with a working-people's quarter or even with workers, that is, so long as he confines himself to his business or to pleasure walks. This arises chiefly from the fact, that by unconscious tacit agreement, as well as with outspoken conscious determination, the working people's quarters are sharply separated from the sections of the city reserved for the middle-class....

Here [in Old Town Manchester] one is in an almost undisguised working-men's quarter, for even the shops and beer houses hardly take the trouble to exhibit a trifling degree of cleanliness. But all this is nothing in comparison with the courts and lanes which lie behind, to which access can be gained only through covered passages, in which no two human beings can pass at the same time. Of the irregular cramming together of dwellings in ways which defy all rational plan, of the tangle in which they are crowded literally one upon the other, it is impossible to convey an idea. Right and left a multitude of covered passages lead from the main street into numerous courts, and he who turns in thither gets into a filth and disgusting grime, the equal of which is not to be found....

In one of these courts there stands directly at the entrance, at the end of the covered passage, a privy without a door, so dirty that the inhabitants can pass into and out of the court only by passing through foul pools of stagnant urine and excrement.... Below it on the river there are several tanneries which fill the whole neighbourhood with the stench of animal putrefaction. Below Ducie Bridge the only entrance to most of the houses is by means of narrow, dirty stairs and over heaps of refuse and filth. The first court below Ducie Bridge, known as Allen's Court, was in such a state at the time of the cholera that the sanitary police ordered it evacuated, swept, and disinfected with chloride of lime....At the bottom flows, or rather stagnates, the Irk [River], a narrow, coal-black, foul-smelling stream, full of debris and refuse....

In dry weather, a long string of the most disgusting, blackish-green, slime pools are left standing on this bank, from the depths of which bubbles of miasmatic gas constantly arise and give forth a stench.... Above the bridge are tanneries, bone mills, and gasworks, from which all drains and refuse find their way into the Irk, which receives further the contents of all the neighbouring sewers and privies. It may be easily imagined, therefore, what sort of residue the stream deposits. Here the background embraces the pauper burial-ground, the station of the Liverpool and Leeds railway, and, in the rear of this, the Workhouse [where the desperately poor found shelter and employment],... which, like a citadel, looks threateningly down from behind its high walls and parapets on the hilltop, upon the working-people's quarter below.

Passing along a rough bank, among stakes and washing-lines, one penetrates into this chaos of small one-storied, one-roomed huts, in most of which there is no artificial floor; kitchen, living and sleeping-room all in one. In such a hole, scarcely five feet long by six broad, I found two beds—and such bedsteads and beds!—which, with a staircase and chimney-place, exactly filled the room. In several others I found absolutely nothing, while the door stood open, and the inhabitants leaned against it. Everywhere before the doors refuse and offal; that any sort of pavement lay underneath could not be seen but only felt, here and there, with the feet. This whole collection of cattle-sheds for human beings was surrounded on two sides by houses and a factory, and on the third by the river....

In almost every court one or even several such pens [of pigs] may be found, into which the inhabitants of the court throw all refuse and offal, whence the swine grow fat; and the atmosphere, confined on all four sides, is utterly corrupted by putrefying animal and vegetable substances....

Such is the Old Town of Manchester.... Everything which here arouses horror and indignation is of recent origin, belongs to the *industrial epoch.*

Source: Friedrich Engels, *The Condition of the Working Class in England in 1844* (London: Swan Sonnenschein & Co., 1892), 45, 48–53.

SOURCE 17.3 Another View of Factory Life ▶

As Engels admitted, early working and living conditions in industrial England had improved by the later nineteenth century, though the debate about factory life had hardly ended. Source 17.3, an 1874 painting by English artist Eyre Crowe, provides a more benevolent view of an industrial factory as it portrays a number of young women workers during their dinner hour outside the cotton textile mill in the industrial town of Wigan.

- How does this depiction of factory life compare with that of Source 17.1? How might you account for the differences?
- How do you respond to Crowe's painting? Do you think it was an honest portrayal of factory life for women? What might be missing?
- Notice the details of the painting—the young women's relationship to one another, the hairnets on their heads, their clothing, their activities during this break from work. What marks them as working-class women? What impression of factory life did Crowe seek to convey? Was he trying to highlight or minimize the class differences of industrial Britain?

EYRE CROWE | *Outside the Factory* | 1874

(The Dinner Hour, Wigan, 1874 (oil on canvas)/Crowe, Eyre (1824–1910)/MANCHESTER ART GALLERY/Manchester Art Gallery, UK/Bridgeman Images)

SOURCE 17.4 A Weaver's Lament

As industrialization generated new work in the factories, it also destroyed older means of livelihood, particularly that of skilled artisans. By the early 1860s, the silk weavers of Coventry, England, a long-established and previously thriving group of artisans, were in desperate straits, owing in part to a decline in the fashion of wearing silk ribbons. Many individual weavers had to sell their looms to the larger manufacturers, who were organizing more efficient production in factories. The song that follows was sung by unemployed weavers as they paraded through the streets of Coventry on their way to relief work, often in stone quarries. It reflects the costs of the Industrial Revolution for a body of proud and skilled artisans and their distress at an economic system that seemed to cast them adrift.

- Who or what does the song blame for the plight of the weavers?
- What does the song mean by mentioning the "commercial plan" and "political economy"? And how do you understand the line "He's only a weaver whom nobody owns"?
- How might you compare the life of an unemployed weaver with that of a factory worker like Elizabeth Bentley?

The Weaver | 1860s

Who is that man coming up the street,
With wearied manner and shuffling feet,
With a face that tells of care and grief,
And in hope seems to have lost belief? . . .
   For wickedness past he now atones;
   He's only a weaver whom nobody owns.
He's coming no doubt from breaking stones,
With saddened heart and aching bones;
But why should he grumble? he gets good pay,
A loaf and sixpence every day. . . .
He thought if he worked both night and day
He ought to receive equivalent pay.
He's evidently an inconsistent man,
Who don't understand the commercial plan. . . .
Political economy now must sway,
And say when a man shall work or play.
If he's wanted, his wages may be high;
If he isn't, why then he may starve and die. . . .
And if you employ him, don't mend the price;
He's starving, you know, and has no choice;
And give him to weave the worst of silk,

For it's only a weaver's time you bilk....
  But take no heed of his sighs and groans,
  His careworn face and agony moans,
  For wickedness past he now atones;
He's only a weaver whom nobody owns.

Source: Joseph Gutteridge, *Light and Shadows in the Life of an Artisan* (Coventry: Coventry, Curtis and Beamish, 1893), 153-55.

■ ■ ■

SOURCE 17.5 Poetry from the Factory Floor

Born around 1835 to a working-class family in an industrializing Scotland, Ellen Johnston worked in a variety of textile mills throughout her life, lived as a single mother, and, most unusually, became a published poet with a modest local reputation under her pseudonym "the factory girl." Johnston had hoped to make her living as a poet, thereby escaping the poverty to which factory wages condemned her. She did receive occasional financial support from upper-class benefactors, including a small gift from Queen Victoria, and a published collection of her work appeared in 1867. Nevertheless, she was aware that both class and gender made it difficult for her to win acceptance among middle- and upper-class members of the literary establishment, a recognition expressed in her writing: "I am so small I cannot shine / Amidst the great that read my rhyme." In 1870, only a year after the publication of the second edition of her book of poetry, Johnston had to apply for "poor relief." In 1874, she died in a Scottish poorhouse, not yet forty years of age.

In her poetry, Johnston did not advocate for socialism or revolutionary upheaval; rather, her poems reflected on the joys and struggles of working people and called for better working conditions, often by appealing to the "master" of the mill to behave in a benevolent fashion towards his employees. Her own experience in working for a caring factory owner is expressed in *Kennedy's Dear Mill*. Nonetheless, Johnston was fully aware of the inequalities and exploitation endemic in industrial life and the need for workers to take action to secure better wages. In *Lines on Behalf of Boatbuilders and Boilermakers*, she highlights the poor treatment of workers in the shipbuilding industry that was so central to Scotland's economy.

- How can one explain the contrasting attitudes toward industrialists in these two poems?
- How might Ellen Johnston have responded to the parliamentary testimony in Source 17.1?
- How would you describe Ellen Johnston's outlook on industrial Britain?

ELLEN JOHNSTON | Poetry | 1867

Kennedy's Dear Mill

OH! Kennedy's dear mill!
To you I'll sing a song
For winter dark and dull;
    For another season's gone,
And summer's bright sunshine
    Thy little shed doth fill.
Prosperity is thine,
    Oh, Kennedy's dear mill!

. . .

Thou hast a secret spell
    For all as well as me;
Each girl loves thee well
    That ever wrought in thee.
They may leave thy blessed toil;
    But, find work they will,
They return back in a while
    To Kennedy's dear mill.

. . .

And freedom's glorious shrine
    Is center'd in thy walls;
No tyrant knave to bind,
    No slavish chain enthrals.
The workers are as free
    As the sunshine on the hill;
Thy breath is liberty
    Oh! Kennedy's dear mill.

We feel no coward fear
    When our dear master comes;
And when he's standing near,
    And gazing on our looms,
He hails us with a smile
    That is a brother's still,
No haughty lord of toil
    Owns Kennedy's dear mill.

. . .

When his workers are in grief,
    It is against his will;
He's the first to send relief
    From Kennedy's dear mill.

. . .

Now, Kennedy's dear mill,
    The best wish of my heart
Shall linger near you still,
    When from you I depart.
Whate'er my fate may be,
    Let me wander where I will,
Peace and prosperity
To Kennedy's dear mill.

Source: Ellen Johnston, *Autobiography, Poems, and Songs*, 2nd ed. (Glasgow: William Love, 1869), 19–21.

Lines on Behalf of the Boatbuilders and Boilermakers of Great Britain and Ireland

O that I could rob fortune of her gold as she has robbed the poor man of his rights, I would give each worthy man his share, and then would thousands live who die for want of that which some of those who are less worthy have too much.— *The Factory Girl*

O gather hay while the sun shines
All ye who wish to be free;
Nip, ere too late, the chain that binds
    The gems of sweet liberty.

Why will ye hesitate longer
    While cruel despotic power
Is working the chain still stronger
    That draws on the evil hour.

Our brothers in prison were cast
    Because like brave men they spoke,
When crushed in the powerful grasp
    of slavery's galling yoke.

Shall our democrats still be slaves—
    Still unknown to fortune's smile—
And drop into premature graves
    The victims of ill paid toil.

Source 17.5 Poetry from the Factory Floor

Shall their children cry out for bread,
    And mothers have none to give,
And die—but ere they are dead
    Curse the hour that saw them live?

Shall tyrants exalt o'er the spoil
    Of gold that was ne'er their own—
Gold obtained by the poor man's toil
    which to his children belong?

. . .

Shall the rich man behold his ship
    With her gallant mast and bow,
Moistened with sweat on the slip
    Wrung out from the poor man's brow?

. . .

Yet still ye would trample him down;
    Yes down to sixpence a day,
For work that is well worth a pound,
    Were justice dealt his pay.

. . .

But now ye'll not spare him a groat
    That he might drink your good health,
And wish speed to the gallant boat,
    to return again with wealth.

. . .

All ye who toil by the river,
    Now is the day and the hour.
Be your watchword—'Union for ever,'
    Till union has gold in its power.

So gather ye hay while the sun shines,
    The Union's harvest secure;
Reap well while yet there's no fierce winds,
'Prevention is better than cure.'

Source: Ellen Johnston, *Autobiography, Poems, and Songs*, 2nd ed. (Glasgow: William Love, 1869), 83–86.

SOURCE 17.6 Railroads and the Middle Class ▶

Among the new experiences of the early industrial era for many people was railroad travel, made possible by the steam locomotive during the early nineteenth century. By 1850, Great Britain had almost 10,000 kilometers of railroad lines and Germany almost 6,000. To Industrial Age enthusiasts, the railroad was a thing of wonder, power, and speed. Samuel Smiles, the nineteenth-century British advocate of self-help, thrift, and individualism, wrote rhapsodically of the railroad's beneficent effects:

> The iron rail proved a magicians' road. The locomotive gave a new celerity to time. It virtually reduced England to a sixth of its size. It brought the country nearer to the town and the town to the country. . . . It energized punctuality, discipline, and attention; and proved a moral teacher by the influence of example.[1]

Like almost everything else, railroads and railway travel were shaped by the social changes of the early industrial era, including the growth of a more numerous and prosperous middle class of industrialists, bankers, and educated professionals of various kinds. Such people invested heavily in railroads, spurring the rapid expansion of railways in Britain. Moreover, travel on the new trains was segregated by class. First-class passengers occupied luxurious compartments with upholstered seats, while second-class travelers enjoyed rather less comfortable accommodations. Third-class travel, which was designed for the poor or working classes, originally took place in uncovered freight wagons, often with standing room only and located closest to the locomotive, where noise and the danger of fire were the greatest. In 1844, regulations required that third-class carriages be roofed.

Source 17.6, dating from the 1870s, illustrates this intersection of an emerging middle class and railway travel, showing a family in a railroad compartment, returning home from a vacation.

- What attitude toward the railroad in particular and the Industrial Age in general does this image suggest?
- What marks this family as middle class and their compartment as "first class"?
- What does the poem at the top of the image suggest about the place of "home" in industrial Britain? How does the image itself present the railway car as a home away from home?

Source 17.6 Railroads and the Middle Class

The Railroad as a Symbol of the Industrial Era | 1870s

> And Papa and Mamma took them home the same day,—
> They were glad to go home, and yet wanted to stay;
> But the train went quite fast, and it seemed a nice change
> To be back in their own home, where nothing was strange:
>
> And always they reckon'd that seeing these sights
> Was a thing to remember—a week of delights;
> And, though they may see them all many times more,
> They'll never enjoy them so much, I am sure.

(Mary Evans Picture Library/The Image Works)

SOURCE 17.7 Inequality

In the early industrial era, almost everyone became acutely aware of the sharp class inequalities of social life. Of course, such differences in status and wealth had characterized all civilizations since ancient Egypt and Mesopotamia. Now, however, those inequalities were experienced within the confined space of city life; they found expression in two relatively new social groups—the urban working class and the growing middle class; and they occurred as democratic ideas and socialist movements challenged the ancient legitimacy of such inequalities. These features of the early industrial era are illustrated in Source 17.7, an image by British artist John Leech, published in 1843 in *Punch*, a magazine of humor and social satire.

- How are the class differences of early industrial Britain represented in this image? Notice the depiction of the life of miners in the bottom panel.

- How does this source connect the Industrial Revolution with Britain's colonial empire? Notice the figure in the upper right reclining in exotic splendor, perhaps in India.

- To what extent does the image correspond to Friedrich Engels's description of industrial society in Source 17.2?

JOHN LEECH | *Capital and Labour* | 1843

(The Granger Collection, New York)

DOING HISTORY

1. **Celebrating industrialization:** Based on these sources, construct an argument in celebration of the Industrial Revolution.
2. **Criticizing industrialization:** Construct an argument based on these sources criticizing the Industrial Revolution.
3. **Considering images and written documents as evidence:** What are the strengths and limitations of visual sources, as compared to written documents, in helping historians understand the Industrial Revolution?
4. **Distinguishing capitalism and industrialization:** To what extent are these sources actually dealing with the Industrial Revolution itself, and in what ways are they addressing the economic system known as capitalism? How useful is this distinction for understanding the early Industrial Age?

HISTORIANS' VOICES

Children and Family during the Industrial Revolution

Few developments in world history have had a greater influence on society and culture than the Industrial Revolution. The two Voices that follow explore the impact of industrialization on that most basic of social relationships—the one between parents and their children. In Voice 17.1, Elinor Accampo examines how industrialization altered the role of the family in preparing children for the world of work. In Voice 17.2, Louise A. Tilly and Joan W. Scott explore how the wages earned by children engaged in industrial work changed the relationship between parents and their offspring.

- What specific changes to family life were the result of industrialization?
- Why were children who worked in factories less reliant on their parents than other children?
- **Integrating primary and secondary sources:** Use the sources and voices in this feature to assess the impact on the family life of those who worked in factories during the Industrial Revolution.

VOICE 17.1

Elinor Accampo on Migration, Industry, and the Loosening of Parental Control | 1989

Migration [to urban areas] also created a gap between generations that mechanization deepened. . . . . Even when the older generation did work in industry of some kind, they could no longer transmit useful skills to their offspring. Children ceased adopting the same occupations as their parents; parents stopped teaching children work skills and passing on traditions associated with work. Certainly, in some cases industrial change opened new doors to the children of these workers, and the break in generational bonds meant upward mobility. . . .

Whether or not the working-class father lost status among his children, the authority and power of the family vis-à-vis employers did decline. Mechanization of work gave employers, the owners of machines, a greater measure of control over the workplace as well as over the worker. The workplace became an arena for discipline and training. . . .

Source: Elinor Accampo, *Industrialization, Family Life and Class Relations: Saint Chamond, 1815–1914* (Berkeley, CA: University of California Press, 1989), 214.

VOICE 17.2

Louise Tilly and Joan Scott on Daughters and Industrial Work | 1978

A teen-aged child's ability to earn wages and, particularly in textiles, the importance of those wages for the family meant that children were no longer as dependent as they once had been on their parents. In fact, the roles might sometimes reverse, with parents depending increasingly on their children. In textile towns, for example, where work was most plentiful and most remunerative for young people in their late teens and early twenties, according to Michael Anderson "children's high wages allowed them to enter into relational bargains with their parents on terms of more or less precise equality." "The children that frequent the factories make almost the purse of the family," observed a contemporary, "and by making the purse of the family, they share in the ruling of it." In France, an observer at a later period bemoaned the decline of apprenticeship training and the easy availability of wage labor for children. As their wages increased and sometimes surpassed their parents', he wrote, children assumed they had the right to a say in family matters. "When the father earns more than his children, he still has the right to his authority; from the day they earn as much as he does, they no longer recognize his right to command." Furthermore, by earning wages a child established a measure of potential independence. She could move elsewhere and still earn her keep. Hence, while the ability to earn wages increased the importance to a family of a daughter's labor, it also created the potential for a daughter to leave home at an early age.

Source: Louise A. Tilly and Joan W. Scott, *Women, Work, and Family* (New York, NY: Holt, Rinehart and Winston, 1978), pp. 120–21.

NOTE

1. Quoted in Francis D. Klingender, *Art and the Industrial Revolution* (New York, NY: Augustus M. Kelley, 1968), 139.

CHAPTER 18

Thinking through Sources

Colonial India: Experience and Response

India was Britain's "jewel in the crown," the centerpiece of its expanding empire in Asia and Africa. Until the late 1850s, Britain's growing involvement with South Asia was organized and led by the British East India Company, a private trading firm that had acquired a charter from the Crown allowing it to exercise military, political, and administrative functions in India as well as its own commercial operations. But after the explosive upheaval of the Indian Rebellion of 1857–1858, the British government itself assumed control of the region until India's independence in 1947.

Throughout the colonial era, the British relied heavily on alliances with established elite groups in Indian society—landowners; the "princes" who governed large parts of the region; and the Brahmins, the highest-ranking segment of India's caste-based society. These alliances strengthened or hardened elements of "traditional" India and brought them under British control. At the same time, colonial rule changed India in a hundred ways. Its schools gave rise to a class of Western-educated and English-speaking Indians; its economic and cultural policies fostered rebellion in the rural areas; its railroads, telegraphs, and postal services linked India more closely together; its racism provoked a growing sense of an all-Indian identity; its efforts to define, and thus control, India's enormously diverse population contributed to a growing divide between its Hindu and Muslim communities.

This collection begins with a group of images that evoke familiar features of British colonial rule in India, followed by a series of documents that present a range of Indian responses to the colonial experience.

SOURCE 18.1 Images of Colonial Rule ▶

The British colonial presence in India has been recorded in a plethora of artistic representations. The four images that follow provide a highly selective glimpse at several features of that experience.

Source 18.1 Images of Colonial Rule

- What information does each of these images convey to you about colonial India?
- How might each of these scenes have been experienced by both British and Indian participants?
- What kinds of interactions between rulers and ruled are suggested in these images?

SOURCE 18.1A

J. BOUVIER | *A British Breakfast in India* | **1842**

British officials and their families sought to re-create as much of English life as possible in the very different environment of India and to maintain a sharp separation between themselves and Indians. In what ways does this engraving, published in 1842, suggest that effort?

(The Breakfast, plate 3 from 'Anglo Indians', engraved by J. Bouvier, 1842 (litho)/Tayler, William (1808–92) (after)/STAPLETON COLLECTION/ Private Collection/Bridgeman Images)

SOURCE 18.1B
Tiger Hunting in Colonial India | 1860s

A favorite sport among British colonial elites and tourists, tiger hunting served to display Victorian era "manliness," "a virile, muscular, patriotic sense of endurance." It also suggested the invincibility of the colonial state in triumphing over such a savage beast as well as its benevolence in ridding villages of their "man-eating tigers."[1]

(British Officers tiger shooting in India, 1860s (colour litho)/English School, (19th century)/PETER NEWARK'S PICTURES/Private Collection/Bridgeman Images)

SOURCE 18.1C

The British and Indian Princes | ca. 1820

In many parts of colonial India, the British governed indirectly, through traditional authorities known as "princes." Here Prince Mahadaji Sindhia entertains two British military officers at a traditional Indian nautch, or dance concert, performed by professional Indian dancing girls around 1820. Stylistically, this illustration differs from the other images in this selection because it was created by an Indian artist rather than a British one. What does this image suggest about British efforts to relate to Indian elites and Indian culture?

(Prince Mahadaji Sindhia entertaining a British army officer and a naval officer to a nautch, c. 1820 (gouache on paper)/Indian School, (19th century)/BRITISH LIBRARY/British Library, London, UK/Bridgeman Images)

SOURCE 18.1D
Blowing from a Gun | 1858

Following Mughal precedents, the British frequently employed a particularly horrific form of public execution for rebels—namely, they tied the victim, or sometimes several victims, to the mouth of a cannon and then fired it. This practice was used quite extensively during the Indian uprising of 1857–1858, as illustrated in this image. The British argued that it served as a deterrent to rebellion, was more humane than the earlier Mughal practice of "flogging to death," and allowed high-caste rebels to avoid the disgrace of being polluted by contact with the untouchables who often conducted hangings. For the families of the victims, both Muslim and Hindu, it proved almost impossible to perform proper funeral and burial rites. The practice was used as late as 1871, but then was discontinued.

(Blowing mutinous Sepoys from the guns, from 'The History of the Indian Mutiny', published in 1858 (engraving)/English School, (19th century)/KEN WELSH/Private Collection/Bridgeman Images)

SOURCE 18.2 Seeking Western Education

Indian understanding of and responses to British rule varied widely and changed over time, involving gratitude, acceptance, disappointment with unfulfilled promise, active resistance, and sharp criticism of many kinds. Sources 18.2 through 18.5 provide four examples, covering almost a hundred years, from the early nineteenth century to the early twentieth century.

The first comes from Ram Mohan Roy (1772–1833). Born and highly educated within a Brahmin Hindu family, Roy subsequently studied both Arabic and Persian, learned English, came into contact with British Christian missionaries, and found employment with the British East India Company. He emerged in the early nineteenth century as a leading advocate for religious and social reform within India, with a particular interest in ending *sati*, the practice in which widows burned themselves on their husbands' funeral pyres. In 1823, Roy learned about a British plan to establish a school in Calcutta that was to focus on Sanskrit texts and traditional Hindu learning. Source 18.2 records his response to that school, and to British colonial rule, in a letter to the British governor-general of India.

- Why was Roy opposed to the creation of this school?
- What does this letter reveal about Roy's attitude toward Indian and European cultures?
- How would you describe Roy's attitude toward British colonial rule in India?

RAM MOHAN ROY | *Letter to Lord Amherst* | 1823

The establishment of a new Sanskrit School in Calcutta evinces the laudable desire of Government to improve the natives of India by education, a blessing for which they must ever be grateful.... When this seminary of learning was proposed ... we were filled with sanguine hopes that [it would employ] European gentlemen of talent and education to instruct the natives of India in Mathematics, Natural Philosophy, Chemistry, Anatomy, and other useful sciences, which the natives of Europe have carried to a degree of perfection that has raised them above the inhabitants of other parts of the world.... Our hearts were filled with mingled feelings of delight and gratitude; we already offered up thanks to Providence for inspiring the most generous and enlightened nations of the West with the glorious ambition of planting in Asia the arts and sciences of Modern Europe.

We find [however] that the Government are establishing a Sanskrit school under Hindu Pandits [scholars] to impart such knowledge as is already current in India. This seminary can only be expected to load the minds of youth with grammatical niceties and metaphysical distinctions of little or no practical use to the possessors or to society. The pupils will there acquire what was known two thousand years ago with the addition of vain and empty subtleties since then produced by speculative men, such as is already commonly taught in all parts of India....

Neither can much improvement arise from such speculations as the following which are the themes suggested by the Vedanta [a branch of Hindu philosophy]: in what manner is the soul absorbed in the Deity? What relation does it bear to the Divine Essence? Nor will youths be fitted to be better members of society by the Vedantic doctrines which teach them to believe that all visible things have no real existence, that as father, brother, etc., have no actual entity, they consequently deserve no real affection, and therefore the sooner we escape from them and leave the world the better....

[T]he Sanskrit system of education would be the best calculated to keep this country in darkness, if such had been the policy of the British legislature. But as the improvement of the native population is the object of the Government, it will consequently promote a more liberal and enlightened system of instruction, embracing Mathematics, Natural Philosophy, Chemistry, Anatomy, with other useful sciences, which may be accomplished with the sums proposed by employing a few gentlemen of talent and learning educated in Europe and providing a College furnished with necessary books, instruments, and other apparatus. In presenting this subject to your Lordship, I conceive myself discharging a solemn duty which I owe to my countrymen, and also to that enlightened sovereign and legislature which have extended their benevolent care to this distant land, actuated by a desire to improve the inhabitants, and therefore humbly trust you will excuse the liberty I have taken in thus expressing my sentiments to your Lordship.

Source: Rammohun Roy, *The English Works of Raja Rammohun Roy* (Allahabad, India: Panini Office, 1906), 471–74.

■ ■ ■

SOURCE 18.3 The Indian Rebellion

In 1857–1858, British-ruled India erupted in violent rebellion. Some among the rebels imagined that the Mughal Empire might be restored to its former power and glory. Such was the hope that animated the Azamgarh Proclamation, issued in the summer of 1857, allegedly by the grandson of the last and largely powerless Mughal emperor, Bahadur Shah.

- What grievances against British rule does this document disclose?
- How does the proclamation imagine the future of India, should the rebellion succeed? How does this compare to Ram Mohan Roy's vision of India's future in Source 18.2?
- To what groups or classes of people was the proclamation directed? What groups were left out in the call to rebellion? Why might they have been omitted?

PRINCE FEROZE SHAH | *The Azamgarh Proclamation* | 1857

It is well known to all that in this age the people of Hindustan, both Hindus and Muslims, are being ruined under the tyranny and oppression of the infidel and the treacherous English. It is therefore the bounden duty of all the wealthy people of India, especially of those who have any sort of connection with any of the Muslim royal families and are considered the pastors and masters of their people, to stake their lives and property for the well-being of the public.... I, who am the grandson of Bahadur Shah, have ... come here to extirpate the infidels residing in the eastern part of the country, and to liberate and protect the poor helpless people now groaning under their iron rule....

Section I: Regarding Zamindars [large landowners]

It is evident the British government, in making [land] settlements, have imposed exorbitant jummas [taxes], and have disgraced and ruined several zamindars, by putting up their estates to public auction for arrears of rent, insomuch, that on the institution of a suit by a common ryot [peasant farmer] yet, a maidservant, or a slave, the respectable zamindars are summoned into court, arrested, put in gaol, and disgraced.... Besides this, the coffers of the zamindars are annually taxed with subscriptions for schools, hospitals, roads, etc. Such extortions will have no manner of existence in the Badshahi [restored Mughal] government; but, on the contrary, the jummas will be light, the dignity and honour of the zamindars safe, and every zamindar will have absolute rule in his own zamindary.

Section II: Regarding Merchants

It is plain that the infidel and treacherous British government have monopolized the trade of all the fine and valuable merchandise such as indigo, cloth, and other articles of shipping, leaving only the trade of trifles to the people, and even in this they are not without their share of the profits, which they secure by means of customs and stamp fees, etc., in money suits, so that the people have merely a trade in name. Besides this, the profits of the traders are taxed with postages, tolls, and subscriptions for schools. Notwithstanding all these concessions, the merchants are liable to imprisonment and disgrace at the instance or complaint of a worthless man. When the Badshahi government is established, all these aforesaid fraudulent practices shall be dispensed with, and the trade of every article, without exception both by land and water, shall be open to the native merchants of India, who will have the benefit of the government steam-vessels and steam carriages for the conveyance of their merchandise gratis....

Section III: Regarding Public Servants

It is not a secret thing, that under the British government, natives employed in the civil and military services have little respect, low pay, and no manner of influence; and all the posts of dignity and emolument in both the departments are exclusively bestowed upon

Englishmen.... But under the Badshahi government, [these] posts ... will be given to the natives.... Natives, whether Hindus or Muslims, who fall fighting against the English, are sure to go to heaven; and those killed fighting for the English, will, doubtless, go to hell; therefore, all the natives in the British service ought to be alive to their religion and interest, and, abjuring their loyalty to the English, side with the Badshahi government and obtain salaries of 200 or 300 rupees per month for the present, and be entitled to high posts in future.

Section IV: Regarding Artisans

It is evident that the Europeans, by the introduction of English articles into India, have thrown the weavers, the cotton-dressers, the carpenters, the blacksmiths, and the shoe-makers, etc., out of employ, and have engrossed their occupations, so that every description of native artisan has been reduced to beggary. But under the Badshahi government the native artisan will exclusively be employed in the services of the kings, the rajahs, and the rich; and this will no doubt insure their prosperity.

Section V: Regarding Pundits [scholars], Fakirs [religious mystics], and Other Learned Persons

The pundits and fakirs being the guardians of the Hindu and Muslim religions, respectively, and the European being the enemies of both the religions, and as at present a war is raging against the English on account of religion, the pundits and fakirs are bound to present themselves to me and take their share in the holy war, otherwise they will stand condemned ... but if they come, they will, when the Badshahi government is well established, receive rent-free lands.

Lastly, be it known to all, that whoever out of the above-named classes, shall ... still cling to the British government, all his estates shall be confiscated, and his property plundered, and he himself, with his whole family, shall be imprisoned, and ultimately put to death.

Source: "The Azamgarh Proclamation," *Delhi Gazette*, September 29, 1857.

SOURCE 18.4 The Credits and Debits of British Rule in India

Dadabhai Naoroji (1825–1917) was a well-educated Indian intellectual, a cotton trader in London, and a founding member of the Indian National Congress, an elite organization established in 1885 to press for a wider range of opportunities for educated Indians within the colonial system. He was also the first Indian to serve in the British Parliament. In 1871, while addressing an English audience in London, Naoroji was asked about the impact of British rule in India. Representing a "moderate" view within Indian political circles at the time, he organized his response in terms of "credits" and "debits."

- According to Naoroji, what are the chief advantages and drawbacks of British rule?
- What is Naoroji seeking from Britain?
- How does Naoroji's posture toward British rule compare to that of Ram Mohan Roy in Source 18.2 or the Azamgarh Proclamation in Source 18.3?

DADABHAI NAOROJI | *Speech to a London Audience* | 1871

Credit

In the Cause of Humanity: Abolition of *suttee* and infanticide. Destruction of *Dacoits, Thugs, Pindarees* [various criminal groups] and other such pests of Indian society. Allowing remarriage of Hindu widows, and charitable aid in time of famine. Glorious work all this, of which any nation may well be proud....

In the Cause of Civilization: Education, both male and female. Though yet only partial, an inestimable blessing as far as it has gone, and leading gradually to the destruction of superstition, and many moral and social evils. Resuscitation of India's own noble literature, modified and refined by the enlightenment of the West.

Politically: Peace and order. Freedom of speech and liberty of the press. Higher political knowledge and aspirations. Improvement of government in the native states. Security of life and property. Freedom from oppression caused by the caprice or greed of despotic rulers, and from devastation by war. Equal justice between man and man (sometimes vitiated by partiality to Europeans). Services of highly educated administrators, who have achieved the abovementioned results.

Materially: Loans for railways and irrigation. Development of a few valuable products, such as indigo, tea, coffee, silk, etc. Increase of exports. Telegraphs.

Generally: A slowly growing desire of late to treat India equitably, and as a country held in trust. Good intentions. No nation on the face of the earth has ever had the opportunity of achieving such a glorious work as this.... I appreciate, and so do my countrymen, what England has done for India, and I know that it is only in British hands that her regeneration can be accomplished. Now for the debit side.

Debit

In the Cause of Humanity: Nothing. Everything, therefore, is in your favor under this heading.

In the Cause of Civilization: As I have said already, there has been a failure to do as much as might have been done, but I put nothing to the debit. Much has been done, though.

Politically: Repeated breach of pledges to give the natives a fair and reasonable share in the higher administration of their own country, which has much shaken confidence in the good faith of the British word. Political aspirations and the legitimate claim to have a reasonable voice in the legislation and the imposition and disbursement of taxes, met to a very slight degree, thus treating the natives of India not as British subjects, in whom representation is a birthright. Consequent on the above, an utter disregard of the feelings and views of the natives....

Financially: All attention is engrossed in devising new modes of taxation, without any adequate effort to increase the means of the people to pay; and the consequent vexation and oppressiveness of the taxes imposed, imperial and local. Inequitable financial relations between England and India, i.e., the political debt of £100,000,000 clapped on India's shoulders, and all home charges also, though the British Exchequer contributes nearly £3,000,000 to the expense of the colonies.

Materially: The political drain, up to this time, from India to England, of above £500,000,000, at the lowest computation, in principal alone, which with interest would be some thousands of millions. The further continuation of this drain at the rate, at present, of above £12,000,000 per annum, with a tendency to increase. The consequent continuous impoverishment and exhaustion of the country, except so far as it has been very partially relieved and replenished by the railway and irrigation loans, and the windfall of the consequences of the American war, since 1850. Even with this relief, the material condition of India is such that the great mass of the poor have hardly tuppence a day and a few rags, or a scanty subsistence. The famines that were in their power to prevent, if they had done their duty, as a good and intelligent government. The policy adopted during the last fifteen years of building railways, irrigation works, etc., is hopeful, has already resulted in much good to your credit, and if persevered in, gratitude and contentment will follow. An increase of exports without adequate compensation; loss of manufacturing industry and skill. Here I end the debit side.

Summary

To sum up the whole, the British rule has been: morally, a great blessing; politically, peace and order on one hand, blunders on the other; materially, impoverishment, relieved as far as the railway and other loans go. The natives call the British system "Sakar ki Churi," the knife of sugar. That is to say, there is no oppression, it is all smooth and sweet, but it is the knife, notwithstanding. I mention this that you should know these feelings. Our great misfortune is that you do not know our wants. When you will know our real wishes, I have not the least doubt that you would do justice. The genius and spirit of the British people is fair play and justice.

Source: Dadabhai Naoroji, *Essays, Speeches, Addresses and Writings* (Bombay: Caxton Printing Works, 1887), 131–36.

SOURCE 18.5 Gandhi on Modern Civilization

Mahatma Gandhi (1869–1948), clearly modern India's most beloved leader, is best known for his theories of *satyagraha*. This was an assertive but nonviolent approach to political action that directly challenged and disobeyed unjust laws, while seeking to change the hearts of India's British oppressors. But Gandhi's thinking was distinctive in another way as well: he objected not only to the foreign and exploitative character of British rule, but also, and more fundamentally, to the modern civilization that it carried. In 1909, he spelled out that critique in a pamphlet titled *Hind Swaraj* (*Indian Home Rule*). In this document, Gandhi assumes the role of an "editor," responding to questions from a "reader."

- What is Gandhi's most fundamental criticism of British rule in India?
- What is the difference between Gandhi's concept of "civilization" and that which he ascribes to the British?
- What kind of future does Gandhi seek for his country?

MAHATMA GANDHI | *Indian Home Rule* | 1909

READER: Now you will have to explain what you mean by civilization.

EDITOR: Let us first consider what state of things is described by the word "civilization."... The people of Europe today live in better-built houses than they did a hundred years ago. This is considered an emblem of civilization.... If people of a certain country, who have hitherto not been in the habit of wearing much clothing, boots, etc., adopt European clothing, they are supposed to have become civilized out of savagery. Formerly, in Europe, people ploughed their lands mainly by manual labor. Now, one man can plough a vast tract by means of steam engines and can thus amass great wealth. This is called a sign of civilization. Formerly, only a few men wrote valuable books. Now, anybody writes and prints anything he likes and poisons people's minds. Formerly, men traveled in wagons. Now, they fly through the air in trains at the rate of four hundred and more miles per day. This is considered the height of civilization. It has been stated that, as men progress, they shall be able to travel in airship and reach any part of the world in a few hours.... Everything will be done by machinery. Formerly, when people wanted to fight with one another, they measured between them their bodily strength; now it is possible to take away thousands of lives by one man working behind a gun from a hill. This is civilization.... Formerly, men were made slaves under physical compulsion. Now they are enslaved by temptation of money and of the luxuries that money can buy.... This civilization takes note neither of morality nor of religion. Its votaries calmly state that their business is not to teach religion. Some even consider it to be a superstitious growth.... This civilization is irreligion, and it has taken such a hold on the people in Europe that those who are in it appear to be half mad. They lack real physical strength or courage. They keep up their energy by intoxication. They can hardly be happy in solitude. Women, who should be the queens of households, wander in the streets or they slave away in factories. For the sake of a pittance, half a million women in England alone are laboring under trying circumstances in factories or similar institutions.

This civilization is such that one has only to be patient and it will be self-destroyed.... I cannot give you an adequate conception of it. It is eating into the vitals of the English nation. It must be shunned.... Civilization is not an incurable disease, but it should never be forgotten that the English are at present afflicted by it.

READER: I now understand why the English hold India. I should like to know your views about the condition of our country.

EDITOR: It is a sad condition.... It is my deliberate opinion that India is being ground down, not under the English heel, but under that of modern civilization. It is groaning under the monster's terrible weight. [M]y first complaint is that India is becoming irreligious.... We are turning away from God.... [W]e should set a limit to our worldly ambition.... [O]ur religious ambition should be illimitable....

EDITOR: Railways, lawyers, and doctors have impoverished the country so much so that, if we do not wake up in time, we shall be ruined.

READER: I do now, indeed, fear that we are not likely to agree at all. You are attacking the very institutions which we have hitherto considered to be good.

EDITOR: It must be manifest to you that, but for the railways, the English could not have such a hold on India as they have. The railways, too, have spread the bubonic plague. Without them the masses could not move from place to place. They are the carriers of plague germs. Formerly we had natural segregation. Railways have also increased the frequency of famines because, owing to facility of means of locomotion, people sell out their grain and it is sent to the dearest markets. People become careless and so the pressure of famine increases. Railways accentuate the evil nature of man. Bad men fulfill their evil designs with greater rapidity....

READER: You have denounced railways, lawyers, and doctors. I can see that you will discard all machinery. What, then, is civilization?

EDITOR: The answer to that question is not difficult. I believe that the civilization India has evolved is not to be beaten in the world.... India is still, somehow or other, sound at the foundation.... India remains immovable and that is her glory. It is a charge against India that her people are so uncivilized, ignorant, and stolid that it is not possible to induce them to adopt any changes. It is a charge really against our merit. What we have tested and found true on the anvil of experience, we dare not change. Many thrust their advice upon India, and she remains steady. This is her beauty: it is the sheet-anchor of our hope.

Civilization is that mode of conduct which points out to man the path of duty. Performance of duty and observance of morality are convertible terms. To observe morality is to attain mastery over our mind and our passions. So doing, we know ourselves.... If this definition be correct, then India ... has nothing to learn from anybody else.... Our ancestors, therefore, set a limit to our indulgences. [They] dissuaded us from luxuries and pleasures. We have managed with the same kind of plough as existed thousands of years ago. We have retained the same kind of cottages that we had in former times and our indigenous education remains the same as before. We have had no system of life-corroding competition. Each followed his own occupation or trade and charged a regulation wage. It was not that we did not know how to invent machinery, but our forefathers knew that, if we set our hearts after such things, we would become slaves and lose our moral fiber.... They were, therefore, satisfied with small villages.... A nation with a constitution like this is fitter to teach others than to learn from others....

The tendency of the Indian civilization is to elevate the moral being; that of the Western civilization is to propagate immorality. The latter is godless; the former is based on a belief in God. So understanding and so believing, it behooves every lover of India to cling to the Indian civilization even as a child clings to the mother's breast.

Source: Mohandas Gandhi, *Indian Home Rule* (Madras: Ganesh, 1922), pts. 6, 8, 9, 10, 13.

DOING HISTORY

1. **Describing alternative futures:** What can you infer about the kind of future for India that the authors or creators of these sources anticipate?

2. **Assessing change through time:** In what ways did understandings of British colonial rule change over time? How might you account for these changes?

3. **Considering visual and written sources:** How do these visual and written sources differ in terms of the understanding they convey about British India?

4. **Noticing what's missing:** What voices are not represented in these sources? How might such people have articulated a different understanding of the colonial experience?

5. **Responding to Gandhi:** How might each of the other authors or artists have responded to Gandhi's analysis of British colonial role and his understanding of "civilization"? To what extent do you find Gandhi's views relevant to the conditions of the early twenty-first century?

HISTORIANS' VOICES

The Great Indian Rebellion

The Great Indian Rebellion of 1857–1858, surely a pivotal event in the history of colonial India, came as a stunning surprise to the British and, in its ferocity and extent, perhaps to many Indians as well. (See Sources 18.1D and 18.3.) Historians have long puzzled over its origins, in particular the relationship between the long-term conditions that set the stage for the rebellion and the immediate trigger that sparked it. Voice 18.1 by Stanley Wolpert, a prominent American historian of India, focuses on an array of upsetting changes introduced by the British, providing a larger context for understanding the outbreak of the rebellion. In Voice 18.2, D. R. SarDesai, an Indian-born historian and professor at the University of California, Los Angeles, describes the "immediate cause" of the rebellion in the issues surrounding the "greased cartridges."

- What do these Voices suggest about the Indian grievances that informed the Great Indian Rebellion of 1857?
- In what ways might the greased cartridges incident, described in Voice 18.2, have expressed or reinforced the long-term tensions described in Voice 18.1?
- **Integrating primary and secondary sources:** How does the Azamgarh Proclamation (Source 18.3) provide support for Stanley Wolpert's argument in Voice 18.1?

VOICE 18.1

Stanley Wolpert on British Innovations and Indian Grievances | 1965

Many were warning that the pace of change was too swift. Important groups within Indian society were being too brashly ignored, too completely alienated. The deposed princes poisoned all ears around with talk of the "faithless" British promises and treaties torn to bits by men without honor. The landed aristocrats, whose estates had always been freeholds, were now assailed by low-born [Indian] tax collectors and bullied by beardless [British] young men in a foreign tongue. Brahmins and Muslim Maulvis [learned teachers of Islamic law] spoke of Christian rulers desirous only of converting all Indians to their English religion. Merchants and craftsmen saw their livelihood undermined by British competition and foreign manufactured goods. Teachers and scholars found the labors of a lifetime no longer valued in a society run in a language they could not understand, according to principles and ideas they feared and hated. Most dangerous of all, the sepoy soldiers [low-ranking Indian troops in Britain's colonial military forces] had grown restive. By 1856 their morale was at an all-time low, just when their number proportionate to British troops in India was at its all-time high.

Source: Stanley Wolpert, *India* (Englewood Cliffs, NJ: Prentice Hall, 1965), 93–94.

VOICE 18.2

D. R. SarDesai on the Greased Cartridges Incident | 2008

The last straw and immediate cause of the army's mutiny centered around the issue of the greased cartridges. More than 90 percent of the troops were Hindu or Muslim. A newly introduced rifle required the user to bite the pouch containing gunpowder before emptying the powder into the barrel. The pouch was coated with grease made from the fat of either pigs, anathema to Muslims, or cows, sacred to Hindus. The British first denied the use of such fat; denial strengthened suspicion of a deliberate conspiracy to have Indian soldiers, Hindus and Muslims, lose their religious affiliation and then convert to the Christian faith. Even though the British stopped using the grease immediately, the damage had been done, and the Indians saw it as another conspiracy by the missionaries and the rulers to convert the troops (and consequently their families) to Christianity. They also believed the withdrawal of the greased cartridges was a sign of weakness and alarm on the part of the British. Many soldiers felt betrayed; they lost respect for their commanders. The effect was more distrust of the rulers on the part of the ruled; every official decision thereafter would be looked upon by the multitudes with palpable suspicion.

Source: D. R. SarDesai, *India: The Definitive History* (Boulder, CO.: Westview Press, 2008), 242–43.

NOTE

1. Kevin Hannam and Anya Diekmann, *Tourism and India: A Critical Introduction* (New York, NY: Routledge, 2011), 69–70.

CHAPTER 19

Thinking through Sources

Japan and the West in the Nineteenth Century

During the nineteenth century, Japan's relationship with the West changed profoundly in a pattern that included sharp antagonism, enthusiastic embrace, selective borrowing, and equality on the international stage. At the time, that changing relationship had implications as well for China, Korea, Russia, and elsewhere, even as it laid the foundation for twentieth-century global conflict in World War II.

In the initial decades of the nineteenth century, the Western world was increasingly impinging upon Japan, which had closed itself off from Europe and America 200 years earlier, with the exception of a small Dutch trading port near Nagasaki. Over time, however, a number of Western whaling ships had penetrated Japanese waters, and suspicions rose. Aizawa Seishisai, a prominent Japanese Confucian scholar, gave voice to these worries in 1825:

> The barbarians live ten thousand miles across the sea; when they set off on foreign conquests, they must procure supplies and provisions from the enemy. That is why they trade and fish. Their men of war are self-sufficient away from home. If their only motive for harpooning whales was to obtain whale meat, they could do so in their own waters. Why should they risk long, difficult voyages just to harpoon whales in eastern seas? Their ships can be outfitted for trading, or fishing, or fighting. Can anyone guarantee that their merchant vessels and fishing boats of today will not turn into warships tomorrow?[1]

SOURCE 19.1 Continuing Japanese Isolation

In response to such concerns about Western intervention, the Japanese government, known as the Tokugawa shogunate, issued an edict that reiterated in the strongest possible terms the country's long-standing posture of isolation from the West.

- What understanding of the West did this edict reflect?
- What actions did the edict prescribe?
- Why might Westerners find the policy offensive and unacceptable?

An Edict of Expulsion | 1825

We have issued instructions on how to deal with foreign ships on numerous occasions up to the present. In the Bunka era [1804–1817] we issued new edicts to deal with Russian ships. But a few years ago a British ship wreaked havoc in Nagasaki, and more recently their rowboats have been landing to procure firewood, water, and provisions. Two years ago they forced their way ashore, stole livestock and extorted rice. Thus they have become steadily more unruly, and moreover seem to be propagating their wicked religion among our people. This situation plainly cannot be left to itself.

All Southern Barbarians and Westerners, not only the English, worship Christianity, that wicked cult prohibited in our land. Henceforth, whenever a foreign ship is sighted approaching any point on our coast, all persons on hand should fire on and drive it off. If the vessel heads for the open sea, you need not pursue it; allow it to escape. If the foreigners force their way ashore, you may capture and incarcerate them, and if their mother ship approaches, you may destroy it as circumstances dictate.

Note that Chinese, Korean, and Ryukyuans [people from a group of islands south of Japan] can be differentiated [from Westerners] by the physiognomy and ship design, but Dutch ships are indistinguishable [from those of other Westerners]. Even so, have no compunctions about firing on [the Dutch] by mistake; when in doubt, drive the ship away without hesitation. Never be caught offguard.

Source: Bob Tadashi Wakabayashi, *Anti-Foreignism and Western Learning in Early-Modern Japan* (Cambridge, MA: Harvard University Press, 1985), 60.

SOURCE 19.2 The Debate: Expel the Barbarians

The arrival of U.S. Admiral Matthew Perry in 1853, demanding that the country open to foreign commerce and navigation, brought to a head the question of Japan's isolationist policy and prompted a considerable debate in Japanese circles. Advocating forceful expulsion of the Americans and sharply opposing any treaty with them was Tokugawa Nariaki, the *daimyo*, or ruler, of a domain on the eastern coast of Japan.

- How does Tokugawa Nariaki characterize Americans?
- What were his arguments for a policy of war?
- What did he fear if Japan tried to accommodate Perry's demands?

TOKUGAWA NARIAKI | *Memorial on the American Demand for a Treaty* | 1853

[W]e must never choose the policy of peace....

[T]he Americans... were arrogant and discourteous, their actions an outrage.... The foreigners, having thus ignored our prohibition and penetrated our waters even to the vicinity of the capital, threatening us and making demands upon us, should it happen not only the Bakufu fails to expel them but also that it concludes an agreement in accordance with their requests, then I fear it would be impossible to maintain our national prestige....

[I]f the people of Japan stand firmly united, if we complete our military preparations and return to the state of society that existed before the middle ages [when the emperor ruled the country directly], then we will even be able to go out against foreign countries and spread abroad our fame and prestige.... [I]f the Bakufu, now and henceforward, shows itself resolute for expulsion, the immediate effect will be to increase ten-fold the morale of the country ... only by so doing will the shogun be able to fulfill his "barbarian-expelling" duty and unite the men of every province in carrying out their proper military functions....

Source: *Selected Documents on Japanese Foreign Policy*, translated by William G. Beasley (1955), pp. 102–7. By permission of Oxford University Press.

■ ■ ■

SOURCE 19.3 The Debate: A Sumo Wrestler and a Foreigner ▶

The debate about Japan's response to Perry's demands not only engaged political and intellectual elites, but also found expression in the popular media of woodblock prints. In 1861, such a print showed a Japanese sumo wrestler tossing a boastful French competitor. The inscription reads: "Hershan, wrestler without peer, comes from Calais in France, a part of Europe. He has traveled to the countries of the world, and nowhere has he been defeated. He is very boastful and came to our country to Yokohama and asked for a match. To the glory of Japan, a Japanese sumo wrestler threw him to the ground."[2]

- Why might this image carry considerable appeal in the middle of a national debate about how to deal with the intrusive foreigners?
- In what ways could it be seen as a visual depiction of Tokugawa Nariaki's point of view?
- What does the inscription add to your understanding of the image?

Source 19.3 The Debate: A Sumo Wrestler and a Foreigner

YOSHIKU UTAGAWA | *Throwing a Frenchman* | 1861

SOURCE 19.4 The Debate: Eastern Ethics and Western Science

The other side of this debate made the case for opening Japan to the West and even embracing aspects of its culture. Ii Naosuke, another *daimyo* and a bitter opponent of Tokugawa Nariaki, wrote in 1853:

> It is impossible in the crisis we now face to ensure the safety and tranquility of our country merely by an insistence on the seclusion laws as we did in former times.... The exchange of goods is a universal practice. This we should explain to the spirits of our ancestors. And we should tell the foreigners that we mean in future to send trading vessels to the Dutch company's factory in Batavia to engage in trade.... As we increase the number of our ships and our mastery of technique, Japanese will be able to sail the oceans freely and gain direct knowledge of conditions abroad.[3]

More generally and more famously, Sakuma Shozan, a Confucian-educated official in the shogun's government, argued that Japan must combine Eastern Confucian-oriented ethics and Western science. He had been briefly imprisoned in 1854 for encouraging one of his students to stow away on one of Perry's ships in an attempt to learn something of Western ways. Shortly after his release, Sakuma Shozan wrote his famous work, *Reflections on My Errors*. It was not really an apology for his actions, but rather a defense of his position.

- How do you understand the metaphor in the first paragraph of this excerpt about "giv[ing] the medicine secretly"?
- What departures from existing practices does Sakuma Shozan advocate? In what ways is he critical of Japan's military and intellectual leaders?
- On what issues might Sakuma Shozan and Tokugawa Nariaki agree? How would you define their differences?

SAKUMA SHOZAN | *Reflections on My Errors* | Mid-1850s

Take, for example, a man who is grieved by the illness of his lord or his father, and who is seeking medicine to cure it. If he is fortunate enough to secure the medicine, and is certain that it will be efficacious, then, certainly, without questioning either its cost or the quality of its name, he will beg his lord or father to take it. Should the latter refuse on the grounds that he dislikes the name, does the younger man make various schemes to give the medicine secretly, or does he simply sit by and wait for his master to die? There is no question about it: ... the feeling of genuine sincerity and heartfelt grief on the part of the subject or son makes it absolutely impossible for him to sit idly and watch his master's anguish; consequently, even if he knows that he will later have to face his master's anger, he cannot but give the medicine secretly....

Source 19.4 The Debate: Eastern Ethics and Western Science

The gentleman has five pleasures, but wealth and rank are not among them. That his house understands decorum and righteousness and remains free from family rifts — this is one pleasure. That exercising care in giving to and taking from others, he provides for himself honestly, free, internally, from shame before his wife and children, and externally, from disgrace before the public — this is the second pleasure. That he expounds and glorifies the learning of the sages, knows in his heart the great Way, and in all situations contents himself with his duty, in adversity as well as in prosperity—this is the third pleasure.... That he is born after the opening of the vistas of science by the Westerners, and can therefore understand principles not known to the sages and wise men of old—this is the fourth pleasure. That he employs the ethics of the East and the scientific technique of the West, neglecting neither the spiritual nor material aspects of life, combining subjective and objective, and thus bringing benefit to the people and serving the nation—this is the fifth pleasure....

The principal requisite of national defense is that it prevents the foreign barbarians from holding us in contempt. The existing coastal defense installations all lack method; the pieces of artillery that have been set up are improperly made; and the officials who negotiate with the foreigners are mediocrities who have no understanding of warfare. The situation being such, even though we wish to avoid incurring the scorn of the barbarians, how, in fact, can we do so?...

Of the men who now hold posts as commanders of the army, those who are not dukes or princes or men of noble rank, are members of wealthy families. As such, they find their daily pleasure in drinking wine, singing, and dancing; and they are ignorant of military strategy and discipline. Should a national emergency arise, there is no one who could command the respect of the warriors and halt the enemy's attack. This is the great sorrow of our times. For this reason, I have wished to follow in substance the Western principles of armament, and, by banding together loyal, valorous, strong men of old, established families not in the military class—men of whom one would be equal to ten ordinary men—to form a voluntary group which would be made to have as its sole aim that of guarding the nation and protecting the people. Anyone wishing to join the society would be tested and his merits examined; and, if he did not shirk hardship, he would then be permitted to join. Men of talent in military strategy, planning, and administration would be advanced to positions of leadership, and then, if the day should come when the country must be defended, this group could be gathered together and organized into an army to await official commands. It is to be hoped that they would drive the enemy away and perform greater service than those who now form the military class....

Mathematics is the basis for all learning. In the Western world after this science was discovered military tactics advanced greatly.... At the present time, if we wish really to complete our military preparations, we must develop this branch of study....

What do the so-called scholars of today actually do? Do they clearly and tacitly understand the way in which the gods and sages established this nation, or the way in which Yao, Shun, and the divine emperors of the three dynasties governed? Do they, after having learned the rites and music, punishment and administration, the classics and governmental system, go on to discuss and learn the elements of the art of war, of military discipline, of the principles of machinery? Do they make exhaustive studies of conditions in foreign countries? Of effective defense methods? Of strategy in setting up strongholds, defense barriers, and reinforcements? Of the knowledge of computation, gravitation, geometry, and mathematics? If they do, I have not heard of it! Therefore I ask what the so-called scholars of today actually do....

In order to master the barbarians there is nothing so effective as to ascertain in the beginning conditions among them. To do this, there is no better first step than to be familiar with barbarian tongues. Thus, learning a barbarian language is not only a step toward knowing the barbarians, but also the groundwork for mastering them.

Source: *Sources of Japanese Tradition*, Volume 2, compiled by William De Bary et al. Copyright © 2001 Columbia University Press. Reprinted with permission of the publisher.

■ ■ ■

SOURCE 19.5 Westernization ▶

The great debate of the 1850s and 1860s, prompted by Perry's arrival, came to an end with the Meiji Restoration of 1868. The shogunate was replaced by a new government, headed directly by the emperor, and committed to a more thorough transformation of the country than Sakuma Shozan had ever imagined. Particularly among the young, there was an acute awareness of the need to create a new culture that could support a revived Japan. "We have no history," declared one of these students; "our history begins today."[4] In this context, much that was Western was enthusiastically embraced. The technological side of this borrowing, contributing much to Japan's remarkable industrialization, was the most obvious expression of this westernization.

But this borrowing also extended to more purely cultural matters. Eating beef became popular, despite Buddhist objections. Many men adopted Western hairstyles and grew beards, even though the facial hair of Westerners had earlier been portrayed as ugly. In 1872, Western dress was ordered for all official ceremonies. Ballroom dancing became popular among the elite, as did Western instruments like the piano and harpsichord. Women in these circles likewise adopted Western ways, as illustrated in Source 19.5, an 1887 woodblock print titled *Illustration of Singing by the Plum Garden*. At the same time, the image includes many traditional Japanese elements. The flowering trees in the background had long been an important subject of study in Japan's artistic tradition, and the flower arrangement on the right represents a popular Japanese art form. Moreover, the dress of the woman in the middle seems to reflect earlier Japanese court traditions that encouraged women to wear many layers of kimonos.

- What elements of Western culture can you identify in this visual source?
- In what ways does this print reflect the continuing appeal of Japanese culture? Pay attention to the scenery, the tree, and the flowers.
- Why were so many Japanese so enamored of Western culture during this time? Why did the Japanese government actively encourage their interest?

Source 19.5 Westernization

TOYOHARA CHIKANOBU | *Women and Westernization* | 1887

(Singing by the Plum Garden (Baien sh_ka zu), Meiji Era, 1887 (ink & colour on paper)/Chikanobu, Toyohara (1838–1912)/MUSEUM OF FINE ARTS, BOSTON/Museum of Fine Arts, Boston, Massachusetts, USA/Bridgeman Images)

SOURCE 19.6 A Critique of Westernization

Not everyone in Japan was so enthusiastic about the adoption of Western culture. Indeed, beginning in the late 1870s and continuing into the next decade, numerous essays and images satirized the apparently indiscriminate fascination with all things European. Source 19.6, drawn by Japanese cartoonist Honda Kinkichiro in 1879, represents that point of view. One caption that accompanied the drawing reads as follows: "Mr. Morse [an American zoologist who introduced Darwin's theory of evolution to Japan in 1877] explains that all human beings were monkeys in the beginning. In the beginning—but even now aren't we still monkeys? When it comes to Western things we think the red beards are the most skillful at everything."[5] A second caption in English below the drawing further develops this theme.

- What specific aspects of Japan's efforts at westernization is the artist mocking?
- Why might the artist have used a Western scientific theory (Darwinian evolution) to criticize excessive westernization in Japan?
- Why do you think a reaction set in against the cultural imitation of Europe?

HONDA KINKICHIRO | *Critique of Wholesale Westernization* | 1879

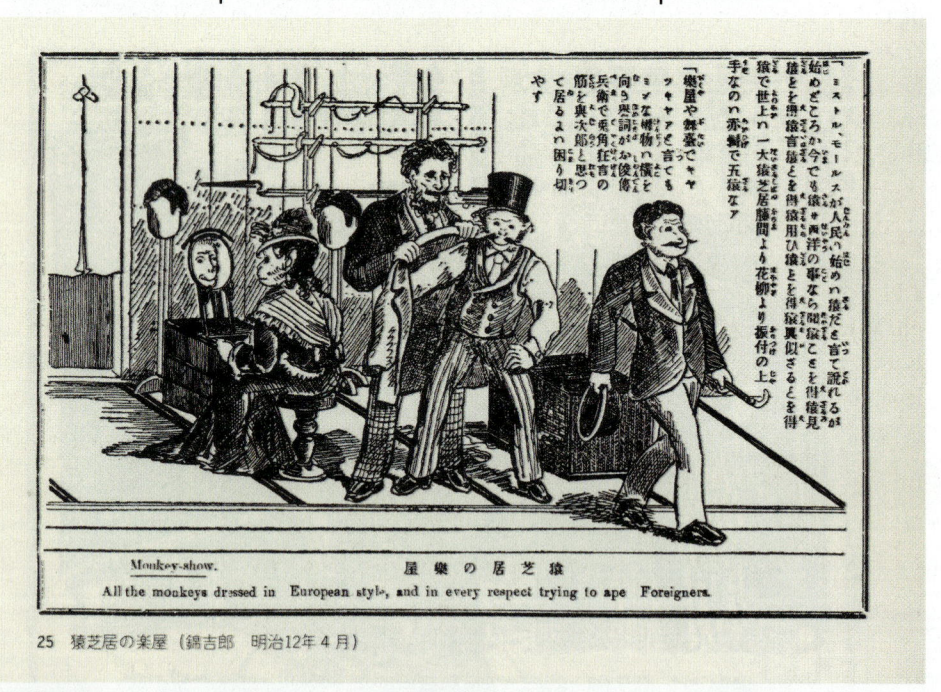

Monkey-show.
All the monkeys dressed in European style, and in every respect trying to ape Foreigners.

25 猿芝居の楽屋（錦吉郎　明治12年4月）

(Library of Congress)

SOURCE 19.7 War and Empire ▶

Behind Japan's modernization and westernization was the recognition that Western imperialism was surging in Asia and that China was a prime example of what happened to countries that were unable to defend themselves against it. Accordingly, achieving political and military equality with the Great Powers of Europe and the United States became a central aim of Japan's modernization program.

Strengthening Japan against Western aggression increasingly meant "throwing off Asia"—a phrase that implied rejecting many of Japan's own cultural traditions and its habit of imitating China, as well as creating an Asian empire of its own. Fukuzawa Yukichi, a popular advocate of Western knowledge, declared:

> We must not wait for neighboring countries to become civilized so that we can together promote Asia's revival. Rather we should leave their ranks and join forces with the civilized countries of the West. We don't have to give China and Korea any special treatment just because they are neighboring countries. We should deal with them as Western people do.... I reject the idea that we must continue to associate with bad friends in East Asia.[6]

Historically the Japanese had borrowed a great deal from China—Buddhism, Confucianism, court rituals, city-planning ideas, administrative traditions, and elements of the Chinese script. But Japan's victory in a war with China in 1894–1895 showed clearly that Japan had emerged from the Chinese cultural shadow in which it had lived for centuries. Furthermore, Japan had begun to acquire an East Asian empire in Korea and Taiwan at the expense of China. Even more dramatically, its triumph in the 1904-1905 Russo-Japanese war illustrated its ability to stand up even to a major European power. This accomplishment was the first modern military victory by an Asian country against a Western power, and its implications resonated widely.

The significance of that victory is expressed in Source 19.7, a 1904 print by Japanese artist Chomatsu Tomisato, created during the Russo-Japanese War. It shows a triumphant Japan, stomping on a Russian battleship and holding aloft a figure representing the Russian czar Nicholas, who carries a white flag of surrender. Korea cowers behind the Japanese figure, while China kneels in submission.

- What overall message did the artist seek to convey in this print? How might you describe the Japanese view of the world that it expresses?
- What do the images of China and Korea evoke?
- How would you describe the posture of Turkey (Tolky), the various European powers, and the United States in this image? Notice that several of them are carrying the Japanese flag.

CHOMATSU TOMISATO | *Japan, Triumphant* | 1904

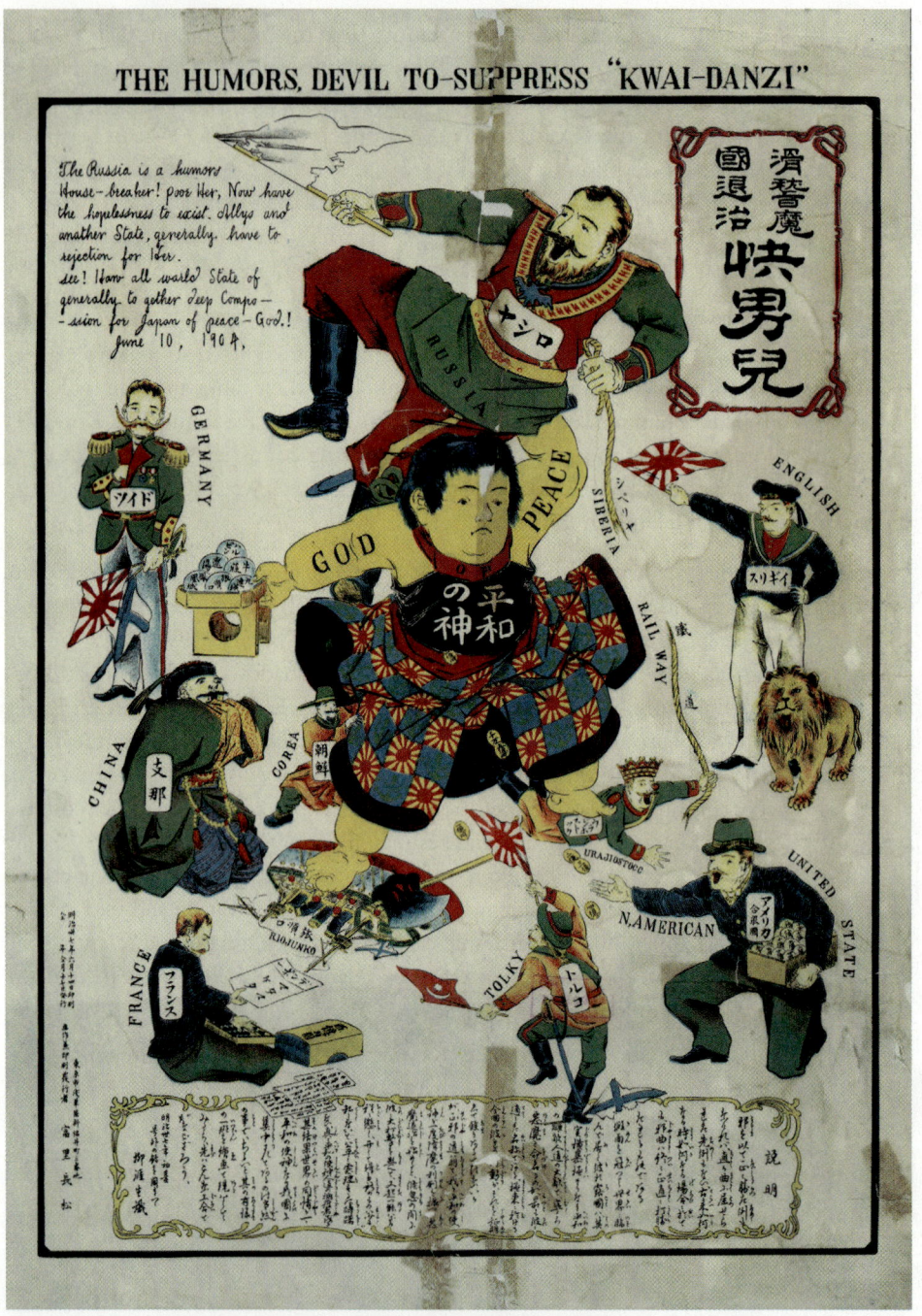

SOURCE 19.8 Japan in the Early Twentieth Century

Early in the new century, a prominent Japanese political figure, Okuma Shigenobu, summed up his view of the country's transformation over the past half-century.

- What were the greatest sources of pride to Okuma?
- To what did he attribute his country's progress?
- In his view, what elements of Japanese tradition were maintained amid all the changes?
- What groups of people might challenge Okuma's description of Japan, and how would they do it?

OKUMA SHIGENOBU | *Fifty Years of New Japan* | 1907–1908

By comparing the Japan of fifty years ago with the Japan of today, it will be seen that she has gained considerably in the extent of her territory, as well as in her population, which now numbers nearly fifty million. Her government has become constitutional not only in name, but in fact, and her national education has attained to a high degree of excellence. In commerce and industry, the emblems of peace, she has also made rapid strides, until her import and export trades together amounted in 1907 to the enormous sum of 926,000,000 yen.... Her general progress, during the short space of half a century, has been so sudden and swift that it presents a rare spectacle in the history of the world.

This leap forward is the result of the stimulus which the country received on coming into contact with the civilization of Europe and America, and may well, in its broad sense, be regarded as a boon conferred by foreign intercourse. Foreign intercourse it was that animated the national consciousness of our people, who under the feudal system lived localized and disunited, and foreign intercourse it is that has enabled Japan to stand up as a world power. We possess today a powerful army and navy, but it was after Western models that we laid their foundations by establishing a system of conscription in pursuance of the principle "all our sons are soldiers," by promoting military education, and by encouraging the manufacture of arms and the art of shipbuilding. We have reorganized the systems of central and local administration, and effected reforms in the educational system of the empire. All this is nothing but the result of adopting the superior features of Western institutions. That Japan has been enabled to do so is a boon conferred on her by foreign intercourse, and it may be said that the nation has succeeded in this grand metamorphosis through the promptings and the influence of foreign civilization....

For twenty centuries the nation has drunk freely of the civilizations of Korea, China, ... yet we remain today politically unaltered under one Imperial House and sovereign, that has descended in an unbroken line for a length of time absolutely unexampled in the world.... They [the Japanese people] have welcomed Occidental civilization while preserving their old Oriental civilization. They have attached great importance to Bushido [the samurai way of life], and at the same time held in the highest respect the spirit of charity and humanity. They have ever made a point of choosing the middle course in everything, and have aimed at being always well-balanced.... We are conservative simultaneously with being progressive; we are aristocratic and at the same time democratic; we are individualistic while also being socialistic. In these respects we may be said to somewhat resemble the Anglo-Saxon race.

Source: Count Segenobu Okuma, *Fifty Years of New Japan*, English version edited by Marcus Huish, vol. 2 (London: Smith, Elder & Co., 1909), 554–55, 571–72.

DOING HISTORY

1. **Explaining change:** How and why did the Japanese people's perceptions of themselves and their relationship to the West change during the nineteenth and early twentieth centuries? What elements of continuity in Japanese traditions are evident in these sources?

2. **Making comparisons:** Based on these sources and those in Chapter 18 (Colonial India: Experience and Response), how might you compare Japanese and Indian perceptions of the West during the nineteenth century? What accounts for both the similarities and differences?

3. **Distinguishing modernization and westernization:** Based on a careful reading of these sources, do you think that technological borrowing (modernization) requires cultural borrowing (westernization) as well? To what extent was Japan able to modernize while avoiding the incorporation of Western culture at the same time?

HISTORIANS' VOICES

Explaining Japan's Transformation

Historians have long struggled to explain Japan's remarkable economic transformation in the wake of the country's Meiji Restoration of 1868. Why was Japan able to accomplish what no other Afro-Asian or Latin American country could do during the second half of the nineteenth century? In Voice 19.1, James L. Huffman, a specialist in modern Japanese history, looks to the country's recent past for an answer as well as to the character and motivations of the men who led the Meiji regime. To these factors, another historian of Japan, James L. McClain, adds a consideration of the unique international circumstances in which Japan was operating in Voice 19.2.

- Do the explanations for Japan's economic transformation identified in these two sources argue with each other, or do they complement one another?

- To what extent do these two historians argue that long-term developments and international circumstances facilitated Japanese modernization? What role do they define for individual historical actors in the modernization process?

- **Integrating primary and secondary sources:** How might the primary sources in this feature be used to support or supplement the arguments of these two historians?

VOICE 19.1

James Huffman on Japan's Historical Legacy and Its Meiji Leaders | 2010

[T]he Meiji rebels did more than survive. They thrived, cobbling together an administration in the name of a shy teen-aged emperor and turning a "restoration" into a revolution of national goals and systems. How did they do it? One answer lies in the Tokugawa legacy. Recall the high literacy rates of that era, the commercial revolution, the bustling cities, and the sophisticated intellectual sphere. Even in its last desperate decade, the *bakufu* [the government of Tokugawa Japan] had engaged Westerners rather than merely resisting them, Chinese style. Big as the problems were, the Meiji innovators inherited a structure with strong foundations.

Another explanation lies in the men who took charge in 1868 ... The oldest ... were only in their early forties and none had top-level administrative experience. What they shared, however, was vision, talent, and realism along with commitment to nation-building... Their pragmatism was illustrated in their approach to the West ... [T]hey realistically concluded that expulsion [of the intruding Westerners] was impossible; Japan must compete with the West on its own terms. So when they issued a "charter oath" ..., they promised: "knowledge shall be sought throughout the world", "matters of state shall be decided by public discussion", and "classes high and low shall unite". They issued the proclamation in a formal Shinto ceremony—evidence that they understood the political wisdom of clothing modern policies in comfortable traditional symbols.

Source: James L. Huffman, *Japan in World History* (Oxford, UK: Oxford University Press, 2010), 76.

VOICE 19.2

James L. McClain on the International Context of Japan's Transformation | 2002

There was also a providential, almost serendipitous quality to Japan's economic accomplishments. In some ways the country was fortunate that the West had started down the path of industrialization a few decades before Perry's arrival, for as a late developer, the newly opened island nation could learn from the experiences of Euro-Americans and make use of their technological innovations. At the same time, the West was not so far ahead in the 1870s and 1880s that the Japanese despaired of catching up; indeed the gap between East and West was narrow enough that it inspired determination to bridge it. It was to Japan's benefit, as well, that it began its economic journey when new marketing networks were emerging on an international scale. A revolution in transportation and communication was transforming the world into a global marketplace in the second half of the nineteenth century, and to their delight the Japanese discovered that they already grew and could soon manufacture a variety of goods that people overseas wanted, from raw tea and raw silk to gold leaf and buttons and cotton textiles. The trend lines of growth arched upward in the early Meiji decades, and Japan was able to build on its initial achievements to become one of the world's leading economic powers at the beginning of the twentieth century.

Source: James L. McClain, *A Modern History of Japan* (New York, NY: W. W. Norton and Company, 2002), 243–44.

NOTES

1. Bob Tadashi Wakabayashi, *Anti-Foreignism and Western Learning in Early-Modern Japan* (Cambridge, MA: Harvard University Press, 1985), 208–9.

2. M. William Steele, *Alternative Narratives in Modern Japanese History* (London: Routledge, 2003), 29.

3. Quoted in Peter Duus, *The Japanese Discovery of America* (Boston, MA: Bedford/St. Martin's, 1997), 100–1.

4. Quoted in Marius B. Jansen, *The Making of Modern Japan* (Cambridge, MA: Harvard University Press, 2000), 460.

5. Quoted in Julia Meech-Pekarik, *The World of the Meiji Print: Impressions of a New Civilization* (New York, NY: Weatherhill, 1986), 182.

6. Quoted in Oka Yoshitake, prologue to *The Emergence of Imperial Japan*, edited by Marlene Mayo (Lexington, MA: D. C. Heath, 1970), 7.

CHAPTER 20

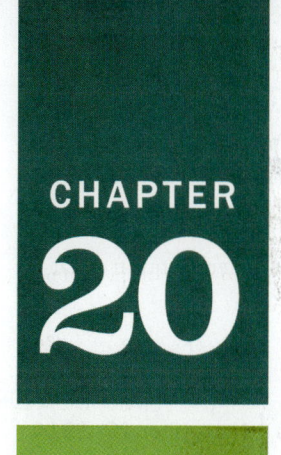

Thinking through Sources

Experiencing World War I

The history of World War I is often told in terms of diplomatic maneuvering, international alliances, altered borders, negotiated treaties, military strategies, battles, and new technologies of war. Here, however, we set aside these important matters to focus on the experience of the Great War as reflected in the accounts of particular individuals, most of them quite ordinary and unknown beyond the circle of their families and friends. Of course, the experience of the war varied greatly. Men and women; Europeans, Asians, and Africans; officers and enlisted men; refugees and prisoners of war; pacifists and militarists—all of these and many others as well encountered the war in quite different ways. Furthermore, the enthusiasm for the war that characterized many at its beginning soon turned to horror and despair as it became apparent that the conflict would drag bloodily on for years. From this immense variety, the following sources provide just a glimpse of the powerful impact of World War I on a number of individuals.

SOURCE 20.1 Experiences on the Battlefront ▶

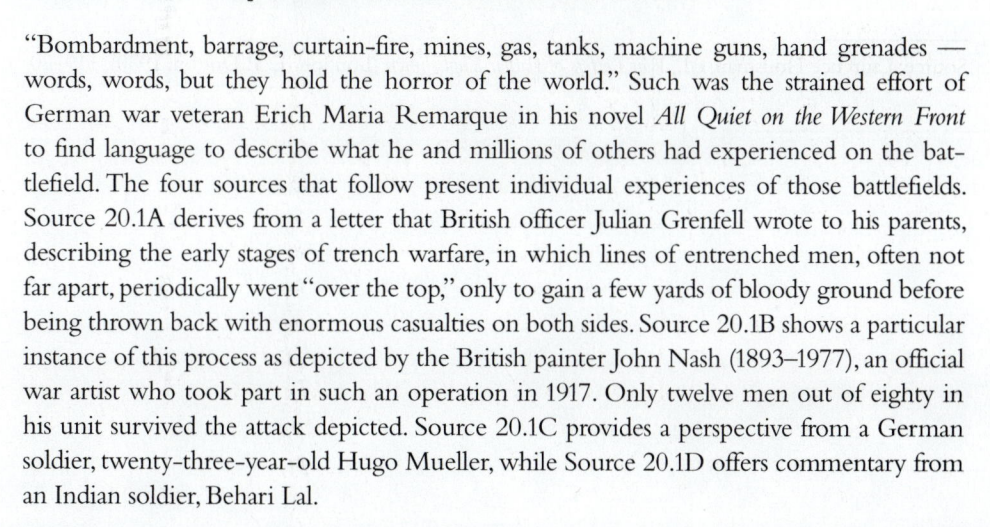

"Bombardment, barrage, curtain-fire, mines, gas, tanks, machine guns, hand grenades — words, words, but they hold the horror of the world." Such was the strained effort of German war veteran Erich Maria Remarque in his novel *All Quiet on the Western Front* to find language to describe what he and millions of others had experienced on the battlefield. The four sources that follow present individual experiences of those battlefields. Source 20.1A derives from a letter that British officer Julian Grenfell wrote to his parents, describing the early stages of trench warfare, in which lines of entrenched men, often not far apart, periodically went "over the top," only to gain a few yards of bloody ground before being thrown back with enormous casualties on both sides. Source 20.1B shows a particular instance of this process as depicted by the British painter John Nash (1893–1977), an official war artist who took part in such an operation in 1917. Only twelve men out of eighty in his unit survived the attack depicted. Source 20.1C provides a perspective from a German soldier, twenty-three-year-old Hugo Mueller, while Source 20.1D offers commentary from an Indian soldier, Behari Lal.

- What insights about the experience of fighting in World War I might you derive from these sources?
- What do they convey about the impact of the war on the outlook of these men?
- To what extent do these sources reveal the horrors of war in general, and in what ways do they reflect the distinctive features of World War I?

SOURCE 20.1A

JULIAN GRENFELL | *Letter from a British Officer in the Trenches* | November 18, 1914

They had us out again for 48 hours [in the] trenches.... After the shells, after a day of them, one's nerves are really absolutely beat down. I can understand now why our infantry have to retreat sometimes; a sight which came as a shock to me at first, after being brought up in the belief that the English infantry cannot retreat.

[We are] in a dripping sodden wood, with the German trench in some places 40 yards ahead....We had been worried by snipers all along and I had always been asking for leave to go out and have a try myself. Well, on Tuesday ... they gave me leave.... Off I crawled through sodden clay and trenches going about a yard a minute.... Then I saw the Hun trench.... So I crawled on again very slowly to the parapet of the trench.... Then the German behind me put his head up again. He was laughing and talking. I saw his teeth glistening against my foresight, and I pulled the trigger very slowly. He just grunted and crumpled up....

[Something similar happened the next day.] I went back at a sort of galloping crawl to our lines and sent a message to the 10th that the Germans were moving up their way in some numbers. Half an hour afterward, they attacked the 10th and our right, in massed formation, advancing slowly to within 10 yards of the trenches. We simply mowed them down. It was rather horrible.

Source: Laurence Housman, ed., *War Letters of Fallen Englishmen* (London: E. P. Dutton, 1930), 119–20.

SOURCE 20.1B

JOHN NASH | *Painting: Over the Top* | 1918

('Over the Top' 1st Artists' Rifles at Marcoing, 30th December 1917, 1918 (oil on canvas)/Nash, John Northcote (1893–1977)/IMPERIAL WAR MUSEUM/Imperial War Museum, London, UK/Bridgeman Images)

SOURCE 20.1C
HUGO MUELLER | Letter from a German Soldier on the Western Front | 1915

It has been extremely interesting to study the contents of the letter-cases of French killed and prisoners. The question frequently recurs, just as it does with us: "When will it all end?" To my astonishment I practically never found any expressions of hatred or abuse of Germany or German soldiers. On the other hand, many letters from relations revealed an absolute conviction of the justice of their cause and sometimes also of confidence in victory. In every letter, mother, fiancée, children, friends . . . spoke of a joyful return and speedy meeting—and now they are all lying dead and hardly even buried between the trenches, while over them bullets and shells sing their gruesome dirge. . . .

War hardens one's heart and blunts one's feelings, making a man indifferent to everything that formerly affected and moved him; but these qualities of hardness and indifference towards fate and death are necessary in the fierce battle to which trench warfare leads. Anybody who allowed himself to realize the whole tragedy of some of the daily occurrences in our life here would either lose his reason or be forced to bolt across the enemy's trench with his arms high in the air.

Source: Philipp Witkop, ed., *German Students' War Letters*, translated by Anne F. Wedd (London: Methuen, 1929), 278–79.

SOURCE 20.1D
BEHARI LAL | Letter from a Soldier in the British Indian Army | 1917

There is no likelihood of our getting rest during the winter. I am sure German prisoners could not be worse off in any way than we are. I had to go three nights without sleep, as I was on a motor lorry, and the lorry fellows, being Europeans, did not like to sleep with me, being an Indian. [The] cold was terrible, and it was raining hard; not being able to sleep on the ground in the open, I had to pass the whole night sitting on the outward lorry seats. I am sorry the hatred between Europeans and Indians is increasing instead of decreasing, and I am sure that the fault is not with the Indians. I am sorry to write this, which is not a hundredth part of what is in mind, but this increasing hatred and continued ill-treatment has compelled me to give you a hint.

Source: David Omussi, ed., *Indian Voices of the Great War* (New York, NY: St. Martin's Press, 1999), 336–37.

SOURCE 20.2 On the Home Front ▶

World War I is often described as an early example of "total war," in which the civilian population was both mobilized for the struggle and deeply affected by it. With so many men away from home, women were engaged with the war in any number of ways. Tens of thousands joined the military in support roles, particularly nursing, while in Russia several "women's battalions," all-female combat forces, were created in 1917, in part to encourage war-weary men to continue the fight. This set of sources highlights some of the ways that women on the home front were involved in the Great War.

Source 20.2A, a British propaganda poster from 1915, and Source 20.2B, a popular British song, both speak to the moral expectation for women in wartime. Source 20.2C, by a young German woman named Editha von Krell, recounts her time working in a factory producing armaments—a common experience of women across Europe during the war. Finally, Source 20.2D, an extract from a police report, describes food riots in the German capital of Berlin as women on the home front dealt with food shortages caused by the Allied blockade of their country.

- For what purposes did male authorities seek to mobilize women during the war?
- What is the message of the British propaganda poster in Source 20.2A to British men? And to British women?
- How is the relationship between social classes in wartime described or implied in Sources 20.2C and 20.2D?

316 CHAPTER 20 • THINKING THROUGH SOURCES

SOURCE 20.2A

British Propaganda Poster: Women of Britain Say—"Go!" | 1915

(Women of Britain say Go, poster for English army's recruitment campaign, World War I, Ingilterra, 20th century/DE AGOSTINI EDITORE/Bridgeman Images)

SOURCE 20.2B

LENA GUILBERT FORD | *Keep the Home Fires Burning* | 1915

They were summoned from the hillside, / They were called in from the glen,
And the country found them ready / At the stirring call for men.
Let no tears add to their hardships / As the soldiers pass along,
And although your heart is breaking, / Make it sing this cheery song:
Keep the Home Fires Burning, / While your hearts are yearning.
Though your lads are far away / They dream of home.
There's a silver lining / Through the dark clouds shining,
Turn the dark cloud inside out / Till the boys come home.

Source: Lena Guilbert Ford, "Keep the Home Fires Burning," music by Ivor Novello (London: Ascherberg Hopewood and the Crew, 1915).

SOURCE 20.2C

EDITHA VON KRELL | *Recollections of Four Months Working in a German Munitions Factory* | 1917

As the war went on, [the government] ordered two large munitions factories to be built right next to our town too. But very soon there was a shortage of male workers there. And so at the end of April 1917, all the town's women and girls were asked to come and work in these factories.... When we heard ... that no one from the educated classes had yet volunteered, and that hundreds of workers were urgently required our decision was made. Together with two friends, my sister and I volunteered for duty immediately.

We began with an eight-hour shift from 3 in the afternoon to until 11 in the evening.... Initially we were all put in the sewing room where day after day we had to sew thousands of little bags which were then filled with barrel powder for the cartridges in another department.... We sewed without interruption—apart from a short coffee break and a half-hour supper break.... Our backs often hurt from this unaccustomed sitting. Our heads often ached terribly in the bad air, which you could almost have cut with a knife.... After a few weeks, at our own request, we were moved on to the "heavy work," where we had to put the howitzer shells together with the cases containing the powder and equip them with fuses....

We were not allowed to air the rooms, even during our meal breaks. Doors and windows had to be kept shut because of the danger of explosions. But we prided ourselves on never slacking, on always keeping up with the professional workers. Here too the harmonious relationships we enjoyed with them was clear. For if ever this completely unaccustomed work proved too much for one of us [the educated women], one of the workers would help out as a matter of course, smiling, "Leave that to me, miss—it's far too hard for you."

Even today we still like to think back to the time when we were able to serve the Fatherland, working with our hands at one with the people.

Source: *Deutsche Frauen, Deutsche Treue* [German Women, German and Loyal], published in 1935. Reprinted in Joyce Marlow, ed., *The Virago Book of Women and the Great War* (London: Virago, 1998), 255–57. Used by permission.

SOURCE 20.2D
Berlin Police Reports | 1915

On the 16th of the month at 5:00 PM thousands of women and children gathered at the municipal market hall ... to buy a few pounds of potatoes. As the sale commenced, everyone stormed the market stands. The police, who were trying to keep order, were simply overrun and were powerless against the onslaught. A life-threatening press at the stands ensued; each sought to get past the next.... Women had their possessions ripped from them and children were trampled on the ground as they pleaded for help.... Women who got away from the crowds with some ten pounds of potatoes each were bathed in sweat and dropped to their knees from exhaustion before they could continue home.

—Report of Officer Rhein

I ... came upon a crowd of several thousand men and women who were howling loudly and pushing the policemen aside.... [T]he crowd had already stormed several buttershops because of the prices.... Several large display windows were shattered, shop doors destroyed, and entire stocks were simply taken.... We cleared the street with fifteen mounted officers.... Various objects such as flower pots were thrown at us.

—Report of Officer Krupphausen

Source: Brandenburgisches Landeshauptarchiv, Potsdam, Provinz Brandenburg, Repositur 30, Berlin C, Titel 95, Polizeipräsidium, Nrs. 15809, 15814, 15821, 15851. Contributed, translated, and introduced by Belinda Davis in *Lives and Voices: Sources in European Women's History*, edited by Lisa DiCaprio and Merry E. Wiesner (Boston, MA: Wadsworth Publishing, 2000), 426–27. Used by permission.

SOURCE 20.3 In the Aftermath of the Great War ▶

Beyond the enormous political, social, and economic changes wrought by World War I lay those transformations of consciousness, outlook, and expectation that registered in the work of artists and writers as well as in the sensibilities of individual people. This set of sources illustrates some of those changes.

Among the many outcomes of the Great War was the presence in every European country of disillusioned, maimed, and disfigured veterans, many of them literally "men without faces." For some intellectuals and artists, they represented the fundamentally flawed civilization that had given rise to such carnage. Often neglected or overlooked, such men were reminders of a terrible past that others wanted to forget. The German artist Otto Dix (1891–1969), who served in his country's military forces throughout the war and was seriously wounded, portrayed this situation in a 1920 painting called *Prague Street*, here as Source 20.3A. Artistically, Dix worked in a style known as New Objectivity, which focused heavily on the horrendous outcomes of the war. Its practitioners deliberately included subject matter that was upsetting and even ugly, and they made little attempt to create unified images, preferring to present disconnected "particles of experience."

Source 20.3B derives from the most famous novel to emerge from the war. Written by the German war veteran Erich Maria Remarque, *All Quiet on the Western Front* describes the experience of a young German soldier and his classmates during the war. Published in 1929, it captured the sense of disillusionment and hopelessness that many returning veterans surely felt as they reentered civilian society. In Source 20.3C, a very different sense of self that derived from the war found expression in the recollections of an African veteran from Senegal, then a French colony in West Africa.

- How does the painting in Source 20.3A describe the situation of the veterans? Notice the leaflet on the skateboard of the legless veteran at the bottom. It reads "Juden raus" (Jews out). What does this suggest about the political views of these men? What do the images in the store windows suggest?

- How does Remarque in Source 20.3B describe the sensibility of those soldiers about to return to ordinary life? In describing the purpose of his book, Remarque wrote: "It will try simply to tell of a generation of men who, even though they may have escaped its shells, were destroyed by the war." How does the excerpt in Source 20.3B reflect that purpose?

- How had the war changed the self-image of the Senegalese soldier in Source 20.3C? How had it altered his standing within his own society and in relationship to Europeans? How and why was his experience so different from that described in Remarque's novel in Source 20.3B?

320 CHAPTER 20 • THINKING THROUGH SOURCES

SOURCE 20.3A

OTTO DIX | *Painting: "Prague Street"* | 1920

(Pragerstrasse, 1920 (oil on canvas) by Otto Dix (1891–1969) / Peter Willi / Staatsgalerie, Stuttgart, Germany / Bridgeman Images / (c) 2018 Artists Rights Society (ARS), New York / VG Bild-Kunst, Bonn)

SOURCE 20.3B
ERICH MARIA REMARQUE | *All Quiet on the Western Front* | 1929

Had we returned home in 1916, out of the suffering and the strength of our experiences we might have unleashed a storm. Now if we go back we will be weary, broken, burnt out, rootless, and without hope. We will not be able to find our way anymore.

And men will not understand us, for the generation that grew up before us, though it has passed these years with us, already had a home and a calling; now it will return to its old occupations, and the war will be forgotten; and the generation that has grown up after us will be strange to us and push us aside. We will be superfluous even to ourselves, we will grow older, a few will adapt themselves, some others will merely submit, and most will be bewildered; the years will pass by and in the end we shall fall into ruin.

But perhaps all this that I think is mere melancholy and dismay, which will fly away as the dust, when I stand once again beneath the poplars and listen to the rustling of their leaves. It cannot be that it has gone, the yearning that made our blood unquiet, the unknown, the perplexing, the oncoming things, the thousand faces of the future, the melodies from dreams and from books, the whispers and divinations of women; it cannot be that this has vanished in bombardment, in despair, in brothels. . . .

I stand up. I am very quiet. Let the months and years come, they can take nothing from me, they can take nothing more. I am so alone, and so without hope that I can confront them without fear.

Source: Erich Maria Remarque, *All Quiet on the Western Front*, translated by A. W. Wheen (New York, NY: Ballantine Books, 1982), 293–95.

SOURCE 20.3C
NAR DIOUF | *A Senegalese Veteran's Oral Testimony* | 1919

I received many lasting things from the war. I demonstrated my dignity and courage, and [I] won the respect of the people and the [colonial] government. And whenever the people of the village had something to contest [with the French]—and they didn't dare do it [themselves] because they were afraid of them—I used to do it for them. And many times when people had problems with the government, I used to go with my decorations and arrange the situation for [them]. Because whenever the *Tubabs* [Europeans] saw your decorations, they knew that they [were dealing with] a very important person. . . . And I gained this ability—of obtaining justice over a *Tubab*—from the war.

[For example], one day a *Tubab* came here [to the village]—. . . (he was a kind of doctor)—to make an examination of the people. So he came here, and there was a small boy who was blind. And [the boy] was walking, [but] he couldn't see, and he bumped into the *Tubab*. And the *Tubab* turned and pushed the boy [down]. And when I saw that,

I came and said to the *Tubab*: "Why have you pushed this boy? [Can't] you see that he is blind?" And the *Tubab* said: "Oh, *pardon, pardon*. I did not know. I will never do it again, excuse me." [But] before the war, [no matter what they did], it would not have been possible to do that with a *Tubab*.

Source: Joe Lunn, *Memories of the Maelstrom: A Senegalese Oral History of the First World War* (Portsmouth, NH: Heinemann, 1999), 232. Used by permission of the author.

DOING HISTORY

1. **Describing the war:** Based on these sources, how would you define the novel or distinctive features of World War I compared to earlier European conflicts?

2. **Considering war and progress:** How do you think the creators of these sources might have responded to the idea of "the perfectibility of humanity" described by Condorcet during the European Enlightenment of the eighteenth century? (See Source 15.3 in Thinking through Sources for Chapter 15.)

3. **Noticing what's missing:** What perspectives on the war are *not* reflected in these sources? Where might you look to find those perspectives?

HISTORIANS' VOICES

The Legacies of World War I

World War I had a profound impact on many aspects of world history over the last century. The voices in this feature explore two of the Great War's most important legacies. In Voice 20.1, John Keegan, a prominent military historian, makes the case that World War II should be considered as part of the legacy of World War I. In Voice 20.2, the world historian Peter Frankopan explores how World War I began a process that brought an end to the "Age of Empires" in Europe.

- Why does Keegan include the destruction wrought in World War II as an integral part of the terrible legacy of World War I?
- According to Frankopan, why did European empires decline in the decades after World War I?
- **Integrating primary and secondary sources:** How might you construct an essay on the legacies of World War I that incorporated both of these Voices and the three items that constitute Source 20.3: In the Aftermath of the Great War?

VOICE 20.1

John Keegan on the Legacies of World War I | 2000

The First World War was a tragic and unnecessary conflict. Unnecessary because the train of events that led to its outbreak might have been broken at any point during the five weeks of crisis that preceded the first clash of arms, had prudence or common goodwill found a voice; tragic because the consequences of the first clash ended the lives of ten million human beings, tortured the emotional lives of millions more, destroyed the benevolent and optimistic culture of the European continent and left, when the guns at last fell silent four years later, a legacy of political rancour and racial hatred so intense that no explanation of the causes of the Second World War can stand without reference to those roots. The Second World War, five times more destructive in human life and incalculably more costly in material terms, was the direct outcome of the First. On 18 September 1922, Adolf Hitler, the demobilised front fighter, threw down a challenge to defeated Germany that he would realise seventeen year later: "It cannot be that two million Germans should have fallen in vain ... No, we do not pardon, we demand—vengeance!"

Source: John Keegan, *The First World War* (New York, NY: Vintage, 2000), 3.

VOICE 20.2

Peter Frankopan on World War I and the Decline of Empire | 2015

[In 1914], Europe was a continent of empires. Italy, France, Austro-Hungary, Germany, Russia, Ottoman Turkey, Britain, Portugal, the Netherlands, even tiny Belgium, only formed in 1831, controlled vast territories across the world. [World War I was when] the process of turning them back into local powers began. Within a matter of years, gone were the emperors, who had sailed on each other's yachts and appointed each other to grand chivalric orders; gone were some colonies and dominions overseas—and others were starting to go in an inexorable progression to independence.

In the course of four years, perhaps 10 million were dead from fighting, and half the same again from disease and famine. Over $200 billion had been spent by the Allies and the Central Powers fighting each other. European economies were shattered by the unparalleled expenditures that were exacerbated by falling productivity. Countries engaged in the fighting posted deficits and clocked up debts at a furious pace—debts they could not afford. The great empires that had dominated the world for four centuries did not slip away overnight. But it was the beginning of the end. Dusk was beginning to descend. The veil of shadows from behind which western Europe had emerged a few centuries earlier was starting to fall once again.

Source: Peter Frankopan, *The Silk Roads: A New History of the World* (New York, NY: Vintage, 2015), 309–10.

CHAPTER 21

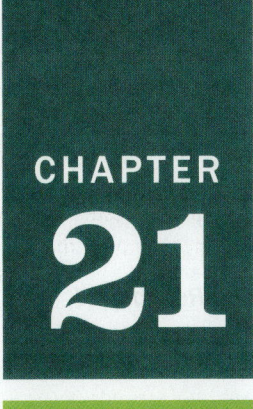

Thinking through Sources

Articulating Independence

For millions of people in Africa, Asia, Oceania, and the Caribbean, the achievement of political independence from colonial rule and foreign domination marked a singular moment in their personal lives and in their collective histories. That achievement took shape in many different ways, with variation in the duration and intensity of the struggle, in the tactics of the independence movements, and in the ideologies that they espoused. Here, we focus less on the process by which independence was acquired, and more on the various meanings ascribed to it. In all of these regions, the moment of independence represented a surprising triumph against great odds and an awakening to the possibility of building new lives and new societies. The sources that follow reflect the hopes, aspirations, and warnings of that remarkable moment. Many of the most ambitious goals subsequently went unfulfilled or were betrayed, fueling immense disappointment. Nonetheless, it is worth reflecting on the varied meanings associated with the coming of independence, for in human affairs, almost always, our reach exceeds our grasp.

SOURCE 21.1 Declaring Vietnam's Independence

Just a few weeks after the end of World War II in Asia, Ho Chi Minh, the nationalist and communist leader of his country's independence movement, declared Vietnam free of both five years of Japanese control and more than sixty years of French colonial rule. The date was September 2, 1945, and the place was Hanoi, the colonial capital of French Indochina. More than thirty more years of struggle lay ahead, first against French efforts to reestablish colonial rule over Vietnam, and then against American military intervention in the country. But the Declaration of 1945 spoke to the meaning of that struggle, largely by referring to the colonial past, to the legacy of the Atlantic revolutions, and to the proclaimed values of the victors in World War II.

- In what ways does the Declaration seek to legitimate Vietnam's independence?
- Why do you think Ho Chi Minh began his Declaration with references to the American and French Revolutions?

325

- What critique of colonial rule is contained in the Declaration?
- How does the Declaration seek to situate Vietnam's independence struggle both historically and in terms of the global politics of 1945?

HO CHI MINH | Declaration of Independence of the Democratic Republic of Vietnam | September 2, 1945

"All men are created equal. They are endowed by their Creator with certain inalienable rights, among them are Life, Liberty, and the pursuit of Happiness." This immortal statement was made in the Declaration of Independence of the United States of America in 1776. In a broader sense, this means: All the peoples on the earth are equal from birth, all the peoples have a right to live, to be happy and free.

The Declaration of the French Revolution made in 1791 on the Rights of Man and the Citizen also states: "All men are born free and with equal rights, and must always remain free and have equal rights." Those are undeniable truths.

Nevertheless, for more than eighty years, the French imperialists, abusing the standard of Liberty, Equality, and Fraternity, have violated our Fatherland and oppressed our fellow-citizens. They have acted contrary to the ideals of humanity and justice.

In the field of politics, they have deprived our people of every democratic liberty.

They have enforced inhuman laws; they have set up three distinct political regimes in the North, the Center and the South of Vietnam in order to wreck our national unity and prevent our people from being united.

They have built more prisons than schools. They have mercilessly slain our patriots; they have drowned our uprisings in rivers of blood.

To weaken our race they have forced us to use opium and alcohol.

In the field of economics, they have fleeced us to the backbone, impoverished our people, and devastated our land.

They have robbed us of our rice fields, our mines, our forests, and our raw materials. They have monopolized the issuing of bank-notes and the export trade.

They have invented numerous unjustifiable taxes and reduced our people, especially our peasantry, to a state of extreme poverty.

They have hampered the prospering of our national bourgeoisie; they have mercilessly exploited our workers.

In the autumn of 1940, when the Japanese Fascists violated Indochina's territory to establish new bases in their fight against the Allies, the French imperialists went down on their bended knees and handed over our country to them.

Thus, from that date, our people were subjected to the double yoke of the French and the Japanese. Their sufferings and miseries increased.... Notwithstanding all this, our fellow-citizens have always manifested toward the French a tolerant and humane attitude.... The Vietminh League helped many Frenchmen to cross the frontier, rescued some of them from Japanese jails, and protected French lives and property.

Source 21.2 An Image of Vietnam's Independence: Fifty Years Later

From the autumn of 1940, our country had in fact ceased to be a French colony and had become a Japanese possession.

After the Japanese had surrendered to the Allies, our whole people rose to regain our national sovereignty and to found the Democratic Republic of Vietnam. The truth is that we have wrested our independence from the Japanese and not from the French.

Our people have broken the chains which for nearly a century have fettered them and have won independence for the Fatherland. Our people at the same time have overthrown the monarchic regime that has reigned supreme for dozens of centuries. In its place has been established the present Democratic Republic.

For these reasons, we, members of the Provisional Government, representing the whole Vietnamese people, declare that from now on we break off all relations of a colonial character with France; we repeal all the international obligations that France has so far subscribed to on behalf of Vietnam and we abolish all the special rights the French have unlawfully acquired in our Fatherland.

The whole Vietnamese people, animated by a common purpose, are determined to fight to the bitter end against any attempt by the French colonialists to reconquer their country.

We are convinced that the Allied nations which at Tehran [where Roosevelt, Churchill, and Stalin met] and San Francisco [where the United Nations was established] have acknowledged the principles of self-determination and equality of nations, will not refuse to acknowledge the independence of Vietnam.

A people who have courageously opposed French domination for more than eighty years, a people who have fought side by side with the Allies against the Fascists during these last years, such a people must be free and independent.

For these reasons, we, members of the Provisional Government of the Democratic Republic of Vietnam, solemnly declare to the world that Vietnam has the right to be a free and independent country—and in fact is so already. The entire Vietnamese people are determined to mobilize all their physical and mental strength, to sacrifice their lives and property in order to safeguard their independence and liberty.

Source: Ho Chi Minh, *Selected Works*, vol. 3 (Hanoi: Foreign Languages Publishing House, 1960–1962), 17–21.

■ ■ ■

SOURCE 21.2 An Image of Vietnam's Independence: Fifty Years Later ▶

In 1995, Vietnam marked the fiftieth anniversary of its earlier Declaration of Independence, an event celebrated by this poster. Pictured on the right side of the poster is Ho Chi Minh, the principal author of the earlier Declaration, who had died in 1969. The caption refers to a "National Day" commemoration for what had become a "unified and socialist" country, almost 20 years after the victory over American forces in the Vietnam war.

- What does the poster suggest have been the country's major achievements since independence?
- What is the significance of the tanks and soldiers shown in red at the upper left of the poster?
- Does the poster emphasize Vietnam's nationalist or its communist achievements?

Fiftieth Anniversary of Vietnamese Independence | 1995

(Poster for the 50th Anniversary of Vietnamese Independence, 1995 (colour litho)/Luong Van, Phuong (fl.1995)/Private Collection/Bridgeman Images)

SOURCE 21.3 India's "Tryst with Destiny"

Just two years after Ho Chi Minh announced Vietnam's independence, Jawaharlal Nehru did the same for India, shortly before midnight on August 14, 1947. Hovering over this joyful event was the tragedy of the bloody partition between India and Pakistan and the absence at the celebration of India's great nationalist leader, Gandhi, who was in Calcutta, praying, fasting, and seeking to stem the violence between Muslims and Hindus.

- How does Nehru's speech compare with Ho Chi Minh's Declaration?
- What kind of India does Nehru foresee emerging from the struggle for independence? How does his vision compare with that of Gandhi? (See Source 18.5 in the Thinking through Sources feature for Chapter 18.)
- What aspects of Indian society posed a challenge for the India of Nehru's hopes?

JAWAHARLAL NEHRU | *Independence Day Speech* | August 14, 1947

Long years ago we made a tryst with destiny, and now the time comes when we shall redeem our pledge, not wholly or in full measure, but very substantially. At the stroke of the midnight hour, when the world sleeps, India will awake to life and freedom. A moment comes, which comes but rarely in history, when we step out from the old to the new, when an age ends, and when the soul of a nation, long suppressed, finds utterance. It is fitting that at this solemn moment we take the pledge of dedication to the service of India and her people and to the still larger cause of humanity....

Before the birth of freedom we have endured all the pains of labour and our hearts are heavy with the memory of this sorrow. Some of those pains continue even now. Nevertheless, the past is over and it is the future that beckons to us now.

That future is not one of ease or resting but of incessant striving so that we may fulfil the pledges we have so often taken and the one we shall take today. The service of India means the service of the millions who suffer. It means the ending of poverty and ignorance and disease and inequality of opportunity. The ambition of the greatest man of our generation [Gandhi] has been to wipe every tear from every eye. That may be beyond us, but as long as there are tears and suffering, so long our work will not be over.

And so we have to labour and to work, and work hard, to give reality to our dreams. Those dreams are for India, but they are also for the world, for all the nations and peoples are too closely knit together today for any one of them to imagine that it can live apart. Peace has been said to be indivisible; so is freedom, so is prosperity now, and so also is disaster in this One World that can no longer be split into isolated fragments.

To the people of India, whose representatives we are, we make an appeal to join us with faith and confidence in this great adventure. This is no time for petty and destructive criticism, no time for ill-will or blaming others. We have to build the noble mansion of free India where all her children may dwell.

The appointed day has come—the day appointed by destiny—and India stands forth again, after long slumber and struggle, awake, vital, free and independent. The past clings on to us still in some measure and we have to do much before we redeem the pledges we have so often taken. Yet the turning-point is past, and history begins anew for us, the history which we shall live and act and others will write about.

It is a fateful moment for us in India, for all Asia and for the world. A new star rises, the star of freedom in the East, a new hope comes into being, a vision long cherished materializes.... On this day our first thoughts go to the architect of this freedom, the Father of our Nation [Gandhi], who, embodying the old spirit of India, held aloft the torch of freedom and lighted up the darkness that surrounded us. We have often been unworthy followers of his and have strayed from his message, but not only we but succeeding generations will remember this message and bear the imprint in their hearts of this great son of India, magnificent in his faith and strength and courage and humility....

The future beckons to us. Whither do we go and what shall be our endeavour? To bring freedom and opportunity to the common man, to the peasants and workers of India; to fight and end poverty and ignorance and disease; to build up a prosperous, democratic and progressive nation, and to create social, economic and political institutions which will ensure justice and fullness of life to every man and woman.

We have hard work ahead. There is no resting for any one of us till we redeem our pledge in full, till we make all the people of India what destiny intended them to be. We are citizens of a great country on the verge of bold advance, and we have to live up to that high standard. All of us, to whatever religion we may belong, are equally the children of India with equal rights, privileges and obligations. We cannot encourage communalism or narrow-mindedness, for no nation can be great whose people are narrow in thought or in action.

To the nations and peoples of the world we send greetings and pledge ourselves to cooperate with them in furthering peace, freedom and democracy.

And to India, our much-loved motherland, the ancient, the eternal and the ever-new, we pay our reverent homage and we bind ourselves afresh to her service.

JAI HIND [Hail India]

Source: Jawaharlal Nehru, "A Tryst with Destiny," August 14, 1947, "Great Speeches of the 20th Century," *Guardian*, http://www.theguardian.com/theguardian/2007/may/01/greatspeeches.

SOURCE 21.4 Another View of India's Struggle for Independence ▶

Nehru's vision of India as a secular and modernizing state that provided a secure home for all of its religious communities was not the only image of the country's struggle for independence. Gandhi was widely viewed as a religious figure, the *mahatma*, or great soul, and the fight against British colonialism, which he led, was often portrayed in distinctly religious and Hindu terms, as Source 21.4, a poster from 1930–1931, illustrates. Here Gandhi is cast as the great Hindu deity Shiva and is portrayed saving a female character representing Mother India from British imperialism, depicted as Yama, the lord of death. This image appropriates the widely known Hindu mythological story of Markandeya, a young and pious sage, who is attacked by Yama, riding a buffalo and seeking to take his soul by casting a rope around the young man. But the great god Shiva rescues Markandeya, grants him eternal life, and slays Yama.

- What features of this legend can you identify in Source 21.4?
- Why might this image be appealing to Indians in the several decades before independence? To what groups in India might this image raise suspicions or be offensive?
- How does this image differ from Nehru's depiction of independent India in Source 21.3?

Gandhi and the Fight against British Colonialism | ca. 1930–1931

(The British Library/The Image Works)

SOURCE 21.5 One Africa

For Kwame Nkrumah, the leader of Ghana's anticolonial movement and the new West African country's first president, independence meant an opportunity to challenge the common assumption that Europe's African colonies should become nation-states within their existing borders. He was convinced that only by forming a much larger union could the African continent achieve substantial economic development and genuine independence. In doing so, Nkrumah was drawing on the notion of a broader African identity, Pan-Africanism, which had emerged among educated people during the colonial era.

- What kind of union did Nkrumah seek?
- Why did he think that union was so essential? What benefits would it bring to Africa in its efforts at modern development?
- What challenges did Nkrumah identify to his soaring vision of a United States of Africa?

KWAME NKRUMAH | *Africa Must Unite* | 1963

There are those who maintain that Africa cannot unite because we lack the three necessary ingredients for unity, a common race, culture, and language. It is true that we have for centuries been divided. The territorial boundaries dividing us were fixed long ago, often quite arbitrarily, by the colonial powers. Some of us are Moslems, some Christians; many believe in traditional, tribal gods. Some of us speak French, some English, some Portuguese, not to mention the millions who speak only one of the hundreds of different African languages. We have acquired cultural differences which affect our outlook and condition our political development....

In the early flush of independence, some of the new African states are jealous of their sovereignty and tend to exaggerate their separatism in a historical period that demands Africa's unity in order that their independence may be safeguarded....

[A] united Africa—that is, the political and economic unification of the African Continent—should seek three objectives: Firstly, we should have an overall economic planning on a continental basis. This would increase the industrial and economic power of Africa. So long as we remain balkanized, regionally or territorially, we shall be at the mercy of colonialism and imperialism. The lesson of the South American Republics vis-à-vis the strength and solidarity of the United States of America is there for all to see.

The resources of Africa can be used to the best advantage and the maximum benefit to all only if they are set within an overall framework of a continentally planned development. An overall economic plan, covering an Africa united on a continental basis, would increase our total industrial and economic power. We should therefore be thinking seriously now of ways and means of building up a Common Market of a United Africa and not allow ourselves to be lured by the dubious advantages of association with the so-called European Common Market....

Secondly, we should aim at the establishment of a unified military and defense strategy.... For young African States, who are in great need of capital for internal development, it is ridiculous—indeed suicidal—for each State separately and individually to assume such a heavy burden of self-defense, when the weight of this burden could be easily lightened by sharing it among themselves....

The third objective: [I]t will be necessary for us to adopt a unified foreign policy and diplomacy to give political direction to our joint efforts for the protection and economic development of our continent.... The burden of separate diplomatic representation by each State on the Continent of Africa alone would be crushing, not to mention representation outside Africa. The desirability of a common foreign policy which will enable us to speak with one voice in the councils of the world, is so obvious, vital and imperative that comment is hardly necessary....

Under a major political union of Africa there could emerge a United Africa, great and powerful, in which the territorial boundaries which are the relics of colonialism will become obsolete and superfluous, working for the complete and total mobilization of the economic planning organization under a unified political direction. The forces that unite us are far greater than the difficulties that divide us at present, and our goal must be the establishment of Africa's dignity, progress, and prosperity.

Source: Kwame Nkrumah, *Africa Must Unite* (London: Heinemann, 1963), 132, 148, 218–21.

SOURCE 21.6 South African "Independence" ▶

Independence in South Africa had a somewhat different meaning than elsewhere in the colonial world, for that country had already ended its colonial relationship with Great Britain in 1910. The struggle in South Africa was against a local entrenched and dominant white minority that had imposed a regime of harsh racial oppression, known as apartheid, which had no parallel in other parts of the world. When that system of government ended in April 1994 with the country's first genuinely democratic elections, its demise marked the conclusion of an era in world history in which Europeans exercised formal political control in the African, Asian, Caribbean, and Pacific worlds. This photograph shows a man standing in line preparing to vote in that historic election by displaying his identification document. Such photographs, of which there were thousands, articulated what was for many the essential meaning of that moment.

- Africans had long resented and resisted the requirement to produce on demand an identity card—a kind of internal passport—during the apartheid era. Why, then, do you think that the man in the foreground is proudly displaying his identification document in this photograph?
- How does the image of several whites, also waiting to vote, enhance the message of the photograph?
- Notice that the two African men in the foreground are shown in clear focus, while the whites in the background are displayed in a somewhat blurred fashion. Do you think this was deliberate on the part of the photographer? How does this feature of the photo contribute to the message it conveys?

Source 21.6 South African "Independence"

Photograph of the First Post-Apartheid South African Election | 1994

(Peter Turnley/Getty Images)

SOURCE 21.7 Independence as Threat

Independence had meaning not only for those who sought it, but also for those who opposed it. In 1961, a Portuguese archbishop in Mozambique, Alvim Pereira, distributed a document to local seminary students and priests that outlined his opposition to independence for Mozambique and other Portuguese colonies.

- How would you summarize the reasons for Pereira's hostility to independence?
- What role does the archbishop prescribe for the Catholic Church in confronting independence movements?
- What kind of future for Mozambique does he imply?

ALVIM PEREIRA | *Ten Principles* | 1961

1. Independence is irrelevant to the welfare of man. It can be good if the right conditions are present (the cultural conditions do not yet exist in Mozambique).

2. While these conditions are not being produced, to take part in movements for independence is acting against nature.

3. Even if these conditions existed, the Metropole has the right to oppose independence if the freedoms and rights of man are respected, and if it [the Metropole] provided for the well-being, for civil and religious progress of all.

4. All the movements which use force (terrorists) are against the natural law....

5. When the movement is a terrorist one, the clergy have the obligation, in good conscience, not only to refrain from taking part but also to oppose it....

6. Even when the movement is peaceful, the clergy must abstain from it in order to have spiritual influence on all people....

7. The native people of Africa have the obligation to thank the colonists for all the benefits which they receive from them.

8. The educated have the duty to lead those with less education from all the illusions of independence.

9. The present independence movements have, almost all of them, the sign of revolt and of Communism; they have no reason....

10. The slogan "Africa for the Africans" is a philosophical monstrosity and a challenge to the Christian civilization, because today's events tell us that it is Communism and Islamism which wish to impose their civilization upon the Africans.

Source: Eduardo Mondlane, *The Struggle for Mozambique* (Hammondsworth, UK: Penguin Books, 1969), 74–75.

DOING HISTORY

1. **Making comparisons:** What do the independence movements described in these sources share? In what ways do they differ?
2. **Defining points of view:** Independence was a widely shared value in the colonial world, but the meanings attached to it varied considerably. How could you use these sources to support this statement?
3. **Imagining a conversation:** Choose three or four of the sources and construct a dialogue between their authors or creators.

HISTORIANS' VOICES

Assessing African Independence

The coming of independence in Africa (1955–1975) was greeted initially with something approaching euphoria. This enthusiastic excitement was captured by the African historian and activist Basil Davidson in Voice 21.1. By the early 1990s, however, that euphoria had turned for many people to disappointment, despair, and anger as widespread corruption, ethnic conflict, political instability, elite enrichment, and mass poverty seemed to betray the great promise of independence. This sensibility found expression in the work of George Ayittey, a Ghanaian economist and historian, and is reflected in Voice 21.2.

- How does Davidson describe the euphoria attending the coming of independence in Africa of the 1960s?
- How does Ayittey account for the rather different mood of the early 1990s?
- **Integrating primary and secondary sources:** To what extent do the primary sources in this feature illustrate the kind of optimism that Davidson describes in Voice 21.1? In what ways are they more cautious?

VOICE 21.1

Basil Davidson on the Promise of Independence | 1978

The coming of independence could in those days seem a climactic moment dividing the past from an altogether different future when all things would be possible . . . [T]he most blatant [European] control was gone or could now be removed. This was the rule that all things must be ordered as though whites were naturally and inherently superior to blacks: the cultural bludgeon of colonial government. Now the bludgeon had no local hand to wield it, and with this there came a profound sense of cultural rebirth. . . .

[T]he overall impression one retains of those sunsets when the imperial flags came down, and the banners of nationhood climbed to mastheads lit with flares and fireworks, stays firm and clear. Independence spelt renewal, the flinging down of racist barriers, the fraught emotion of swaying crowds, dancing, drumming, for whom their own ideas, beliefs, and abilities could now be clothed in a new respect and value.

This may be seen as the chief achievement of the 'political classes'. They had asserted the right of Africans to stand level with other peoples in all ways cultural or psychological. They had struck down the old spectre of a 'natural' inferiority, and banished the haunting fear that racist teachings, so grimly argued over so many decades, might after all contain a truth . . . [T]he doorway to equality was open. There came a vivid consciousness of having grasped destiny by the hand so that Africa's history could begin again.

Source: Basil Davidson, *Let Freedom Come* (New York, NY: Little Brown, 1978), 283–84.

VOICE 21.2

George Ayittey on the Betrayal of Independence | 1992

Three decades of independence from colonial rule have produced nothing but economic misery and disintegration, political chaos, and institutional and social disintegration. The decline in per-capita income has been calamitous for many African countries. Agricultural growth has been dismal, producing chronic food shortages and an ever-present threat of famine.... The proportion of state spending devoted to health and education fell....

For most Africans, independence did not bring a better life or even greater political or civil liberties.... Since independence in the 1960s, there has been a systematic curtailment and virtual banishment across Africa of freedom and civil liberties.... One word of criticism of an African government may earn a death sentence.

Africa has been betrayed. Freedom from colonial rule has evolved into ghastly tyranny, arbitrary rule, denial of civil liberties, brutal suppression of dissent, and the wanton slaughter of peasants.... But the most painful was the cultural insult.... African elites who replaced them [colonial rulers] deprecated the indigenous as "backward" and "primitive." In many places the elites sought the destruction of the indigenous by imposing alien systems on Africa.... To replace western institutions, many African leaders marched off to the East and adopted socialist and communist systems for transplantation into Africa....

Most analysts now agree that although colonialism was evil, it offered comparatively more freedom than did many independent African countries in the 1980s.

Source: George Ayittey, *Africa Betrayed* (New York, NY: St. Martin's Press, 1992), 8–10, 12.

CHAPTER 22

Thinking through Sources

Reflections on Technology

The past century has witnessed an astonishing pace of technological innovation, transforming practically every domain of human life: work and play; making war and making love; transportation and communication; commerce and consumption; politics and private life. Accompanying these transformations has been an endless commentary on all matters technological, which took shape in many ways . . . as celebration and criticism, as prediction and propaganda, as professorial essays and parental warnings. The sources that follow provide just a tiny sample of this vast conversation about the role of technology in contemporary life since 1900.

SOURCE 22.1 Postcards of the Future: A French Artist Imagines Technological Change ▶

The turn of the twentieth century prompted widespread speculation about the shape of the future, which focused heavily on technology, at least in the West. In 1900, an article in the *Ladies Home Journal*, an American women's magazine, predicted "What May Happen in the Next Hundred Years." Those predictions included cities "with all hurry traffic below or high above ground . . . free from all noises"; automobiles cheaper than horses; "aerial war-ships and forts on wheels"; "photographs will be telegraphed from any distance"; "strawberries as large as apples"; "wireless telephone . . . will span the world"; the end of coal for heating and cooking; and much more.[1] In 1910, the French artist Maximilian Villemard gave visual expression to such predictions in a series of postcards depicting life in Paris in the year 2000. Five of the many available images are shown here.

- What aspects of Parisian life does Villemard think will be transformed during the twentieth century? To what extent did his imaginative predictions come to pass?
- To what extent, if at all, are the predicted technological changes matched by imagined changes in gender roles?
- How might you describe Villemard's posture toward the technological future?

Source 22.1 Postcards of the Future: A French Artist Imagines Technological Change

SOURCE 22.1A
MAXIMILIAN VILLEMARD | *Air Battles and Air Freight in the Future* | 1910

Un Combat aérien.

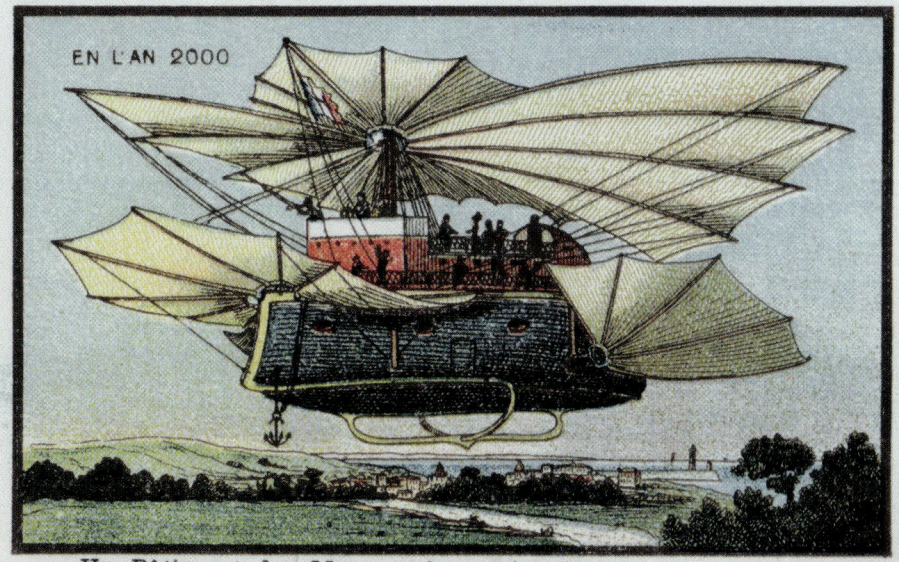

Un Bâtiment des Messageries aériennes.

(Fantasy depictions of an air battle and of an aircraft for transporting freight in the year 2000, c.1910 (colour litho)/French School, (20th century)/INDIVISION CHARMET/Private Collection/Bridgeman Images)

SOURCE 22.1B
MAXIMILIAN VILLEMARD | *The Horse as a Curiosity* | 1910

(A curiosity in the year 2000 (chromolitho)/French School, (19th century)/LOOK AND LEARN (M IMAGES)/Private Collection/Bridgeman Images)

Source 22.1 Postcards of the Future: A French Artist Imagines Technological Change

SOURCE 22.1C
MAXIMILIAN VILLEMARD | *The School of the Future* | 1910

('At School in the Year 2000', c.1910 (colour litho)/French School, (20th century)/LOOK AND LEARN (M IMAGES)/Private Collection/Bridgeman Images)

SOURCE 22.1D
MAXIMILIAN VILLEMARD | *A Video-Telephone in the Year 2000* | 1910

(Photo telephone in the year 2000 (chromolitho)/European School, (19th century)/LOOK AND LEARN (M IMAGES)/Private Collection/Bridgeman Images)

SOURCE 22.2 Depicting Communist Technology ▶

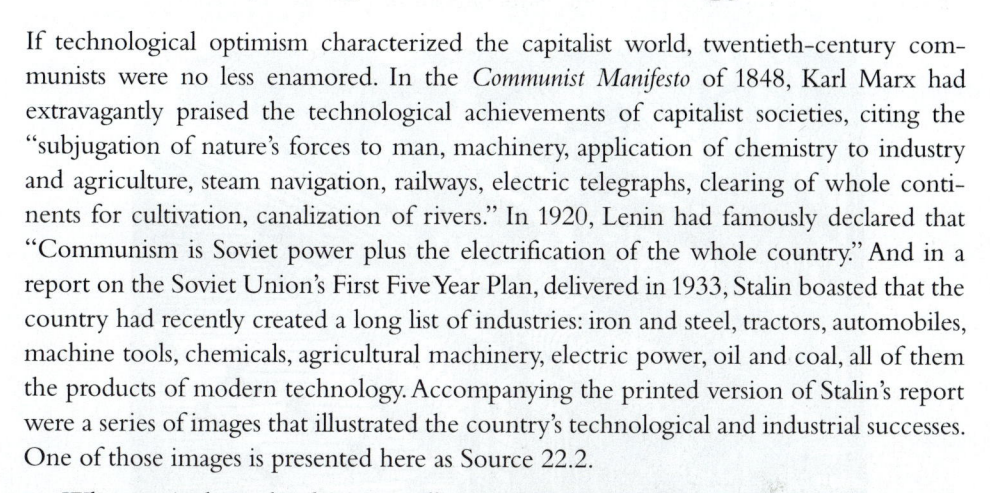

If technological optimism characterized the capitalist world, twentieth-century communists were no less enamored. In the *Communist Manifesto* of 1848, Karl Marx had extravagantly praised the technological achievements of capitalist societies, citing the "subjugation of nature's forces to man, machinery, application of chemistry to industry and agriculture, steam navigation, railways, electric telegraphs, clearing of whole continents for cultivation, canalization of rivers." In 1920, Lenin had famously declared that "Communism is Soviet power plus the electrification of the whole country." And in a report on the Soviet Union's First Five Year Plan, delivered in 1933, Stalin boasted that the country had recently created a long list of industries: iron and steel, tractors, automobiles, machine tools, chemicals, agricultural machinery, electric power, oil and coal, all of them the products of modern technology. Accompanying the printed version of Stalin's report were a series of images that illustrated the country's technological and industrial successes. One of those images is presented here as Source 22.2.

- What particular technologies are illustrated in this image?
- What overall impression is this image intended to convey?
- How do the technologies illustrated in this image differ from those in Source 22.1? What similarities and differences can you identify between capitalist and communist attitudes toward technology?

Soviet Industry and Technology | 1933

SOURCE 22.3 Nehru and Gandhi on Technology and Industry

The leaders of anticolonial movements throughout Asia and Africa were virtually unanimous that modern technology, science, and industrialization were essential for the new nations they sought to create. No one expressed these sentiments more clearly than Jawaharlal Nehru, a leading figure in India's independence movement and the country's first Prime Minister. But Nehru had to take account of the rather different views held by his leader and mentor, Mahatma Gandhi (see Source 18.5 in Chapter 18 of this book). Almost alone among major political figures, Gandhi was highly skeptical about industrialization and "the machine": "Industrialization is, I am afraid, going to be a curse for mankind," he declared. "God forbid that India should ever take to industrialism after the manner of the West.... It is machinery that has impoverished India."[2] Source 22.3, taken from Nehru's book, *The Discovery of India*, was written while he and Gandhi were in prison during World War II because of their political activity. In this passage, Nehru outlines his own hopes for technology in India even as he seeks to understand, explain, and accommodate Gandhi's quite different outlook.

- Why does Nehru feel that industry and modern technology are essential for India's future as an independent country?

- How does he explain Gandhi's views on the subject? Does he perceive a major difference in their outlooks or merely a matter of emphasis?

- How might Gandhi respond to Nehru's views?

- While Gandhi has been widely admired and celebrated in India, his views on technology and industrialization have been largely ignored, as the country followed Nehru's path of embracing the "latest technical achievements of the day." How might you explain this situation?

JAWAHARLAL NEHRU | *The Discovery of India* | 1946

The Congress [Party], under Gandhiji's [Gandhi's] leadership, had long championed the revival of village industries, especially hand-spinning and hand-weaving. At no time, however, had the Congress been opposed to the development of big industries, and whenever it had the chance ..., it had encouraged this development....

It is true, I think, that there is a fundamental difference between his [Gandhi's] outlook on life generally and what might be called the modern outlook. He is not enamoured of ever-increasing standards of living and the growth of luxury at the cost of spiritual and moral values.... Above all he is shocked at the vast gulf that stretches between the rich and the poor, in their ways of living, and their opportunities of growth. ...This vast difference between the few rich and the poverty-stricken masses seemed to him to be due to two principal causes: foreign rule and the exploitation that accompanied it, and the capitalist industrial civilization of the west as embodied in the big machine. He reacted against both. He looked back with yearning to the days of the old autonomous and more-or-less self-contained village community....

There is no necessary conflict between this [village-based handicraft manufacturing] and the introduction of machinery on the largest scale, provided that machinery is used primarily for absorbing labour and not for creating fresh unemployment....

I am all for tractors and big machinery, and I am convinced that the rapid industrialization of India is essential to relieve the pressure on land, to combat poverty and raise standards of living, for defence and a variety of other purposes. But I am equally convinced that the most careful planning and adjustment are necessary if we are to reap the full benefit of industrialization and avoid many of its dangers....

[T]he problem before us in India during recent decades has been how, in the existing circumstances and restricted as we were by alien rule and its attendant vested interests, we could relieve the poverty of the masses and produce a spirit of self-reliance among them....

[Gandhi's views on technology] forced India to think of the poor peasant in human terms, to realize that behind the glitter of a few cities lay this morass of misery and poverty, to grasp the fundamental fact that the true test of progress and freedom in India did not lie in the creation of a number of millionaires or prosperous lawyers and the like, or in the setting up of councils and assemblies, but in the change in the status and conditions of life of the peasant....

Gandhiji's attitude to the use of machinery seemed to undergo a gradual change. 'What I object to,' he said, 'is the craze for machinery, not machinery as such.' 'If we could have electricity in every village home, I shall not mind villagers plying their implements and tools with electricity.' The big machines seemed to him to lead inevitably, at least in the circumstances of to-day, to the concentration of power and riches.... He even came to accept the necessity of many kinds of heavy industries and large-scale key industries and public utilities, provided they were state-owned and did not interfere with some kinds of cottage industries which he considered as essential. Referring to his own proposals, he said: 'The whole of this programme will be a structure on sand if it is not built on the solid foundation of economic equality.'

It can hardly be challenged that, in the context of the modern world, no country can be politically and economically independent, even within the framework of international interdependence, unless it is highly industrialized and has developed its power resources to the utmost. Nor can it achieve or maintain high standards of living and liquidate poverty without the aid of modern technology in almost every sphere of life. An industrially backward country will continually upset the world equilibrium and encourage the aggressive tendencies of more developed countries. Even if it retains its political independence, this will be nominal only, and economic control will tend to pass to others. This control will inevitably upset its own small-scale economy which it has sought to preserve in pursuit of its own view of life. Thus an attempt to build up a country's economy largely on the basis of cottage and small-scale industries is doomed to failure. It will not solve the basic problems of the country or maintain freedom, nor will it fit in with the world framework, except as a colonial appendage....

The economy based on the latest technical achievements of the day must necessarily be the dominating one. If technology demands the big machine, as it does today in a large measure, then the big machine with all its implications and consequences must be accepted. Where it is possible, in terms of that technology, to decentralize production, this would be desirable. But, in any event, the latest technique has to be followed, and to adhere to out-worn and out-of-date methods of production, except as a temporary and stop gap measure, is to arrest growth and development....

Source: Jawaharlal Nehru, *The Discovery of India* (Delhi: Oxford University Press, 1946), 402–8.

■ ■ ■

SOURCE 22.4 "Technology with a Human Face"

By the mid-twentieth century, a highly positive and optimistic view of modern technology had become firmly inscribed in global culture—in capitalist, communist, and colonial/developing countries alike—and to a large extent it has remained so to the present day. And no wonder! For billions of individuals, this technology has lengthened life spans substantially, improved health, enabled travel and communication, diminished poverty, and greatly enriched the material conditions of life. For businesses large and small, that technology has created vast markets and spawned no end of profit-making possibilities. For governments, it has enhanced military power and international prestige, while generating economic growth, which has become a major source of legitimacy and popularity for political elites everywhere.

And yet, as the twentieth century wore on in its second half and as the twenty-first century dawned, more skeptical voices appeared, even as technological innovations of all kinds multiplied many times over. In 1972, for example, an international think tank, the Club of Rome, published the highly controversial *The Limits to Growth*, a report that sharply questioned the earth's ability to accommodate continued economic and population growth. Criticizing "technological optimism," the report declared, "Faith in technology as the ultimate solution to all problems can thus divert our attention from the most fundamental problem—the problem of growth in a finite system—and prevent us from taking effective action to solve it."[3]

A year later, the German-born British economist E. F. Schumacher published his classic text, *Small Is Beautiful*. Widely read around the world, it was dubbed one of the 100 most influential books since World War II. Challenging what he called "gigantism," "mass production," and "unlimited economic growth," Schumacher called for "technology with a human face" and "economics as if people mattered." His thinking on questions of technology is reflected in Source 22.4.

- What is Schumacher's critique of the prevailing technology he observed?
- How does his proposal for "intermediate technology" or "technology with a human face" differ from that which Schumacher observed during his lifetime? How does he distinguish between "mass production" and "production by the masses"?
- How might Gandhi and Nehru respond to Schumacher's views?

E. F. SCHUMACHER | *Small Is Beautiful* | 1973

[T]he modern world, shaped by modern technology, finds itself involved in three crises simultaneously. First, human nature revolts against inhuman technological, organisational, and political patterns, which it experiences as suffocating and debilitating; second, the living environment which supports human life aches and groans and gives signs of partial breakdown; and, third . . . the inroads being made into the world's non-renewable resources, particularly those of fossil fuels, are such that serious bottlenecks and virtual exhaustion loom ahead in the quite foreseeable future. . . .

What is quite clear is that a way of life that bases itself on materialism, i.e. on permanent, limitless expansionism in a finite environment, cannot last long. . . .

The type of work which modern technology is most successful in reducing or even eliminating is skillful, productive work of human hands, in touch with real materials of one kind or another. . . . We may say, therefore, that modern technology has deprived man of the kind of work that he enjoys most, creative, useful work with hands and brains, and given him plenty of work of a fragmented kind, most of which he does not enjoy at all.

The threefold crisis of which I have spoken will not go away if we simply carry on as before. It will become worse and end in disaster, until or unless we develop a new lifestyle which is compatible with the real needs of human nature, with the health of living nature around us, and with the resource endowment of the world. . . .

[T]he poverty of the poor makes it in any case impossible for them successfully to adopt our technology. Of course, they often try to do so, and then have to bear the more dire consequences in terms of mass unemployment, mass migration into cities, rural decay, and intolerable social tensions. They need . . . a different kind of technology, a technology with a human face, which instead of making human hands and brains redundant, helps them to become far more productive than they have ever been before. . . .

The system of *mass production*, based on sophisticated, highly capital-intensive, high energy input dependent, and human labour-saving technology, presupposes that you are already rich, for a great deal of capital investment is needed to establish one single workplace. The system of *production by the masses* mobilises the priceless resources which are possessed by all human beings, their clever brains and skillful hands, and supports them with first-class tools. The technology of *mass production* is inherently violent, ecologically damaging, self-defeating in terms of non-renewable resources, and stultifying for the human person. The technology of *production by the masses*, making use of the best of modern knowledge and experience, is conducive to decentralisation, compatible with the laws of ecology, gentle in its use of scarce resources, and designed to serve the human person instead of making him the servant of machines. I have named it intermediate technology to signify that it is vastly superior to the primitive technology of bygone ages but at the same time much simpler, cheaper, and freer than the super-technology of the rich. One can also call it self-help technology, or democratic or people's technology — a technology to which everybody can gain admittance and which is not reserved to those already rich and powerful. . . .

[T]he direction which modern technology has taken and is continuing to pursue—towards ever-greater size, ever-higher speeds, and ever- increased violence, in defiance of all laws of natural harmony—is the opposite of progress.... Hence the call for taking stock and finding a new orientation. The stocktaking indicates that we are destroying our very basis of existence, and the reorientation is based on remembering what human life is really about.

I have no doubt that it is possible to give a new direction to technological development, a direction that shall lead it back to the real needs of man, and that also means: to the actual size of man. Man is small, and, therefore, small is beautiful. To go for gigantism is to go for self-destruction.

Source: E. F. Schumacher, *Small Is Beautiful* (London: Blond and Briggs, 1973), 139, 141–42, 144–46, 149–50.

■ ■ ■

SOURCE 22.5 Nuclear Technology and Fears of a Nuclear Holocaust

Yet another source of anxiety and skepticism about modern technology derived from growing fears about nuclear weapons and their likely consequences, which took shape during the 1980s as a nuclear arms race, driven by Cold War hostilities, picked up speed. In the United States, such concerns found expression in the "nuclear freeze" movement, which called for a Soviet–American "freeze on testing, production, and further deployment of nuclear weapons." Massive peace demonstrations in the United States, Europe, and the Soviet Union as well as widespread global support for a "freeze" in the United Nations likewise reflected this mounting fear of a nuclear holocaust. The scientific case for the fearful consequences of a major nuclear war appeared in the prestigious American periodical *Scientific American* in 1984. Source 22.5A contains its somber conclusions, which include the possibility of human extinction. In Source 22.5B, the writer, scholar, and activist Jonathan Schell muses on the philosophical implications of that possibility in a widely read and controversial book entitled *The Fate of the Earth,* published in 1982.

- According to Source 22.5A, what outcomes of a major nuclear war might lead to "nuclear winter" and the possible extinction of the humankind?
- In what larger contexts does Jonathan Schell frame the question of nuclear holocaust?
- How does the tone of Schell's reflections differ from that of the scientists who wrote the *Scientific American* article?

SOURCE 22.5A
"The Climatic Effects of Nuclear War" | 1984

Since the beginning of the nuclear arms race four decades ago, it has generally been assumed that the most devastating consequences of a major nuclear war between the U.S. and the U.S.S.R. would be a gigantic number of human casualties in the principal target zones of the Northern Hemisphere. Although in the wake of such a war the social and economic structure of the combatant nations would presumably collapse, it has been argued that most of the noncombatant nations—and hence the majority of the human population—would not be endangered, either directly or indirectly. Over the years questions have been raised about the possible global extent of various indirect, long-term effects of nuclear war, such as delayed radioactive fallout, depletion of the protective ozone layer in the upper atmosphere and adverse changes in the climate. Until recently, however, the few authoritative studies available on these added threats have tended to play down their significance. . . .

This comparatively optimistic view of the potential global impact of nuclear war may now have to be revised. Recent findings by our group, confirmed by [scientific] workers in Europe, the U.S. and the U.S.S.R. suggest that the long term climatic effects of a major nuclear war are likely to be much severer and farther-reaching than had been supposed. In the aftermath of such a war, vast areas of the earth could be subjected to prolonged darkness, abnormally low temperatures, violent windstorms, toxic smog and persistent radioactive fallout—in short the combination of conditions that has come to be known as "nuclear winter." The physical effects of nuclear war would be compounded by the widespread breakdown of transportation systems, power grids, agricultural production, food processing, medical care, sanitation, civil service and central government. Even in regions far from the conflict, the survivors would be imperiled by starvation, hypothermia, radiation sickness, weakening of the human immune system, epidemics, and other dire consequences. Under some circumstances, a number of biologists and ecologists contend, the extinction of many species of organisms—including the human species—is a real possibility.

Source: Richard P. Turco et. al., "The Climatic Effects of Nuclear War," *Scientific American* 251, no. 2 (August 1984), 33.

SOURCE 22.5B
JONATHAN SCHELL | *The Fate of the Earth* | 1982

A nuclear holocaust, because of its unique combination of immensity and suddenness, is a threat without parallel. . . . Our species is caught in the same tightening web of technical success that has already strangled so many other species. . . . The peril of human extinction . . . is, in a word, an *ecological* peril. The nuclear peril is usually seen in isolation from the threats to other forms of life and their ecosystems, but in fact it should be seen as the very center of the ecological peril. . . . Both the effort to preserve the environment and the effort to save the species from extinction by nuclear arms would be enhanced and strengthened by this recognition....

According to the Bible, when Adam and Eve ate the fruit of the tree of knowledge God punished them by withdrawing from them the privilege of immortality and dooming them and their kind to die. Now our species has eaten more deeply of the fruit of the tree of knowledge, and has brought itself face to face with a second death—the death of mankind....

The possibility that the living can stop the future generations from entering into life compels us to ask basic new questions about our existence, the most sweeping of which is what these unborn ones . . . mean to us. [N]o generation before us has ever held the life and death of the species in its hands.... In what court is such a crime to be judged? Against whom is it committed? And what law does it violate? . . .

Death cuts off life; extinction cuts off birth. . . . We have always been able to send people to their death, but only now has it become possible to prevent all birth and so doom all future beings to uncreation....

Source: Jonathan Schell, *The Fate of the Earth* (New York, NY: Alfred A, Knopf, Inc., 1982), 111, 115–17.

■ ■ ■

SOURCE 22.6 Technology and Climate Change ▶

By the early 1990s, the Cold War had ended and the danger of nuclear war had diminished, at least temporarily. But that existential threat to the planet and its many inhabitants—human and otherwise—was soon replaced by another such threat: climate change or global warming. Both the threat of nuclear war and the risks associated with climate change are rooted in the vast capacities of modern technology, and both hold the very real possibility of engendering social collapse on a global scale. Climate change, however, is even more deeply embedded in the entire fabric of modern life, because the greenhouse gases that cause it derive from endless demands of individuals, corporations, and governments alike for more energy to meet the growing needs and desires of a mounting population. Furthermore, climate change is a rather more gradual process compared to the spasm of destruction with which nuclear war is often imagined. Moreover, climate change has generated—at least in the United States—a small industry of denial that had no counterpart in the discourse around nuclear war. The sources that follow explore the relationship of technology and climate change.

The challenge that climate change presents has been described by the eminent ecological philosopher Thomas Berry as that of "moving modern industrial civilization from its present devastating influence on the Earth to a more benign mode of presence."[4] One approach to this challenge relies heavily on technology itself: rapidly ramping up alternative energy sources not dependent on fossil fuels, such as solar, wind, geothermal, nuclear, or fusion technologies; developing electric cars; pursuing carbon capture and storage possibilities; constructing more energy efficient buildings; and much else. Among the more exotic technological proposals for addressing global warming is "geoengineering," sometimes called "climate engineering." Such technologies represent deliberate human efforts to intervene massively in the earth's climate system to remove existing carbon dioxide from the atmosphere and to reduce the solar radiation reaching the earth's surface. Various geoengineering possibilities are depicted visually in Source 22.6A.

But can technology alone allow humankind to maintain its high-energy, industrialized way of living while protecting the planet as well? Many observers have their doubts and argue that any effective response to global warming will require major adjustments and painful sacrifices in both personal and public life. These potential sea-changes include lower standards of living, higher taxes, greater regulations, less driving and flying, wealth transfers from the rich to the poor, and, most fundamentally, changes in the modern values and habits of thought that have led us into an unsustainable way of living. Such an outlook is reflected in Source 22.6B, derived from a recent book by Jeffrey Kiehl, a prominent American climate scientist and a Jungian analyst.

- What kinds of technologies are suggested in Source 22.6A? How do you respond to such technologies? What negative consequences might they generate?
- Why does Jeffrey Kiehl in Source 22.6B believe that "we need to look beyond a technological transformation"? What kind of changes does he envisage?
- How might Kiehl and the creators of "geoengineering" technologies respond to one another?

SOURCE 22.6A
PIERS FORSTER | *Reversing Climate Change . . . Technologically* | 2014

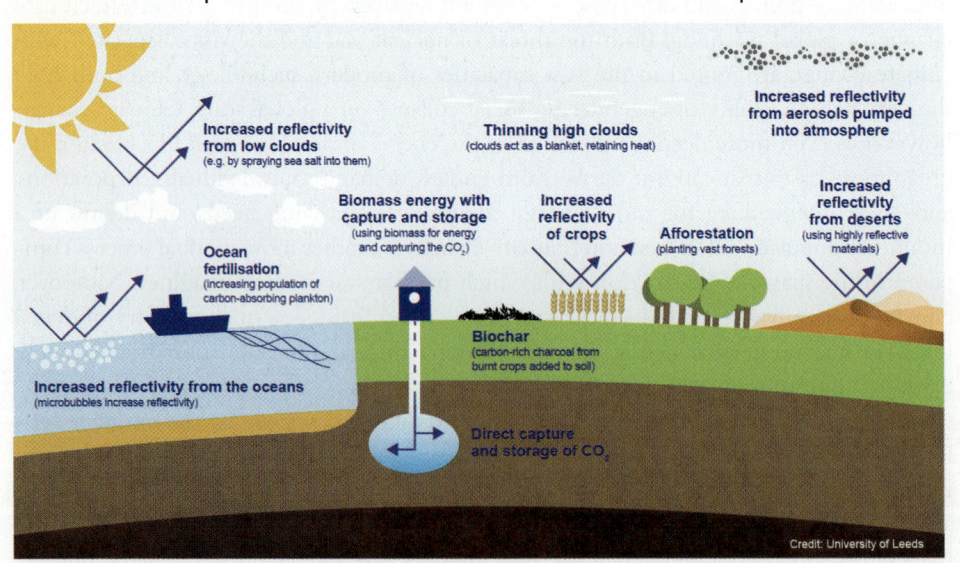

(Courtesy Professor Piers Forster, Faculty of the Environment, School of Earth and Environment, Leeds University)

SOURCE 22.6B
JEFFREY T. KIEHL | *Facing Climate Change* | 2016

Our commitment to burning fossil fuels arises from our need for more and more energy. The critical social factors that drive this need are the increasing number of people on the planet, the increasing consumption of energy, and technological innovations that require more energy.... The explosion of consumerism has led to owning more things that require energy.... [U]ntil we rein in this desire to consume recklessly we will continue to place the world out of balance....

We need to imagine a world without fossil fuels, a world where we tread lightly on the earth, and in which food is distributed more equally. A world where we are living in cooperation, rather than competition, with nature.... We have drifted far away from seeing a living world, and we view the material world as existing to serve our endless needs and wants.... It is time to recognize our active participation in a fully animate world.... To live a balanced life requires us to consider how we relate to the world around us....

Global warming exists because of our excessive consumption of energy.... Often global energy consumption is used as an important measure of human "progress." To address the problem of climate change will require us to redefine our measure of meaning beyond this single factor. As long as we view consumption as a significant source of meaning, we commit ourselves to a life of depletion and destruction.... Our current living myth of unconstrained economic growth pushes the world ever closer to catastrophic collapse. Eternal growth must give way to meaningful sustainability.

We are called to make sense of our being in the world.... Historically we have met this call by defining ourselves in terms of something greater, perhaps reflecting our innate need to be contained or held by something larger than ourselves....

Today we live in a world where the greater is defined by economic growth and the accumulation of wealth and power. In our process of "development" we have moved farther from a sense of meaning that allowed us to feel like an integral part of the greater.... The material things in the world, seen as dead and disconnected objects, will never provide us with a meaningful sense of the greater....

Overcoming this self-defeating and dying myth requires us to move beyond a meaning rooted in senseless materialism to one truly representing the greater, one transcending the "I" and even the "we." We must discover and connect with the transpersonal [the "something greater"] within ourselves, to rediscover our place in a living, dynamic cosmos. Here the transpersonal is not just spiritual but also the greater social good, the animate natural world, and the sense of holistic well-being....

[W]e find ourselves in a situation calling out for transformation, a situation in which we know that our uncontained consumption of the Earth's natural resources is morally wrong.... Equally unjust is burdening future generations with the immense disruption caused by global warming.... As usual, the world is full of voices proclaiming the impossibility of such change because the fossil-fuel industry is too strong, politicians are too weak, and worst of all, humans are too self-centered.... Fortunately ... today we hear some arguing that rampant consumption and environmental destruction cannot continue....

We require a transformation unique in human civilization, a transformation in which we relinquish our dependence on something to which we are highly addicted. It is for this reason that we need to look beyond a technological transformation. . . . We need to look toward a transformation of consciousness; our behavior toward the world and toward one another needs to change. We need to recognize our interconnectedness. . . . We need to enter onto a *path of compassionate action* to avoid the worst consequences of human-induced climate change.

Source: Jeffrey T. Kiehl, *Facing Climate Change* (New York, NY: Columbia University Press, 2016), 78, 80–82, 111–13, 132–34, 143.

DOING HISTORY

1. **Considering change:** What changes in attitudes toward technology since 1900 do these sources reveal? How might you account for these changes?

2. **Distinguishing between technology and human uses of technology:** To what extent are differing postures toward technology more about human uses of these innovations rather than about the nature of the technologies themselves?

3. **Imagining a conversation:** Construct a conversation among the authors or creators of these sources. What issues or arguments might arise? What areas of agreement might surface?

4. **Engaging in speculation about the future:** Might you be willing to risk some speculation about the shape of technology and its impact over the next century as the artist in Source 22.1 did?

HISTORIANS' VOICES

Technological Change in the Twentieth Century

The rapid pace of technological change over the course of the twentieth century transformed the lives of people across the planet in increasingly profound ways and played a central role in ushering in the Anthropocene—the "age of man." The two voices that follow take stock of the global impact of these developments at two different points in the century. In Voice 22.1, Trevor I. Williams, a scientist and historian writing in the 1980s, assesses the impact of technological change on humankind by the mid-twentieth century. In Voice 22.2, J. R. McNeill, one of the most prominent environmental historians of his generation, assesses the historical constraints on humankind that had been overcome during the twentieth century and the new constraints that had emerged by the end of the century.

- What do these two assessments share and where do they differ?
- According to McNeil, how have natural constraints on humankind changed over the past century?
- **Integrating primary and secondary sources:** How might Williams and McNeill use the sources in this feature to support their arguments?

VOICE 22.1

Trevor Williams on the Impacts of Technology in the First Half of the Twentieth Century | 1982

First, . . . was a very great increase in man's material wealth. For many this encouraged the hope that the long-sought brotherhood of mankind would be brought demonstrably nearer; the elimination of poverty and disease, it was argued, would remove the main causes of strife and create a milieu favourable to universal peace. In the event no such thing happened: nine years of our half-century were given over to two World Wars and the peace between and after was uneasy in both the military and the industrial sphere. The new wealth was not evenly distributed: if anything the rich became richer and the poor became poorer. . . . Understandably, new technology brought not only the fear but also the reality of unemployment, and led to bitter disputes not only between unions and employers but also between unions. . . . While it can be argued convincingly that new technology created rather than diminished employment, in the sense that at mid-century a very large number of people worked in industries that in 1900 did not even exist, individuals made redundant were often unfitted by age or training to grasp the new opportunities. . . .

Equally important was the fact that wealth provided a degree of security that made it possible to stand back and question the means by which it had been created. Technology was no longer satisfying merely basic needs—food, clothing, shelter—for a growing population, but had created new ones. Abundant and sophisticated foods out of season; non-stop entertainment by radio and, later, television; . . . were all pleasant new adjuncts to life but certainly not necessities. Paradoxically perhaps, the first half of this century witnessed the beginning of an anti-technology movement that was quickly to represent a political force too powerful to be ignored.

Source: Trevor I. Williams, *A Short History of Twentieth-Century Technology c. 1900–c. 1950* (Oxford, UK: Clarendon, 1982), 397.

VOICE 22.2

J. R. McNeill on Challenges Overcome and Challenges Created in the Twentieth Century | 2000

According to the Hebrew Bible, on the fifth day of creation God enjoined humankind to fill and subdue the earth and to have dominion over every living thing. For most of history, our species failed to live up to these . . . injunctions, not for want of trying so much as for want of power. But in the twentieth century the harnessing of fossil fuels, unprecedented population growth, and a myriad of technological changes made it more nearly possible to fulfill these instructions. The prevailing political and economic systems made it seem imprudent not to try: most societies, and all the big ones, sought to maximize their current formidability and wealth at the risk of sacrificing ecological buffers and tomorrow's resilience. The general policy of the twentieth century was to try to make the most of resources, make Nature perform to the utmost, and hope for the best.

With our new powers we banished some historical constraints on health and population, food production, energy use, and consumption generally. Few who know anything about life with these constraints regret their passing. But in banishing them we invited other constraints in the form of the planet's capacity to absorb the wastes, by-products, and impacts of our actions. These latter constraints had pinched occasionally in the past, but only locally. By the end of the twentieth century they seemed to restrict our options globally. Our negotiations with these constraints will shape the future as our struggles against them shaped our past.

Source: J. R. McNeill, *Something New under the Sun: An Environmental History of the Twentieth-Century World* (New York, NY: W. W. Norton, 2000), 361–62.

NOTES

1. John Elfreth Watkins Jr., "What May Happen in the Next Hundred Years," *Ladies' Home Journal*, December 1900, 8.

2. Mahatma Gandhi's Writings, Philosophy . . . , "The Curse of Industrialization", http://www.mkgandhi.org/momgandhi/chap49.htm; Mahatma Gandhi, *The Penguin Gandhi Reader*, edited by Rudrangshu Mukherjee (Delhi: Penguin Books, 1993), 58.

3. Donella Meadows et.al, *The Limits to Growth* (New York, NY: Universe Books, 1972), 154.

4. Thomas Berry, *The Great Work* (New York: Bell Tower, 1999), 7.

CHAPTER 23

Thinking through Sources

Experiencing International Migration

The long-distance movement of people has been a prominent feature of the human story, and never more so than in the seven decades since the end of World War II. This immense stream of people in motion has been and remains the product of many elements in recent world history: an awareness of global inequality and the perceived promise of a better life abroad; the pressures of population growth and the harsh realities of poverty; environmental degradation; war, repression, and political crises. These and other factors have given rise to many kinds of migrants: economic migrants seeking work in new lands; political migrants or refugees seeking safety or freedom; legal and undocumented migrants; migrant victims of sex trafficking. These migrant streams have moved in many directions. Russia has been the destination for many millions, many of them Russian speakers from the countries of the former Soviet Union. Small but wealthy states such as Hong Kong, Singapore, Kuwait, and the United Arab Emirates have attracted large numbers of immigrants, who represent now a substantial proportion of their populations—some 88 percent in the United Arab Emirates and 73 percent in Kuwait. Global sex trafficking has become a big and profitable business, moving millions of women and girls across international boundaries. Western retirement migrants, seeking warmer and inexpensive locations for their later years, have generated expatriate communities in various countries of Latin America and Asia.

But the largest stream of international migrants has involved people from the Global South of Africa, Asia, the Middle East, and Latin America seeking new homes and new lives in the more developed countries of the Global North, including Europe and North America. The United States has been the target destination for the largest number of the world's migrants; by 2015, it was home to some 46.6 million migrants, or approximately 14.5 percent of the total U.S. population. For many of the world's migrants, the journey to their new homes has been harrowing and often deadly—trekking across burning deserts of northern Mexico, the southwestern United States, or the Sahara, or navigating the treacherous Mediterranean Sea in flimsy boats.

The sources that follow focus less on these journeys and more on the experience of the migrants in their new homes, the response of the host societies, and the impact of migration on those left behind in their countries of origin.

SOURCE 23.1 Hana in Holland

Once migrants arrive in their new location, many questions arise about how to live, fit in, accommodate, or resist the new and alien culture. Source 23.1 provides one example. Hana was a "multiple migrant." Born in Eritrea (then part of Ethiopia) around 1970, as a young girl she fled with her family to Sudan because of her father's political involvements. She spent some time in a Somali prison after being accused of spying for Ethiopia, and in 1990 made her way to Holland. There, her story, told to a British researcher, picks up.

- What particular difficulties did Hana experience in Holland?
- How did the events of September 11, 2001, affect Hana?
- What does Hana imply about her expectations when she arrived in Holland?

HANA | *Adapting to Holland* | 2016

In Holland of course when I came it was a bit of a shock. After all that, you expect to come to a country which people will understand your situation or will support you, but when I came to Holland it was so shocking. I was put in a camp very far away from all other people. We were just us, all different kind of people, and most of them were from white European country or other. There was only one black woman from Somalia where I stayed....

So it was the most depressing time of my life. Being locked in one place and then what you see is only from the window and you don't have enough clothes or enough warm jackets to go outside because when I came it was October 1990.... It took me I think nine months until I came to live in Amsterdam in a room with other Ethiopians and other nationalities.

Hana lived in the Netherlands for 14 years, during which time she lived with a partner who was also Muslim, with whom she started a family. She worked in an accountancy firm until 2005.

I started to put a scarf on [a sign of Islamic modesty] and I was more deepened in my religion so at that time I was kicked off my job. And things got really really tough. First of all they found somebody who is Dutch [to replace her], and also kind of they didn't accept that I put on a scarf and I'm different, so that was my experience in Holland....

In Holland you get stuck. There is a roof on your head, if you just move your head up more than you should, you just get pushed and you get pushed into a black hole that you never come out of. And after the incident of 11 September it was much worse.

All even my neighbors they tried to, they started to treat my children differently and some of my friends in the road they were pulled and pushed and they took off their scarves and pulled their hair on the street and that is while the police is watching. And there are, where my child used to go was the Islamic school, that school had been bombed.

Imagine, you think you came to safe country to live safely and to have happiness at last in your life and it is being discriminated and you know I had to leave Holland.... And now I've started my life again here in England since 2005 March.

Source: Linda McDowell, *Migrant Women's Voices* (London, UK: Bloomsbury Publishing, 2016), 49–50.

■ ■ ■

SOURCE 23.2 Ayaan Hirsi Ali in Holland

A very different immigrant response to life in Holland can be seen in the experience of Ayaan Hirsi Ali, a Somali immigrant to the Netherlands and later to the United States who repudiated much of her Somali culture and its Islamic faith. Born in 1969, Hirsi Ali was the daughter of a prominent political opponent of the Somali government. Fleeing the country with her family, she spent much of her childhood in Saudi Arabia, Ethiopia, and Kenya, where she was attracted for a time to a strict form of Islam. As a teenager, she willingly wore a *hijab*, the traditional covering for modest Muslim women.

But in 1992, fleeing an arranged marriage to a man she regarded as a "bigot" and an "idiot," Hirsi Ali found political asylum in the Netherlands and was disowned by her father. As an immigrant, she flourished, moving from work as a cleaner to that of a translator in a refugee center and obtaining a master's degree in the process. Her encounter with Western individualism and Enlightenment thought produced a growing disenchantment with Islam, and Hirsi Ali came to see herself as an atheist. She got involved in politics, was elected to the Dutch parliament, and participated in the making of a film highly critical of Muslim treatment of women, for which she received numerous death threats. In 2006, she relocated to the United States, "in search of an opportunity to build a life and livelihood in freedom" and became an American citizen in 2013. By then a prominent public figure both in Europe and in North America, Hirsi Ali described her remarkable personal transformation as an immigrant in a number of books, articles, and interviews. In one of them, she penned "A Letter to My Grandmother," from which Source 23.2 is taken.

- How would you describe the difference between Hirsi Ali's response to life in Europe and that of Hana in Source 23.1?
- What elements of Western life does she appreciate?
- What criticisms of Islam are disclosed in this passage?

AYAAN HIRSI ALI | *"From a Letter to My Grandmother"* | 2010

I am sorry Grandmother that I was not there in your old age.... I would have summoned the spirits of my new world. Here they have salves to cleanse and sooth the itch in folded skin; they have hearing aids; they have walking sticks on wheels...;

I have lived with the infidels for almost two decades. I have come to learn, appreciate, and adopt their way of life....

Gone with you are the rigid rules of custom.... Gone with you is that bloodline [clan or tribal loyalties], for better or worse, and gone is the idiot tradition that meant you cherished mares and she-camels more than your daughters and granddaughters....

The secret of the Dutchman's success is his ability to adapt, to invent.... We bow to a God who says we must not change a thing; it is he who has chosen it.

The infidel does not see life as a test, a passage to the hereafter, but as an end and a joy in itself. All his resources of money, mind, and organization go into making life here, on Earth, comfortable and healthy.... He is loyal to his wife and children; he may take care of his parents, but has no use for a memory filled with an endless chain of ancestors. All the seeds of his toil are spent on his own offspring, not those of his brothers or uncles.

Because the infidel trusts and studies new ideas, there is abundance in the infidel lands.... the birth of a girl is just fine.... The little girl sits right next to the little boy in school.... she gets to eat as much as he does ... and when she matures, she gets the same opportunity to seek and find a mate as he does....

Grandmother, I no longer believe in the old ways....

Source: Ayaan Hirsi Ali, *Nomad: From Islam to America* (New York, NY: Atria Paperback, 2010), 86, 88–90, 92.

■ ■ ■

SOURCE 23.3 Left Behind

Migration had repercussions well beyond the circle of the migrants themselves, for those who remained in their homelands also felt the impact of those who had departed. One young Moroccan woman, whose new husband left for work in Europe in the early 1970s, expressed her anguish at his leaving. "I am afraid, afraid that my love forgets me in your paradise", she wrote. "With you he stays one year, with me just one month.... I am like a flower that withers more each day."[1]

More broadly, the repercussions of extensive migrations also echoed in fears within developing countries about the social and economic impact of losing many young, well-educated professional people to higher-paying and more prestigious positions in Europe and North America. Many who went abroad to study did not return home. Others were recruited—or seduced—by professional opportunities not available in their own countries. Frustration with such people boiled over in a novel by the Zimbabwean neurosurgeon and writer J. Nozipo Maraire. In her novel, *Zenzele: A Letter for My Daughter*, the leading character sharply criticizes a friend who left Zimbabwe for a better life in the West.

- What is her fundamental criticism of those who do not return home?
- What does she fear for Africa if such practices continue?
- Who does she feel is responsible for this situation?

J. NOZIPO MARAIRE | *Zenzele: A Letter for My Daughter* | 1996

Africa needs the hearts and minds of its sons and daughters to nurture it. You were our pride. . . . When you did not return, a whole village lost its investment. Africa is all that we have. If we do not build it, no one else will. . . . Yes, you are just one, but it is thousands like you, whom our churches and governments pour money into, who ultimately drain our resources. If our brightest minds go and never return, then it is no wonder that we have poor leadership to guide our nations, that we have no engineers to run our machinery, no doctors to staff our hospitals, no professors to fill our universities, and no teachers to educate the generations to come. How can we move forward if our future Mandelas are content to spend their days sipping cappuccinos on Covent Gardens? If our potential Sembene's [a Senegalese film director] are happier shooting French films in Paris or our Achebes-to-be [a leading Nigerian novelist] prefer to tell stories of Americans, is it surprising that we appear to be culturally void? Who is left? You are the epitome of the brain drain.

Source: J. Nozipo Maraire, *Zenzele: A Letter for My Daughter* (New York, NY: Delta Books, 1996), 64–65.

■ ■ ■

SOURCE 23.4 The Politics of Immigration: A Cautious Welcome in Europe

Immigration has long found expression as a political issue in the receiving countries, and never more so than in early twenty-first century Europe. Fleeing civil war, poverty, drought, and oppression, a massive wave of desperate migrants from the Middle East and Africa, some 1.3 million people in 2015 alone, sought refuge in Europe. In many places, they received a warm and hospitable welcome. Angela Merkel, the chancellor of Germany and a citizen of the former communist state of East Germany, emerged as a spokesperson for a compassionate approach to this enormous humanitarian tragedy. That sensibility found expression in a speech she gave to the European Parliament in October of 2015.

- How might you describe Merkel's posture toward the immigration crisis in Europe?
- In what ways does her speech respond to those opposed to large-scale immigration in Europe?
- What does she expect from those who seek a new home in Europe?

ANGELA MERKEL | *Speech to the European Parliament* | October 7, 2015

Not since the Second World War have so many people fled their homes as today—the number has now reached around 60 million.... We can rightly expect the people who come to us in Europe to become integrated into our societies. This requires them to uphold the rules that apply here, and to learn the language of their new homeland.

But, conversely, we also have a duty to treat the people who come to us in need with respect, to see them as human beings and not as an anonymous mass—regardless of whether they will be allowed to stay or not.... [T]his means that we must be guided by the values we have enshrined in the European treaties: human dignity, the rule of law, tolerance, respect for minorities and solidarity....

....Today Europe is a region on which many people from all over the world pin their hopes and aspirations...We have to deal responsibly with Europe's gravitational pull. In other words, we have to take greater care of those who are in need today in our neighbourhood.

Source: Statement by Federal Chancellor Angela Merkel to the European Parliament, October 7, 2015. Accessed at https://www.bundesregierung.de/Content/EN/Reden/2015/2015-10-07-merkel-ep_en.html?nn=393812.

■ ■ ■

SOURCE 23.5 The Politics of Immigration: Resentment and Resistance in Europe

A welcoming posture was not the only European response to the recent influx of immigrants, as a backlash against large-scale immigration, fueled by fears of a threat to national cultures, of the loss of jobs, and of terrorism, took shape across much of Europe. That backlash was reflected in Great Britain's decision to exit the European Union in 2015, and it was encouraged by the 2016 election of Donald Trump in the United States and his subsequent effort to restrict immigration from Muslim countries. That sensibility was articulated in a speech by Geert Wilders, a prominent Dutch politician and a leading figure in European anti-immigrant circles, delivered in early 2017 at a "Europe of Nations and Freedom" Conference in Germany.

- What fears does Wilders articulate?
- Who does he hold responsible for the influx of Muslims into Europe?
- What is his posture toward the European Union? What kind of Europe does he favor?
- How might Chancellor Merkel respond to Wilders' speech?

GEERT WILDERS | Speech at the "Europe of Nations and Freedom" Conference | 2017

[A]ll our European countries are faced with the question of their existence. My friends, the United Nations expects that the population of Africa will quadruple by the end of the century.... Many of them want to come to Europe in the future.

The question that none of our ruling politicians now ask is: How do we protect our country and our identity against mass immigration? How do we protect our values? How do we protect our civilization? Our culture? The future of our children? These are the fundamental questions we have to answer.

In recent years, our governments have allowed millions of people to flow uncontrollably into our countries. Our governments have conducted a dangerous open-borders policy....

Our leaders ... no longer value freedom.

Politicians from almost all of the established parties are promoting our Islamization. Almost the entire Establishment, the elite universities, the churches, the media, politicians, put our hard-earned liberties at risk....

Day after day, for years, we are experiencing the decay of our cherished values. The equality of men and women, freedom of opinion and speech, tolerance of homosexuality—all this is in retreat....

And then there is also the great danger of Islamic terrorism. A German undercover journalist recently revealed that some refugee housing centers have become breeding-grounds for terrorists. The consequences are visible to everyone....

We are fed up with the elites, who offer you a beautiful ideal world, in which all cultures are morally equivalent....

History calls on you to save Germany. History calls on us all to save Europe. To save our own humanistic Judeo-Christian culture and civilization, our liberties, our nations, the future of our children.

We are fed up with the Europhiles in Brussels, who want to abolish our countries and impose an undemocratic super-state, in which we become a single multicultural society.

To this Europe we say no! We stand for a Europe of national states and freedom! We will take our countries back. We will make sure that our countries will stay ours....

My friends, we live in historic times. The people of the West are awakening. They are casting off the yoke of political correctness. They want their freedom back. They want

366   CHAPTER 23 • THINKING THROUGH SOURCES

their sovereign nations back. And we, the patriots of Europe, will be their instrument of liberation!

Source: Geert Wilders, "Speech at the 'Europe of Nations and Freedom' Conference," January 22, 2017. Accessed at https://www.gatestoneinstitute.org/9812/geert-wilders-koblenz-enf.

■ ■ ■

SOURCE 23.6 From the Holocaust to Israel ▶

During the post–World War II era, and especially since the 1960s, the industrialized countries of Europe and North America have been the chief destinations for many millions of the world's migrants. Pakistanis, Indians, and West Indians moved to Great Britain; North Africans and West Africans to France; Turks and Kurds to Germany; Filipinos, Vietnamese, Koreans, Cubans, Mexicans, and Haitians to the United States. But there was one highly significant migrant stream moving outward from Europe — that of European Jews heading to Palestine/Israel. That migrant stream, known as Zionism, had begun in the late nineteenth and early twentieth centuries, but it expanded greatly in the wake of the Holocaust and the creation of the newly established State of Israel in 1948. There, these European migrants were joined by millions of other Jews hailing from the Islamic world and later from the former Soviet Union. Altogether, more than 3 million Jews have migrated to Israel since 1948, with the active support and encouragement of the Israeli government. Source 23.6 illustrates the connection between the Holocaust and this mass migration of European and other Jews. It was a fund-raising poster from circa 1950 for a Jewish settlement or *kibbutz* in northern Israel.

- What is happening in the action of the poster? Note: The yellow armband worn by the older man was one of the signs of Jewish identity that the Nazis required Jews to wear. It served to isolate and dehumanize Jewish people.
- How might this poster serve to encourage migration to Israel?
- What image of the new Israeli state did the poster seek to convey?

Source 23.6 From the Holocaust to Israel

Fund-Raising Poster from Israel | 1950

SOURCE 23.7 The Palestinian Diaspora

This large-scale Jewish migration to Israel prompted yet another migratory stream, as some 750,000 Palestinian Arabs fled or were expelled from their homes during the 1948 war that established the State of Israel. Many of them moved to often squalid refugee camps in Gaza, the West Bank, Syria, Lebanon, and Jordan, where millions of their descendants remain to this day. This forced migration of 1948, known to Palestinians as *Al-nakba* or "the catastrophe," is commemorated every year, with marchers carrying Palestinian flags and a key, symbolizing their "right to return" to the lands and homes from which they had been expelled. These two migrations have together generated one of the most intractable conflicts of the contemporary world—that between Israel and the Palestinians. Source 23.7 shows a Palestinian man from a refugee camp in the West Bank town of Hebron tenderly touching a poster announcing the sixty-seventh anniversary of Nakba in 2015.

- What message is the poster intended to convey?
- How might you imagine the thinking of the man touching the poster?
- How might you compare the migratory journeys reflected in Sources 23.6 and 23.7? Construct a conversation between the creators of these two posters. What common ground might they share? On what issues might they never agree?

"The Catastrophe" Memorialized | 2015

(HAZEM BADER/Getty Images)

DOING HISTORY

1. **Comparing experiences:** In what different ways has migration been experienced by individuals during the past century?
2. **Considering consequences:** In what ways has migration had consequences well beyond the stories of individual migrants?
3. **Practicing empathy:** History, we often say, serves to awaken our empathy with people in a wide variety of circumstances. To what extent can you enter sympathetically into the experience of the people whose lives are depicted in these sources?

HISTORIANS' VOICES

Immigration to the United States and Europe

The principal destinations of twentieth-century migrants were the United States and, from the 1960s, Western Europe. The two voices that follow assess attitudes toward migrants in these two regions. In Voice 23.1, Konrad H. Jarausch, a specialist in twentieth-century Europe, examines the societal tensions associated with Europe's shift from a continent of emigrants to an immigration continent. In Voice 23.2, Tobias Brinkmann and Annemarie Sammartino, specialists in migration and German history, compare American and German attitudes toward migration during the twentieth century and question common interpretations of both.

- According to Jarausch, what fears inspired a nativist backlash toward immigration? In what ways have European governments and supporters of immigration reacted to this nativist backlash?
- What differences between American and German attitudes toward migration and immigrants do Brinkmann and Sammartino identify?
- **Integrating primary and secondary sources:** How might the primary sources presented earlier illustrate or explain the European and American reactions described in these Voices?

VOICE 23.1

Konrad Jarausch on Europe's Shift from Emigration to Immigration | 2015

The increasing pressure for immigration in the wake of globalization caught Europeans unprepared, because they continued to think of themselves as emigrants. Since the Old Continent had produced more hungry people than it could feed, migrants . . . had left for centuries populating distant shores from the United States to Australia. . . . But with fertility declining below replacement and longevity increasing substantially, an aging Europe turned from emigration to an immigration continent, needing foreign migrants to survive.

In response to growing immigration and economic downturn [after ca. 1970 and especially in the early twenty-first century], an ugly nativist backlash formed in many European countries. . . . Much of the motivation stemmed from irrational fear of losing one's job to the newcomers, envy of their purported welfare benefits or ignorance of their different customs. . . . Various rightist groups . . . capitalized on this widespread resentment to score surprising electoral victories. . . . While civil society groups of the Left rallied for tolerance, schools encouraged acceptance of strangers, and sports clubs tried to celebrate difference, established conservative parties profited from popular anger by proposing restrictive legislation.

The conflicting pressures of fear of foreigners and need for skilled immigration engendered a contradictory set of immigration policies. On the one hand, nativist backlash forced a tightening of ethnic remigration, family immigration, and recognition of asylum, decreasing the yearly influx. To stop the flow of illegal immigrants the EU agreed on a joint border regime, which sent asylum seekers back to "safe countries.". . . On the other hand, business lobbying forced the initiation of various "blue card" programs permitting university graduates to remain or professionals to enter. . . .

Source: Konrad H. Jarausch, *Out of Ashes: A New History of Europe in the Twentieth Century* (Princeton, NJ: Princeton University Press, 2015), 732–36.

VOICE 23.2

Tobias Brinkmann and Annemarie Sammartino on American and German Attitudes toward Immigration | 2010

There is no German counterpart to the image of the Statue of Liberty welcoming the "huddled masses" to America's shores. Yet behind the myths of American inclusion and German exclusion lurks a much more complicated portrait of two nations struggling with the challenges and opportunities of immigration.

The image of the United States as a beacon of freedom and tolerance for immigrants is a myth. From the earliest days until the present, forces of exclusion, deep-rooted racism and discrimination, and even brutal violence, especially against "non-white" immigrants, have been part of American history. For most of the twentieth century, U.S. immigration policy was restrictive, and the most deserving refugees and immigrants were excluded. Still, American immigration history proves the enormous potential of immigration from around the world.... Ethnic groups are not perceived as minorities but as distinctive parts of the dynamic and pluralist American mosaic. Since the late nineteenth century, immigrants have made America "their" home. Hyphenated identities are really an expression of a deeper link between a specific ethnicity and America....

In contrast, Germans have never accepted immigration as part of their national identity, even as the long twentieth century bears witness to the reality of a large population of immigrants living and working on German soil. In Germany, as in many other countries, immigrants were and often still are expected to accommodate to their respective host societies, although prejudice has made such assimilation difficult if not impossible. Germans have rarely been entirely hospitable to migrants, but except for the Nazi years, they cannot be characterized as being completely unwelcoming either. As in the United States, economic, political, social, legal, and cultural imperatives all complicate any simple narrative of the German encounter with immigrants.

Source: Tobias Brinkmann and Annemarie Sammartino, "Immigration: Myth versus Struggles," in Cristof Mauch and Kiran Klaus Patel, *The United States and Germany during the Twentieth Century: Competition and Convergence* (Cambridge, UK: Cambridge University Press [German Historical Institute Copyright], 2010), 100.

NOTE

1. Quoted in Hazel Johnson and Henry Bernstein, *Third World Lives of Struggle* (London, UK: Heinemann Educational Books, 1982), 173–74.

Acknowledgments

Chapter 12
Source 12.1: "On Meeting with Budomel, 1455," in G. R. Crone, *The Voyages of Cadamosto and Other Documents on Western Africa* (Farnham, UK: Hakluyt Society, 1937), 35–52. Used by permission David Higham on behalf of the Hakluyt Society.

Chapter 13
Source 13.2: James Lockhart, ed. and trans., *Repertorium Columbianum Volume 1: We People Here: Nahuatl Accounts of the Conquest of Mexico.* Reprinted by permission of Wipf and Stock Publishers.

Source 13.4: Excerpts from Patricia de Fuentes, ed. and trans., *Conquistadors.* Copyright © 1963 by Penguin Random House LLC. Used by permission of Viking Books, an imprint of Penguin Publishing Group, a division of Penguin Random House LLC. All rights reserved.

Source 13.5: James Lockhart, ed. and trans., *Repertorium Columbianum Volume 1: We People Here: Nahuatl Accounts of the Conquest of Mexico.* Reprinted by permission of Wipf and Stock Publishers.

Source 13.7: Miguel León-Portilla, *The Broken Spears.* Copyright © 1962, 1990 by Miguel León-Portilla. Expanded and updated edition © 1992 by Miguel León-Portilla. Reprinted by permission of Beacon Press, Boston.

Chapter 16
Source 16.1: Lynn Hunt, *The French Revolution and Human Rights: A Brief History with Documents,* 2nd ed. Copyright © 2016 by Bedford/St. Martin's. All rights reserved. Used by permission of the publisher, Macmillan Learning.

Source 16.3: "The Jamaica Letter," 1815, in Francisco Javier Yanes y Cristóbal Mendoza Montilla: *Colección de documentos relativos a la vida pública del Libertador de Colombia y del Perú Simón Bolívar para servir a la historia de la independencia de Suramérica, Caracas,* 1833, T. XXII, pp. 207–29. Translated by Suzanne Sturn. Used by permission of Suzanne Sturn.

Chapter 19
Source 19.4: William De Bary et al., *Sources of Japanese Tradition, Volume 2.* Copyright © 2001 Columbia University Press. Reprinted with permission of Columbia University Press.

Chapter 20
Source 20.3C: Joe Lunn, *Memories of the Maelstrom: A Senegalese Oral History of the First World War* (Portsmouth, NH: Heinemann, 1999), 232. Used by permission of the author.

Chapter 22
Source 22.4: Excerpts from pp. 156, 158, 160, 162–3, 167, 169 from E. F. Schumacher, *Small Is Beautiful: Economics As If People Mattered.* Copyright © 1973 by E. F. Schumacher. Reprinted by permission of HarperCollins Publishers and The Random House Group, Limited.

Source 22.5A: Richard P. Turco et al., "The Climatic Effects of Nuclear War," *Scientific American* 251, no. 2 (August 1984). Copyright © 1984 Scientific American, a division of Nature America, Inc. All rights reserved. Reprinted with permission.

Source 22.5B: Jonathan Schell, *The Fate of the Earth.* Copyright © 1982 by Jonathan Schell. Reprinted by permission of the author.

Source 22.6B: Jeffrey T. Kiehl, *Facing Climate Change.* Copyright © 2016 Columbia University Press. Reprinted with permission of Columbia University Press.

Chapter 23
Source 23.1: Copyright © Linda McDowell, 2016, *Migrant Women's Voices.* Berg Publishers, an imprint of Bloomsbury Publishing Plc. Reprinted by permission.

Source 23.5: Geert Wilders, "Speech at the 'Europe of Nations and Freedom' Conference", January 22, 2017, https://www.gatestoneinstitute.org/9812/geert-wilders-koblenz-enf. Used by permission of The Tweede Kamer der Staten-Generaal.

Voice 23.2: Tobias Brinkmann and Annemarie Sammartino, "Immigration: Myth versus Struggles", in Cristof Mauch and Kiran Klaus Patel, *The United States and Germany during the Twentieth Century: Competition and Convergence.* Copyright © The German Historical Institute, 2010, published by Cambridge University Press, reproduced with permission.